SO-BHR-255

First Edition £25=

I FOLLOW ST. PATRICK

Kevin A. Ryan

31. X. '44.

By the same author:

AS I WAS GOING DOWN SACKVILLE
   STREET

OTHERS TO ADORN. (POEMS)

I FOLLOW SAINT PATRICK

OLIVER ST. JOHN GOGARTY

RICH & COWAN
LONDON MCMXXXVIIJ

First published 1938

MADE IN GREAT BRITAIN

PRINTED AND BOUND BY RICHARD CLAY AND SONS, LIMITED, BUNGAY, SUFFOLK,
FOR MESSRS. RICH AND COWAN, LIMITED, 37 BEDFORD SQUARE, LONDON, W.C.I,
ON PAPER SUPPLIED BY GERALD JUDD, LIMITED

" The savage people free and yet despised,
    The outlying parts where still the Tribesmen fight,
You drew to better things and civilised,
    Loading the Roman arch with greater might."

LINDSAY, from the Latin : *Anon.*

THIS BOOK FOLLOWS THE JOURNEYS OF ST. PATRICK AS far as they are traceable at the present time. It is by no means a " Life." The writer has not the qualifications for such a work, nor the ambition to step in where, with all his advantages, the earliest biographer, Muirchu, left much to conjecture and uncertainty.

The writer can sympathise with that biographer and can bring his mind into agreement with him when he states :

But these writers never attained to one sure track of history, on account of the extreme difficulty of the task of story-telling, and because of conflicting opinions, and the very many surmises of very many persons. Therefore, if I mistake not, as our popular proverb has it, " Like bringing boys into a council meeting," I have brought the infantile rowboat of my feeble brain into this most dangerous and deep ocean of sacred story, where mountainous seas rage and swell, amidst sharpest rocks lying in unknown seas, an ocean on which no boat has as yet ventured, save only that of my father Cogitosus. However, that I seem not to make a great thing out of what is small, I shall essay, in obedience to the command of thy holiness and authority, to unfold, piecemeal and with difficulty, these few out of the many actions of St. Patrick. My skill is small ; my authorities are uncertain [or, anonymous] ; my memory is treacherous ; my intelligence is worn out ; my style is poor ; yet the feeling of my love is most pious.

The present writer's object is not biography so much as geographical history. And his aim is, by describing the places which the Saint visited and sanctified in our island, to draw from these, as from well-springs, inspirations which shall be truly traditional, pure, and undiluted by modern distractions and fatuous ideas of patriotism ; and shall again be as much part and parcel of our race as the rivers, seas, valleys, fields, and mountains are part of our country.

CONTENTS

LIST OF ILLUSTRATIONS
By BIP PARES

RDIGA

HEN

▲ CARN

AINT PATRICK

□
MENAPIA

Carn Carswig ▲

S

THE M
EN
Showing

CHAPTER I

ST. DAVID'S HEAD IS THAT PART OF WHAT ONCE WAS Roman Britain which juts furthest out into " our sea," as the biographer of St. Patrick calls St. George's Channel. This promontory is made a peninsula by an inlet from the north-west, which forms a deep division of sea-water, one hundred and fifty feet below, as crystal clear as Ogof Crystal itself—another but less-indenting inlet, some furlongs to the east. The neck thus formed could be easily fortified, and anyone with an eye for archæology can promptly recognise a promontory fort such as the neolithic men made of the Baily at Howth, County Dublin, and indeed at all parts of the coast where the land lent itself to such a natural acropolis of the sea. This basic intrusion of Cambrian rock which is St. David's Head has been the home of human beings from time out of mind. The remains of the primitive fortresses which gave men shelter from manifold dangers are easily to be seen and their succession may be easily traced. When one sits on the summit of St. David's Head, the bay which, when viewed from either crescent of white sand, appeared to be a gently curving arc, is now seen to be more than a semi-circle, almost an amphitheatre. Beheld from the sea, the Head is lost against the greater range of Carn Llidi and other hills, and except at low tide, the silver sands are invisible against the green of the Valley of the Roses which ends in Whitesands Bay. To the south of the Head in Porth Melgan a good-sized ship or little steamer can find anchorage, but the vessel must be prepared for beaching when the tide, which runs to twenty feet, ebbs away to leave a lovely sheltered cove with a cave in the folds of a rock which forms the cliff that sinks to sea level towards the south.

The valley rises gently from the sea, and as it rises the view extends until the eye can look far beyond Ramsey Island and sweep an unbroken horizon. The whole district from Haverfordwest to the coast, where there are seventeen hills in sixteen miles, is full of valleys filled in summer with wild flowers ; and with its rills and glimpses of the sea, a long arm of which indents at Solva, it forms one of the most fertile and lovely places in Britain. One of the valleys is cup-shaped, and in it lies, a mile and a half from the shore, the cathedral which makes a city of St. David's which is the oldest diocese in Britain and the nearest to Ireland, sixty miles away.

Of an evening from the high ground, the hills of Wicklow, purple against the setting sun, seem to gain height as they hide behind them the " ultimate places of the earth," mysterious, unknown, in which no Roman legionary had ever set foot, unless as a captive or as a soldier returning from service with one of the legions, a " galeatus," one who had worn the Roman helmet—an ex-service man ; a land which, to those dwelling on this fringe of empire, was magical, barbarous, and menacing—an ever-present danger to law and order, liberty and life, when it moved as one man and its sea-kings made the water fume with their

oars. To those coming from Ireland, St. David's or Demetia or Dyfed was the gate of the Roman Empire. The tribe of the Dési inhabiting it came from Meath in the third century of our era. Its kings were descended from Irish kings.

CHAPTER II

A SEARCH FOR THE ARMS OF KING NIAL OF THE NINE HOSTAGES, AND FOR THE IRISH SEA-KINGS' SHIPS THAT BORE PATRICK AWAY IN THE FIRST YEARS OF THE FIFTH CENTURY

DIFFICULT AS IT IS TO IMAGINE ONESELF IN ANOTHER person's position, it is harder still to reverse the reel of Time and to fit oneself into another period. For here imagination is a hindrance rather than a help. It is liable to be prejudiced by ideas from one's own day; and it is far harder to dissociate ideas than to combine them. So when I try to project myself into the fifth century, not only have I to throw overboard a great deal that I have learnt, but also to take on board a great deal that has not been within the reach of those educated in Ireland, as education here is known. And in addition to this there is the tendency of past things to appear to run together, as railway lines seem to meet in the distance. I find myself suffering from a mental limitation which regards things long past as having happened all at once or suddenly, and I am unable to extend to the men of old what I may call the benefit of Time. Even worse, I am apt to forget what that under-appreciated poet Longfellow pleads: "That in all ages every human heart is human." Life, Love, and Death touch all mortal men in the march of Time. It is the ages and beliefs that change more than the heart. But:

> Let change as may the names of God,
> Let alter all this social frame,
> For mortal men the ways of Life
> And Death are still the same.

So although slavery existed and cruelty was rampant, the natural affections between parents and children and men and country were as they have always been. What is it, then, from which I have to clear my mind ? From the notion that the men of old were haphazard, unorganised and undisciplined, that they were restricted in their movements, and that colonies and settlements were made in a day, and not by the process of centuries. And what have I to take on board ? That which until recently could be obtained nowhere in Ireland under the various systems of education : knowledge enough to form a judgment of the strength and importance of our heroic period.

Ignorance of our history is one of the root causes of our Irish troubles. In Ireland the heroic period is historical, a fact which adds to its importance as a ground from which to arrive at a new assessment of history. To realise a bygone time to which our heroic period may be compared you will have to stand under the Lion Gate of Mycenæ, " rich in gold," or by its covered well, or go to Tiryns, with its tunnelled wall that looks to Nauplia, where lay the ships that brought to Troy Agamemnon and his men with their chariots and their horses. As I stood by the wall of Mycenæ under the Lion Gate, I thought of Ard Macha and of Nial of the Nine Hostages. He too had ships which could travel far, sea-worthily, and bear many captives away. As early as A.D. 290 the Roman Britons were already " accustomed " to invasions from Ireland. St. Patrick leads one to believe that he considered such piratical raids a normal

B

condition of life by " our sea." Centuries later our
sea-kings were imitated by Norsemen, in that these
raided for two generations before colonising. To
Dr. Bøe of Oslo I owe this information about the
colonising methods of his fellow-countrymen. And
no doubt it was a practice arising from the nature of
things : raids to find out weak spots in a coveted
territory and colonies to hold it when surveyed.

Three kings before King Leary of Tara were sea-
kings, and the period from the date of the preliminary
raids at the end of the third century to the middle of
the fifth covers the time of Irish settlements along the
west coast of Britain. The first colonies were in
Argyllshire, but gradually they extended southwards.
But domination of the Irish Sea did not cease with
Leary, though he, deterred by an equivocal prophecy,
never went abroad—for in the sixth century a king of
Tara is found threatening the men of Wales that he
will harry their coasts if they continue to extend
sanctuary to an Irish refugee.

But of all these men who tackled Rome and ruled its
western seas, not a word to Irish children in the
schools ! It was left to adults, to those who have time
and inclination for such lore, to find out and to piece
history together for themselves. It may seem strange
that a knowledge of his own past was not at the disposal of any Irishman who cared to study it. If it
seems strange, one has only to recall the state of the
National Museum of Ireland in the days of old.
Some brass guns from India decorated its porch,
which also contained a more or less modern and

cumbersome gun-carriage and an exhibit of a cast-iron drinking-fountain. Within, the student was confronted by a fine specimen of a coach and a plaster statue of that Venus on the bottom of whom John Elwood inscribed his name in lead pencil. As for Irish remains, an Irishman in bronze in the uniform of a British officer was bestriding the fallen body of a Sikh and vigorously using a revolver. A case of French miniatures lent by Dr. Sigerson gave the place an air of home. A spade was never put in the soil of Ulster, which was in those days a separate part of Ireland, as it is to-day, and as it had been from time immemorial until the British took over the country and ignored its boundaries. There was absolutely no archæological field-work done in any part of Ireland.

The Director waited for " finds " to be sent in, and then waited an historical period to acknowledge them. I presented a collection of flint arrows, celts, and spearheads to the Museum. Some years elapsed, during which I received no recognition of my gift. As I had purchased them to save them from being dispersed by auction, I began to think that after all they would be better in many collections than to be buried unnoticed in Kildare Street.

But now all things are changed for the better, the National Museum of Ireland is a treasure-house of Irish remains as well as a university for the student of archæology. The war-horns of the men who harried West Britain, and raided first and colonised for generations afterwards the western shelf of Wales

until there came to be more Irish on that side of the
Irish Sea than on the west, can be seen, arranged and
displayed according to their periods. As one goes
round the Museum, well-informed, scholarly attendants assist the visitor. I had the good fortune to
meet Dr. Mahr, from whom I learned how meagre is
the information that exists regarding the very period
in which I was interested—that of the fifth century.
Of the older times we know more, but this century
continues to elude and to lend itself to speculation.
And it is with some conjecture and much deduction
that I must endeavour to furbish it out. It is the
Dark Age of Archæology. Nothing can be said with
exactitude regarding the weapons of its warriors. Dr.
Mahr suggested that " either they had no weapons at
all, or the Late Bronze existed in Ireland down into
the fifth century." There are the short swords, as
that in the left hand of a warrior represented on the
carven cross of Muredach, 900–923. In panel two,
on the west face, is a figure holding a sword in his left
hand. Another holds one in his right. The two
soldiers are supposed by Kingsley Porter to be exiling
St. Columcille. The importance of the sword may
be guessed by bringing it forward, even though it
makes the soldier left-handed.

" Is it a Scandinavian sword ? "

" No. It is Irish. There is the round brooch on
the right shoulder of that figure in the centre."

I looked closely and could make out the circle of a
great brooch half a shoulder in width, such a brooch

as we have outlined in that unique masterpiece, the
" Tara " brooch.   I thought of the vigilance and
knowledge with which these archæologists follow every
line and carving of these monuments of weathered stone.
In the ninth and tenth centuries, the centuries when the
triumph of monastic Christian art was at its height,
our country put out its best artistic blossom : represented by these great and detailed and symbolically
carven crosses, every one of which is the work of an
original master—and this at a time when the country
lay prone before the very raids and harryings that a
few centuries before it had inflicted ruthlessly on others.
St. Patrick, looking down from on high, might have
reflected (if such a thought had not been paradoxical
for him) that he was well avenged for the fierce raids
his own Welsh countrymen endured.

I lamented the fact to Dr. Mahr that, with so much
writing about himself, St. Patrick managed to say the
least about either his condition or the topography of
the country of his apostolate.   A Chinese prince
journeying through China could not have eschewed
as bad form any reference to the actual details of
the journey.   The only place-names he mentions—
and they are but two—are subjects of conjecture and
discussion.

" St. Patrick was not a curator of a museum,"
Dr. Mahr answered, with his pleasant, quizzical
smile.

We went to inspect the shields.   There is a great
round shield of bronze, much fretted and holed.   And

one of leather made of hide from the chest of a mature bull. It has behind its central boss rivets for a leather handle. But it is the front portion which is interesting. On the margin are two concentric rings interrupted on the right side by two entering chevrons which make two notches in the circular rings. I imagined, judging by the thick elder-wood shield near by, that this was to enable the warrior to peep out. But no. That shield is much warped, because it was allowed to dry too quickly after its removal from the bog where it was found. Another, sent to the Museum with more despatch, shows no shrinking of the rim. What, then, were these chevrons? To break perfection as represented by the circles, as the Persians introduce a fault deliberately in their carpet-weaving lest they tempt the jealous gods? Wrong! An indentation on a shield was a mark of honour. It was presumed to have been made by the spear of an enemy. It was a mark of honour much the same as the wounds on the face of a German student duellist were considered honourable. Well, those chevrons represent the dints already there and those to come. " Wound-stripes," thought I. And in spite of its wry appearance, I thought with respect of the wizened bull-hide shield that has retained its shape through fifteen hundred years. For of Hector and Æneas has not Homer sung : " And the twain went straight forward, their shoulders clad with shields of bull's-hide, dry and tough, and abundant bronze had been welded thereon ? "

The amazing war-horns! They were found intact. Could St. Patrick have heard them "growl and snarl" from the ships as the pirates sprang into the water and waded ashore? "Certainly he could," said Dr. Mahr. Immediately I became fascinated by the great curved horns, eight feet long, riveted marvellously, whose sound was terrible to those living near the shore. More terrible when the fierce kilts of Ulster drew inland, different from other marauders "partly in their habits, yet alike in one and the same thirst for bloodshed—in a preference also for covering their villainous faces with hair rather than the immodest parts of their bodies with decent clothing." Now, if I can get some information about the ships of the time, will he agree, I wonder, with my suggestion that our sea-kings had no mean ships: ships, shall I say, as good as those that bore Cæsar to Britain and across the Adriatic—a ship stout enough to carry the fortunes of a man who never feared or hesitated to put them to the touch? Ships fit to carry Cæsar! After all, the Ictian Sea—that is, the English Channel—was patrolled. And the builders of ships such as these were, like shipbuilders in our time, and in every time for all we know, quite prepared to do a deal with the "small nations." And few nations were richer in gold than our own. It does not necessarily mean that no one of us, man or nation, can go to sea unless we build our own ships. The Irish sea-kings must have had . . . ?

" In the *Journal of the Royal Society of Antiquaries*

of Ireland there is a description by Dr. Macalister of a huge coracle or Irish ship found a few years ago."

I felt slightly crestfallen.   I had it all so well worked out, or, rather, imagined I had, that I was full of self-satisfaction, thinking of great ships.   And now this enormous coracle.   I remembered the mention and stipulation about a boat " of more than one hide " in a life of St. Patrick.   The sizes or the displacements of boats like that must have been measured by the number of hides that went to their making. I had yet to learn of boats of forty hides and two masts.

I asked !   " But had they not wooden ships ? "

" They may have had ; they may have used—if they continued into this period—wooden canoes hollowed out."

Wooden canoes !   Who wouldn't be crestfallen ? However, I recovered my spirits instantly, as is the way with me, and I quoted the Poet of the Decline, Claudian, at the Director :

> " *Totam cum Scottus Hivernen*
> *Movit et infesto spumavit remige Tethys.*"

It took some ships to make the sea foam with their oars.   And I might go on with the quotation in order to get a hint of what kind of weapons our piratical ancestors used :

> " *Illius effectum curis ne tela timerem*
> *Scottica . . .* "

" *Tela   Scottica.*"   What   were   they   like ?   But

considering that there is only one specimen of a Roman pilum to be found (that is on view in the museum at Wiesbaden), and one-third of these six-foot spears was of iron, out of all the tens of thousands that must have been forged for the legions and only two to be seen on monuments, we are not in too bad a way if we can point to hundreds of swords and darts in our many specimens of the Bronze Age.

Show me a long-bow of the Welshmen who won Crecy and Agincourt.   None exists.

If the Bronze Age lingered until the fifth century, why could not the weapons of that era linger on until the ninth ?   So I examined the ninth-century crosses, which are pillars of history—the news chroniclers and army gazettes of their time—for an idea of what the swords of King Nial's marines were like.   True, the swordsmen on the ninth-century cross are said by some to be Roman soldiers, but their weapons are exactly like those in the case which holds the long trumpets and a Scandinavian sword or two.   After all, the artists who made these recording crosses were unaware of historical perspective, and drew Romans and others almost like contemporaries.   Or could the figures not be Norse raiders holding up a monk ?   If so, the artist had first-hand knowledge of the Vikings' dress !   One thing so far is certain.   Dr. Mahr's jocular premise, " either they had no arms at all," is untenable.   They had arms, and here they are.   But it is a pity that they could not have carried on with no arms at all or have conducted war after the newly-invented method of that British

Tilbury battalion, a salutary and revolutionary method, to use an adjective that becomes somewhat ambiguous in the context I am about to unfold. A "revolutionary" form of war might suggest war in connection with a revolution. So it could and so it does ; but this was a form of war that revolutionised all war known to us. When Peace was raging at home a battalion commander led his men abroad in army a thousand strong to a foreign war, and came back after six months with one thousand and fifty, and none of them prisoners ! Now, if this great captain were still with us to take charge of all wars, what a difference it would make to the world ! Things would be reversed. Peace would be deadlier than war—a menace to humanity—unless, of course, it were a Peace to end Peace. War would be more procreant than peace. Both Mr. Churchill and Herr Hitler assure us that it is by arming and re-arming that peace is assured— so, conversely, when men had no arms, war must have raged continuously. Then truly it would be "the mother of all good things " (discipline maintained). The chief could reply, " I have defeated Death. But do you think it is the chief function of a general to lose his army ? " He could confound you there ! And we would come to wishing each other not " long life " but a piping time of War. That was the greatest marshal whoever walked on earth. The only one under whom I would not be afraid to serve. " He never lost an English gun," was sung of the Duke of Wellington. But how much better if he never lost an English man ! As for our Thousand-Fighter . . . " either they (the enemy) had no weapons, or . . ." From this it will seem manifest, even to a member of the Society of Friends, that what we want is a Peace to end Peace. If Peace broke out and interrupted the piping times of War, we would be thrown back again under the wheels of buses or under the surgeons' knives—more deadly than the bayonet—or back into Clubs to die of a surfeit or, what is worse, of some disease we should not have brought on ourselves. " Nothing is more disconcerting," my old friend the Doctor used to say, " than a disease we have *not* brought on ourselves."

In spite of the pious wish of the Director, the Irish raiders had swords, and swords of iron. There is documentary evidence in that great epic of ours, *The Cattle Raid of Cualnge*, a La Tène romance, where we find the Ulster hero hacking through a spear-shaft which had stuck in his shield, and, later, of his enemies cutting down a spinney with their swords. From the fourth century B.C. the legends tell of a folk who invaded Ireland and were invincible because of their " swords of light," their gleaming iron blades.

But documentary evidence is not proof. I wished to satisfy myself once and for all about the weapons that they who carried off Patrick wore. What if I made a sword of bronze and tried it out on a sapling and on the ash-handle of a pitch-fork ? I went and put the problem before that great metallurgist Dr. Lane-Joynt. So thoroughly did he enter into the test, that there and then he took me to the basement of his house in Harcourt Street, where he had a forge and a

large workshop.   He knew all about the archæology of
Irish swords, spears and bells.

" No bronze sword exceeded twenty inches in length.
True, there is a rapier, but I am talking about bronze
swords.   I have some copied exactly from those in the
Museum—so exactly that I have been requested to
cease from making them lest later on they be sold to the
Museum when I am dead and gone.   I will show you
where they break.   They break exactly at the same
places as those which are broken in the Museum :
nine inches up the blade just behind the first swelling
and inside the hilt where the rivet-holes (usually six
in number) are."

Very generously he took a bronze sword nineteen
inches long and beautifully shaped, with its swelling
leaf-like blade.   The handle was very small.   I
remarked that it was too small for my hand to hold
firmly.

" The men of old were smaller than we.   They have
been magnified by romance.   Look at the armour of
Crecy or Agincourt. . . ."

" Yes," I said, " even the skulls of the wolf-hounds
which have been found preserved in bogs are smaller
than those of their descendants to-day."

We went into the garden to try the blade against a
bough of laburnum about three inches in diameter.
The sword remained intact while not used as strongly
as we could wield it.   Perhaps the continued hammer-
ing affected the rivets.   Anyway, it came out of its
hilt, the flange that held it was broken.   We patched
it up with a hilt that lapped over the blade ; and with a

shrewd stroke broke it exactly nine inches from the improvised hilt.   There was no need to try it on an ashen shaft.

The question was settled.   Bronze swords never carried rapine and ruin to the western verge of the Imperium Romanum.

Lane-Joynt was one of the most knowledgeable of men.   His dissertations on ancient weapons : how the bronze sword warriors had recourse to scabbards longer than their blades to affect the bearing of a steel sword-owner, and how civilisation followed arms would have delighted those who were interested.   But he had proved my case.

Praise to him.   He was a great Irishman.   He is in the world that holds Cuchullin and Maeve and McRoy, and those fierce men who lived by the sword and perished thereby.

More suggestive than a search for the weapons contemporary with the sea forays, more even than a realisation of the power and range of their fleets, is one short quotation from the poet who pre-eminently praised Rome, unaware of the imminence of her ruin.   Claudian, in a fine figure, in that line of his already quoted, sees foam added to that of the sea by the oars of the long-ships from Ierne : when the men of Ireland moved as one man and the sea fumed with hostility.   That line is like a window opening on the foam of the fleets of the fifth century, the ships of the Scots, the wild men from Ulster.   It does more to show the Irish Fleet in action than all my attempts born of wandering through coastwise villages, and a study of

the weapons in our own Museum.   And in other lines
from the panegyric by the same poet on Honorius's
third consulate there is an account of the counter-
blows that disintegrating and exasperated Britain
struck :

> *Ille leves Mauros nec falso nomine Pictos*
> *Edomuit Scottumque vago mucrone secutus*
> *Fregit Hyperboreas remis audacibus undas.*

Theodosius pursued the Irish and broke with his
daring oars the waves of the hyperborean sea, actually
following the pirates as far as the mouth of their
stronghold in the salt marshes of Strangford Lough, if
we may read that into a line from Pacatus :

> *Redactum ad paludes suas loquar ?*

Back to the bogs with a vengeance !   No, but back to
the securest harbour in Ulster for those familiar with
it—Strangford Lough, with its salt marshes where
none could pursue vessels of light draught.   I see it
better now through the eye of the poet : fleet upon
fleet, and advantage taken instantly of any relaxation
of the vigilance of the legions that guarded Britain.
After all, I might just as well have expected myself to
reconstruct the Great War from the inspection of a
few of the guns captured and on show on village greens,
as to bring up a vision of long-lost ships from a study
of their fighting-men's weapons.

I believe in Claudian, even allowing for poetic
licence.   He paints a picture that must have had a
model.   But wait ; I also believe in Julius Cæsar, for
whom no one need make allowance for poetic licence—
that unruffled mind which subordinated storms and

tides and warring tribes alike to its inhuman, cold omnipotence. He was accurate to the point of boredom, and his attention to detail was as thorough as himself. True, he wrote more than four hundred years before the time of Nial, but if weapons from an older day continued unchanged down the centuries, can it not be the same with ships ? And here is what Cæsar says of the ships of a Celtic tribe who used to sail to Britain from across the Ictian Sea from the Loire :

> For their ships were built and equipped after this manner. The keels were somewhat flatter than those of our ships, whereby they could more easily encounter the shallows and the ebbing of the tide ; the prows were raised very high, and, in like manner the sterns were adapted to the force of the waves and storms (which they were formed to sustain). The ships were built wholly of oak, and designed to endure any force and violence whatever ; the benches were made of planks a foot in breadth, were fastened by iron spikes the thickness of a man's thumb ; the anchors were secured fast by iron chains instead of cables, and for sails they used skins and thin dressed leather. These [were used] either through their want of canvas and their ignorance of its application, or for this reason, which is more probable, that they thought that such storms of the ocean, and such violent gales of wind could not be resisted by sails, nor ships of such great burden be conveniently enough managed by them.

And they lacked not for numbers or equipment :

> ". . . about 220 of their ships, fully equipped and appointed with every kind of [naval] implement, sailed forth from the harbour, and drew up opposite to ours. . . ."

If Nial, fighting four hundred and fifty years *later*, had ships like those, it is easy to understand how St. Patrick was captured with " *tot milia*," so many thousand, as he himself says when describing the raid, and

carried beyond hope of rescue.   And even allowing for
the recession of the waves of progress which occurs
every five hundred years, we must not forget that the
freebooters on the other side of Britain, the Saxons,
when they did come to the island, arrived, as Gildas
tells us, in three long-ships.*

In another place Cæsar refers to the handicap of the
great leather-sailed ships of the Veneti in that they had
no oars.   The Roman galleys had the advantage of
oars in speed and in manœuvring.   They were not at
the mercy of the wind.   And if I am true to my belief
in Claudian, I cannot shut my eyes to the picture he
calls up which must have had a model : " *Spumavit
Tethys.*"   The sea foamed to their oars.   So they
had oars, those boats of the Irish sea-kings.   Oars
are always mentioned.   And what sea-worthy boats
have oars ?   Pre-eminently the very type of boat I
myself used when hunting seals over the waves of the
Atlantic near Cahir Island, twelve miles off the
extreme edge of Europe, the most westerly point
reached by St. Patrick " *ubi nemo ultra erat.*"   What
was it but a Connemara curragh ?   Instead of skins,
now they have canvas stretched on frames and tarred :
the oldest and still the most sea-worthy boats that
exist anywhere where men have business with the sea ;
shaped like half a cylinder brought to a point in an
upraised and pointed prow and, being keel-less, balanced
by long, narrow-bladed oars.   Two men can row them
and carry them ashore, and place them upside down in

* It seems worth noting that the modern Irish word for ship is
long = *longa navis.*

the traditional manner so that they could lie safe from the wind. I remember that we had our choice of two wooden vessels—a pookawn, twenty-five feet long, and a glothoge, longer still, masted and rigged like a yacht to carry three sails against the pookawn's one. Would my men put out in those ?

" Ah, no. They might go down."

But the curraghs skimmed the seas and were independent of winds, however great, for they lay low in the water and moved slantwise to the breakers, stabilised by the great depth to which their sweeps sank in the waves. A willow peg two feet long made a rowlock. It passed through a hole in a flange, fitted one-fifth down the loom of the oar. The oars could not be " feathered," but we were sailing where birds could not flock. Never into a wind, but a few points off; and twelve sea miles were only two hours to the men who lay back to their oars. An oar and the puddle it made were invisible in the raging water through which it slipped as easily as the pared blade of some Etonian favourite of the trainer who wished him to get his blue; for the curraghs skimmed the surface keel-less and rudderless in the sea, and the winds passed overhead with nothing on which to get a purchase. An eighteen-footer could carry seventeen hundredweight well bestowed, as well as two oarsmen. I had too much faith in the men of the West, any old prophecy or poem concerning whom demands and gets respect, to be unmindful of the Gaelic line, " There never was an O'Māille not master of the sea." It may have referred to the galley-slaves of Granuaile, which

c

is Grace O'Māille, the sea-queen of Connemara, but I
took it as referring to the man who was a postman for
twenty years, voyaging twice weekly in all weathers to
Inis Turk, which is, if anything, farther into the
Western Ocean than the island called Cahir.

Great for fishing and for carrying cattle and for
trading,—I should have remembered Breccan's fleet
of fifty curraghs which traded between Antrim and
Kantire. And he was Nial's grandson. And I
should have remembered that there was nothing to
prevent their being made for three or even six oars
aside, and that there was no more lack of stout-
hearted fellows in Nial's day in Ulster than there is
now on the seaboard of the West. I realised now that
there was no need for our sea-kings to use wooden
ships, which would actually have put them at a disadvantage, because of the dependence of such ships
on sheltering harbours and the depth of their draught.

It mattered little what I remembered, for I am no
authority on nautical history. Wishing to get the best
information I could so as to arrive at some idea of
what the ships of Nial were like, I wrote to the greatest
living authority on the subject. I can do no better
than to reproduce his answer. For this he has very
kindly given me permission.

" DEAR SIR,
        " In reply to your enquiry, I may say
that the character of the ships (or galleys as is more
probable) used by Nial is a difficult problem to
solve, especially in view of the definite knowledge

we have that the Veneti had excellent wooden galleys and that the Norsemen were also using wooden galleys from the fifth century A.D. On the other hand, we have the equally definite statement of Gildas, who wrote in the middle of the sixth century that when the Romans left Britain, no sooner were they gone than Scots (*i.e.* Irish) and Picts ravaged the British coasts and that they came in curraghs; for he uses the phrase '*de curicis*' to describe their boats. A curragh is an ideal vessel for short-distance raiding; it is independent of the winds and has a great turn for speed when manned by many oarsmen. I do not doubt that the ancient raiding curraghs were far larger (longer) than those of the present day, though some of these are fairly large. In the article which I send you are a few other references that I have picked up, and these may be of use to you. When the Norse and Danes invaded or traded with Ireland it is almost certain that their long-ships set a new fashion in Eastern Ireland and probably in Ulster as well, and that the sea-going curragh gradually faded out of existence on all the coasts save the wild Western coasts, where timber was scarce and difficult to procure—thereby contributing effectively to the survival of the skin-boat.

" Trusting this will help you; any further assistance in my power is at your service.

" Yours faithfully,

(*Signed*) " JAMES HORNELL."

Now, that is the whole thing in a nutshell. But we don't want things in a nutshell, for ancient history is too prone to crystallise itself into nutshells, and so prevent an expansive view. I was saved from this by the masterly paper which Mr. Hornell wrote, and here are extracts which touch the period very intimately :

For us its value lies chiefly in the fact that the tale describes the principal features of an Irish curragh of the sixth century. The account, which is in Latin (Moran, 1872), tells how the Saint and his companions " using iron tools, prepared a very light vessel, with wickerwork sides and ribs, after the manner of that country (Ireland) and covered it with cow-hide, tanned in oak bark (*rubricatis in cortice* roborina), tarring its joints : and they put on board provisions for forty days, with butter * enough to dress hides for covering the boat (whenever the covering needed repair), and all utensils necessary for the use of the crew " (Joyce, 1903, 11, 424). A tree (mast) was fitted amidships and a sail and the equipment requisite for the steering of a boat were provided. There is no discrepancy in regard to the number who accompanied St. Brendan. In the " Life " in the Book of Lismore, three curraghs are mentioned, each carrying twenty persons ; in the Metrical Life the number is raised to thirty in each. Accepting the lower figure, the size of the curraghs would be considerably larger than any of the present day.

Among the places which the Saint and his companions probably visited was Iceland, reached after forty days sailing northward. Afterwards they seem to have touched at the Shetlands on their way south to the coast of Brittany. At the end of five years Brendan returned to Ireland, only to be advised by his foster-mother Itha to keep away from Ireland for some time longer to avoid the still-active resentment of the family of a lad drowned through an inadvertent act of the Saint. Itha disapproved of navigation in flimsy curraghs : she advised the use of boats made of wood. Brendan agreed, so on his second voyage the craft he used was a wooden ship as recommended by the thoughtful Itha.

* *Cf.* Homer for the preparation of a hide.

St. Brendan's first or curragh voyage probably occurred A.D. 519–24; his second or wood-built boat voyage, 525–27.

He was born in the Fenit, a township of Kerry, the county distinguished to-day as having the finest curraghs used by Irish fishermen.

St. Columba used curraghs in his voyages to and from Iona. In his first voyage to the island in A.D. 563, he was accompanied by twelve companions in one large curragh. He landed at a little bay called Port na Curaich, the Bay of the Curragh, and is said to have buried his curragh in the sand, satisfied that his beloved home, Ireland, was out of sight —to see it always before his eyes would have disturbed his thoughts.

St. Cormac, one of his disciples, used a curragh in his three voyages in search of a sea-girt solitude—" desert as these would-be anchorites termed such a place." Adamnan, who wrote the Life of St. Columba a century after his death, describes how Cormac on his third attempt, having set up sail in his curragh, was carried swiftly northward for fourteen days and nights before a strong southerly wind. Ever driving towards the Arctic, they found themselves beset by unfamiliar dangers. Of these the most terrifying was the attack by myriads of loathsome stinging creatures about the size of frogs, which struck the sides of the curragh with such violence " that it seemed as if they would wholly penetrate the leather covering " (Reeves, 1874, 72). They had begun to despair of life when at last, in seeming answer to their prayers, the wind suddenly veered round, enabling them to return home.

These instances show how sea-worthy these old voyagers considered the curraghs of their time. That this was not due to lack of acquaintance with the wooden-hulled boats is evident from Adamnan's account of the boats possessed by the monks of Iona in Columba's time (Adamnan, himself a successor of Columba as Abbot of Iona). Besides curraghs of wicker and hide, he enumerates a variety of wooden craft known to or used by the monks. These include dug-out canoes and several types of plank-built vessels. The dug-outs were of large size; they appear to have been employed for the transport from the mainland of timber required for buildings and boat construction.

In the extremely ancient Brehon Laws we have a nearly similar classification into (a) *ler-longa* (sea-ships), large wooden vessels fit for oversea trade, (b) *barca*, smaller wooden vessels used in coasting trade, and (c) curraghs of wicker. Dug-outs were plentiful on lakes, but these required little technical skill to dub out, and so were ignored in the rates of payment prescribed by the Laws to the master craftsmen (*ollaves*) who constructed them.

The lightness and shallow draft of the curragh made for speed. It therefore became the favourite of the hordes of plundering Irish who descended on the shores of Britain from time to time during Roman rule and increasingly thereafter until checked by rival bands of Saxon plunderers. Irish raids were particularly active during the fourth, fifth and sixth centuries ; they were always made in curraghs.

The British monk Gildas, who wrote in the middle of the sixth century, describes vividly their raids following the departure of the Romans in the preceding century. Habington (1638) translates the passage in picturesque language. He gives it thus :

" They (the Romans) were notwithstanding no sooner gone home, but as the brownish bands of wormes and eamots, which in the heighth of Sommer, and encreasing heate, doe swarming breake out of their most straight and darkesome dens, the dreadful routes of Scots and Picts . . . land out of their ships, wherein they were transported over the ' Titicham vallem ' (St. George's Channel)."

In this translation " ships " should be rendered " curraghs," for in the Latin text Gildas wrote *de curicis*. The Scots here referred to were actually Irish from Ireland ; the term Scot continued to mean " Irishman " as late as the ninth century.

The most famous of these Irish invaders was Niall of the Nine Hostages, King of Ireland from A.D. 379–405. He ravaged Wales repeatedly and even effected settlements there. Eventually he was chased away by the Roman general Stilicho.

Commerce between Ireland and Scotland was considerable, for Scots from northern Ireland were in occupation of much of the western Highlands; instead of the raids we hear of upon Wales, intercourse with Scotland was peaceful. In Cormac's *Glossary*, compiled in the ninth century, we read that Breccan, grandson of Niall above mentioned, had a fleet of fifty curraghs trading between Ireland and Scotland. One tragic day the whole fleet were caught in a great tidal whirlpool in the neighbourhood of Rathlin Island; all were lost, and thenceforward the whirlpool or tide rip has gone by the name of Coire-Breccain (Corrie-vrekan), " Breccan's cauldron."

Again, when the fugitive Irish chieftain Lughaid, surnamed MacCon, found asylum in the Scottish Court, the King of Scotland, according to the tale, promised not only his own help for an invasion of Ireland, but also that of the King of Britain and the King of the Saxons. The number of small craft supplemented to the ships, galleys and barks thus requisitioned to convey the invading host across the sea was so great that the chronicler says, " men do affirm that betwixt Ireland and Scotland was a continuous bridge of curraghs " (O'Grady, *Silva Galdelica*, II, 352). To give one more instance : In the story of " The Siege of Etar," when the Ulster forces were besieged in Ben Adair (Howth) by Leinstermen, they implored their friends in the north to come to their relief either by land or " in curraghs " (*i curchaib*) (Joyce, II, 426).

The last of these old references that I shall quote is in an entry in the *Annals of Ulster*, under the year 621. Referring to the drowning in this year of Conaing, son of Aedhan mac Gabhrain, of the Irish Kingdom in Scotland, the chronicler sings:

> The great clear waves of the sea
> And the sand have covered them—
> Into his frail wicker curragh
> They flung themselves over Conaing.
> The woman has cast her white tresses
> Into his curragh upon Conaing ;
> Hatefully she has smiled her smile
> To-day upon the Tree of Torta.

Here " the woman " is the sea; the reference to the " Tree of Torta " is obscure in this context.

Although curraghs figure prominently in many old accounts of Ireland until and including the Age of Saints, records subsequent to the seventh century have scarcely any contemporary references to their use.   The appearance of the Norsemen and Danes on the eastern seaboard of Ireland in the eighth and ninth centuries and their seizure of all sea trade entailed a complete revolution in the design of Irish oversea trading-ships.   Thenceforward the planked ship of wood drove the curragh off the high seas, and the curragh survived only on the wild western and north-western coasts for fishing and local coastal trade, and for traffic on some of the inland waters.

The only early English record is the well-known story mentioned in the Anglo-Saxon Chronicle of three pious Irishmen (so-called Scots) in a hide-covered boat in the year 891.   Their vessel was of good size, for the chronicler relates two hides and a half were sewn together to form the cover ; this would allow a length of about 15 feet.   This curragh, abandoned by its occupants to the guidance of God, took seven days to drift to the Cornish coast; on landing, the men took their way to the Court of King Alfred, who received them graciously and set them on their way to Rome.   The prominence given to this event does not mean, I believe, that the English were unaware of the use of curraghs by the Irish; it is probable that this voyage was chronicled as being a notable instance of the providence of God guiding the drifting craft to a haven of safety

Now it remains for me to apply that great principle which made England what it is—Compromise.   I conclude that the mariners of Nial had both curraghs *and* wooden ships.   They at all events had ships with sails.   This does not exclude curraghs, as Mr. Hornell has shown.   Let me give the passage from Gildas to which Mr. Philip Graves drew my attention.   It shows the invaders coming in rowing-boats and sailing vessels.

> (Cap. XVI.) *Illi priores inimici ac si ambrones lupi pro-*
> *funda fame rabidi siccis faucibus ovile transilientes non*
> *comparente pastore, alis remorum remigiumique brachus ac*
> *Velis vento sinuatis vecti terminos rumpunt coeduntque*
> *omnia.*

These latter may have been those " hired " of which
Archbishop Healy writes (I cannot trace his authority)
—ships hired from the men of Norway rich in woods.

But if they had only the curragh, " an ideal vessel
for short-distance raiding," as Mr. Hornell remarks,
it is all the more likely that they would take their prey
from the land nearest to them and which could be
soonest surprised : another argument in favour of the
Pembroke peninsula being the scene of that fateful
raid in 405.   After all, if I find myself making excuses
for the curraghs, from a fear that anything covered
only with skins could not be sea-worthy, I must
not forget that the highest-speed boats of to-day,
heavily engined, are covered only with a thin " skin "
of cedar or of mahogany.

CHAPTER III

WHERE WAS THIS WELSH VALLEY? IF I KNEW THAT I could solve the much-discussed and still-unanswered problem. Where was St. Patrick taken? If I knew that I could give a good guess at the place of his birth, though it does not follow that he was taken away by the Irish pirates from the exact place wherein he was born. His father's villa may have been a sea-side villa, for his father held rank equivalent to one of our knights, and the youthful Patrick was thus the son of a noble who had menservants and maidservants and who might be expected to follow the Roman fashion of sojourning by the sea in due season. Patrick's nobility appears indubitably from his letter to the soldiers of one Coroticus, a Pict, who ruled from the Rock of Clyde in Dumbarton as a petty *tyrannus* or king tolerated by the Romans. The passage deserves greater publicity than it gains from the schools.

> Is it from me that springs that goodly compassion which I exercise towards that nation who once took me captive, and made havoc of the menservants and maidservants of my father's house? I was free born according to the flesh; I am born of a father who was a decurion; but I sold my noble rank—I blush not to state it nor am I sorry—for the profit of others; in short I am a slave in Christ to a foreign nation for the unspeakable glory of the eternal life which is in Christ Jesus our Lord.

"Goodly compassion"! What excellent writing that is for one who in his modesty dubbed himself "rusticus"! A *decurion* was a member of a town's

42

curia, which consisted of well-to-do landowners, and
it is possible that Patrick's father, who from indirect
evidence was a man of considerable means, maintained a villa by the sea. Apparently he was absent
from it at the moment of the raid, or was left behind
with his father Potitus as being over age for the
hardships of slavery. But though to be a member
of a *curia* or town council might presuppose a town or,
if not a *municipium*, at least a *conciliabula* which could
be managed by a council, it is not necessary to suppose that Patrick's father could not retain the rank of
decurion without even a *conciliabula* in the neighbourhood of his villa. Even if he possessed the property
which necessitated his becoming a *decurion* under the
Roman land system, he could, by taking Orders in
the Church, presumably be exempted from the
decurion's thankless and unpopular duties of tax-
collecting. Thus it would not be necessary to live
in the vicinity of even a small town to maintain the
rank and title of *decurion*. This is a way out that
Dr. Bury, who described the status of the *decurions*,
did not take when he made the location of the birthplace of Patrick depend on the presence or nearness
of a *municipium* or a *forum* or *prefectura*. A little
village would have sufficed, such as that described in
the *Confessio*. This is all the more extraordinary
because it is he who so enlightenedly expounds the
status of *decurions* in the latter days of Rome, and
points out that by taking Orders they could escape
from the onus of the *decurion's* position. He goes on
to say that while Maxentius punished Christians by

promoting them to the dignity of *decurions*, here was one class of *decurions* which caused Christian emperors considerable perplexity—those who took Holy Orders.

" Theodosius the Great laid it down that the estates of *decurions* who had become deacons before a certain year should be exempt from municipal obligations, but that those who had taken Orders after that year should forfeit their lands to the State. He qualified this law, however, by a later enactment which provided that if the presbyter or deacon had a son who was not in Orders, the son might keep the paternal property. Now, Calpurnius, the father of Patrick, belonged to this class of deacons who had sought ordination. He was a Christian deacon, and his father (Potitus) before him had been a Christian presbyter. And it would seem as if they found it feasible to combine their spiritual with their worldly duties. In any case we may assume that the property remained in the family—it was not forfeit to the State."

And may I not presume that Patrick's father could live anywhere he wished, provided that there was a church to attend in his capacity as deacon? But if a likely place can be found where undoubtedly a church and a little town once existed, it will not be necessary to presume even this.

CHAPTER IV

THIS QUESTION WILL SEEM VERY HIGHLY PRESUMPTUOUS,
coming as it does from one so ill-equipped as myself
with either scholarship or the knowledge of exegesis.
When scholars are divided, contradictory, and uncertain, the only appeal that remains is to what is not
yet fully appreciated, and that is the veracity of legend
and local tradition. I may dare to affirm that no
legend associated with a particular place where a
strong local tradition persists has ever been wholly
discredited in the light of modern research. We find
facts distorted and monstrosities added by the mytho-
pœic faculty among all peoples, yes ; but in the final
analysis there is always a ground foundation of fact
which could sustain the most grotesque superstructures.
This was borne in on me in the most impressive
manner lately by two instances of the truth and, I
may say, accuracy of legend. By " lately," I mean
within the experience of the last ten years. I will
take the younger of the legends or traditions which
came to be justified by modern research first.

Since our school days we were told that the poet
Kit Marlowe died as a result of a brawl in a public-
house—a likely place for a brawl. It was stated that
he died from a dagger wound in his eye, after a scuffle
with one Francis Archer or Freiser—what else the
name might be was obscure. Literary men in England had the little bit of parchment evidence before

their eyes, with its letters just in transition from the characters of Gothic writing, and though an immediate example of the long " F " was afforded in the next line, the experts who pored over it missed the example. They missed the evidence which was hidden away ready to be disclosed amply to justify local tradition. What was the evidence ? Not any literary find or poetic record, but the hard matter-of-fact record of the inquest on Marlowe, and the Queen's pardon for those who were associated with his death. He had been stabbed after a day's debauch with gamester companions in a half brothel, half public house in Deptford, and stretching from the pallet whereon he lay to take the dagger from the belt of a companion, he was wounded in the struggle which ensued after he had hit his friend twice on the back of the head. But nobody until the advent of Professor Hotson of Harvard thought of going to law reports for the doings of poets in the reign of Elizabeth. All the names were written down and " Archer " became the possible Freiser, *i.e.* called after the craftsman who puts the freise on cloth.

That is within three hundred years ago ; but what of the legend more than three thousand years old : the tale of that impossible monster, the Minotaur. How could there be a minotaur, a merger of man and bull, and a devourer of youth at that ? A carnivorous bull who dwelt in a labyrinth and devoured a tribute of youths and maidens sent annually from Athens. " Hard to tell," an Irish bard would call it. Yet nine inches of earth alone prevented the solution of this

problem from going with the solution of the Marlowe
legend to the credit of the United States of America.
An American archæologist gave up digging, so I was
told in Crete, when he was within nine inches of un-
covering what is surely the most stupendous and
enlightening story ever spelt out by the spade of the
antiquarian : nothing less than the very palace of the
Minotaur ! The palace of Minos, who delighted in
bull-baiting, but who was, for all his three millennia
B.C., more humane in recreations than the modern
Spaniard who baits and fights bulls. For Minos employed youths and young girls much as a circus or
music-hall proprietor would take on acrobats, to
vault, tumble, and to somersault over the heads of the
animals, and doubtless to exhibit marvellous skill in
eluding them when infuriated. It is a bull's business
to be more or less infuriated (frustration or what not,
but we think cautiously of a bull). The lithe girls
somersaulted over their horns. You can see their
shapes, with waists of incredible and anatomically
impossible slimness, in the sea-green frescoes which
adorn the ruined walls. Girls with a cable-like ring
no wider than a quoit round their waists. There is
no sign of a sword or even of a banderillo. Nothing
but grace and agility appear in the rendering by
some long-lost artist of the athletes who eluded the
bulls of the Hundred-Citied Island. It may be true,
and presumably it is, that a tribute of supple youths
was taken every year and that they were trained un-
willingly to this dangerous exhibition. Their grace
justifies almost any training, however rigorous. How

much better it is than boxing, and how much more dangerous and much less crude! You have only to see the frescoes to realise what grace informed the lives of the youths and maids who "lived dangerously" three thousand years before Our Lord. And so the discovery, to which Sir Arthur Evans devoted his life and treasure, explains the confused tale about a bull who devoured the flower of Athenian youth! Fundamentally it had the seeds of truth, but it became sinister in the long restrospect of Time.

Therefore, when not one of the authorities on St. Patrick can satisfactorily prove where he was born, is it any wonder that I, with no scholarship, should, remembering the value of tradition, go where I could find tradition most lively and most strong?

CHAPTER V

Patrick was born at Nemthur.
(Author of Fiacc's Hymn.)

IN A PHOTOGRAPHIC ENLARGEMENT OF THE SCRIBE'S handwriting in the *Confession* of St. Patrick I read:

qui fuit vico Bannavem
Taberniæ, villulam enim prope habuit.

The words, as may be seen, are in Latin, but the letters are Irish letters. This also is the practice in the Book of Kells. Before I begin, let me presume to translate " Confessio Patricii " by " The Testimony of St. Patrick." " Testimony " is less misleading than the word " Confession." But, however we translate it in conformity with the modern meaning of the word, let us not forget that it is the oldest and perhaps the most important document in British history.

The cause of all the uncertainty regarding the locality from which Patrick was taken resides in the last word of line seven and the first word of line eight: " *bannavem tabernæ*." It is the cause of my wanderings in the paths of the Saint. Not one of the scholars knows for certain where Bannavem Taberniæ was. Where is Bannavem of the Tavern? Where is Tavern Town? If we knew this, we would know where Patrick was born and whence, presumably, he was taken. Five scholars hold five different opinions. Each fondles his own; just as every balladist of Robin

D   49

Hood clings to his own version of his hero's birth-place. Each repudiates each. Only the singer, the bard with the audience for the time being, knows.

> Some sings of the grass, the grass,
>   And some sings of the corn;
> But them wha sings of Robin Hood
>   Kens little where he was born.
>
> It was not in the hall, the hall,
>   Nor in the painted bower;
> But it was in the good green wood
>   Amang the lily-flower.

So which of the five places will you choose? All will agree that Patrick can have been carried off from only one place at once. Here is where, facts lacking, we must go on by conjecture and inductive reasoning.

One claims *Daventry* as the most assured place that bore the name Bannavem. But though Daventry may fit the name, it is far from fitting the description of the place by Patrick's biographer, Muirchu', who writes, about as far from Patrick's life-time as we from Shakespeare's, of " the town of Bannavem Thaburinde *not far from our sea*." Now, Daventry is deeply inland in Northamptonshire; and though there was a station called Bannaventa on the Roman Watling Street, a few miles from Daventry, it was not the only possible Bannaventa. And as for prob-abilities? Would the Irish raiders have to penetrate so far inland for booty and prey? Why take the risk of being cut off by the garrisons of many a camp between them and their return to the sea? For instance, one, Deva (Chester), where the XXth Legion was. And what would have become of " *tot milia hominum*," all those thousands of prisoners, after the first nightfall? Unless they were tethered they would have made off. They knew the lie of the land. To the mind of Bury of Trinity College, Dublin, Daventry won't do. It is true that Nial, the sea-king, razed Chester, Cearleon, Wroxeter, and Cearwent in the year 395 (destruction was his badge), ten years before the capture of Patrick. But this does not mean that all the survivors could be driven into a huddle as far inland as the little Town of the Road House near Daventry. The resources of Roman civilisation were not at so low an ebb as that. Daventry's Bannavem Taberniæ will not do. And here is a reason of my own (and do not disregard it though it appear facetious): " What would—to use an expressive Irish construction—thousands of people be doing with only one tavern?" I must confess that my peregrinations did not lead me to Daventry.

But here I am at the Roman Wall. I am at the western end of it, and I am in the fifth century. And backwards to older times still, I make my mind a citizen of that Age of Gold when the sword yielded to the shovel and the limits of Empire were set, for all men to see, in another and greater wall, the first double dyke and wall (fence), fourteen feet high and eight feet thick, between what is Scotland now and what was civilisation then. This the Senate and the Roman people who were Publius Ælius Hadrianus decreed. The Roman Empire desired to expand no more. Its limits were set. The *Pax Romana* blessed the universal and

civilised world. The Golden Pomp had come. It
was high noon! That was in the year 122. How
far have we, in 405, fallen from the Roman *lux
perpetua*? The life of a Roman citizen on the out-
posts of Empire now is anything but secure. Aye,
even in most of the " five Britains " life is unassured.
The shorter, more northern Aurelian Wall which
Septimus Severus strengthened by stone has been
abandoned for 225 years. The Picts pass over it;
while behind it, from the sea, raiders harass the
Empire's western coast. Nothing is secure.

Things were better and life was fairer in accomplished Hadrian's day, that Emperor who, in spite of
his Roman *gravitas*, could be gentle and gay and turn
a lyric (Herrick-like) with the best. All the world
knew that pleasant poem of his, so sweetly and so
lightly poignant—his address to his departing soul.
Presumptuous would he be who would try to translate
it! It cannot be translated. I, who am still in the
fifth century, need no translation; but for those who
will not follow, or whom I am unable to bring with
me into St. Patrick's period, I will try to convey its
meaning. In spite of my affected modesty, I might
have known that I would be unable to resist attempts
at a translation. That better men had been at it
before only eggs me on. Thus I while away the time
journeying through Valentia and falling back on the
comparative security of Hadrian's Wall.

He was a great fellow, Hadrian. He had the in-
defatigable Roman virtues, the manhood and the
capacity at all times and in all places to play the

man. He marched with his men, 20,000 Roman
miles, they say. He hunted with the best. He was
at heart an Hellene, and his mind was open, liberal,
and unprejudiced. And, like a Roman, he faced
death without this latter-day and outlandish fear of
ours. But what endears him to me is his skill with
the lyric. Who can beat (outside Chinese poetry)
the tenderness and terseness of this address to his
poor little soul? It may for all I know be touched
with a little cynicism and a little irony at the expense
of the soul. Here it is once again, though most
people know it. I like to see even the shape of its
lines and letters in print.

> Animula, blandula, vagula,
> Hospes comesque corporis;
> Quæ nunc abibis in loca?
> Pallidula, rigida, nudula,
> Nec ut soles dabis joces.

We would have to go to the French for such a series
of diminutives. We cannot call the soul a " sprite "
or a goblin, but something between these is his meaning. And " kindly little leprechaun " would not be
understood outside Ireland.

But just because I am proving to myself and perhaps
to others, that it is untranslatable, I am caught by the
" fascination of what's difficult "; and here I try,
failing of course, but clearing the mind meanwhile
from its undischarged " creative stress."

No; after all I will not step in with my translation.
It has been done much better 100 years ago and by a
Dublin man. He succeeded in spite of the scarcity
of diminutives in the language and he had a great

understanding of the original. Look at the essential artistry : he is not afraid to repeat " shiv'ring " to get the necessary shrinkage, so to speak, and the uncertain movement.

THE EMPEROR HADRIAN TO HIS SOUL

Poor, gentle, wavering thing,
The body's friend and guest ;
You fly from that to which you'd cling,
Scar'd from the flutt'ring breast.

Poor, paly, shiv'ring sprite,
You leave the shivering frame ;
Say whither now thy cheerless flight ?
Your wonted mirth is tame.

M. GORDON, 1836.

I could never equal that simplicity.

But still it fails to equal the Emperor who, in his directness and his lightness, can be so carefree as to make us, even us whom Eternity stalks while noting our idlest words and most thoughtless actions, envious of his unequivocal Roman despair.

The hopeless and splendid Roman resignation of it all !

He built a wall between Rome and Scotland. What was on the farther side of it, and what " goings on " took place between 122 and 142, between the seventy-mile-long wall and the dyked isthmus of the Clyde and the Forth ? The era of conquest had not ceased after all. Punitive expeditions wear out an Empire's patience, and either a " clean up " took place or " representations " were made by the peoples dwelling on the Border to the acting Commander-in-Chief to save them from forays and to bring them within the vigilance of the Eagles. Camp followers, traders, and sergeants' wives had made a kind of colony at the end of the civilised world on the shore where the Firth of Clyde meets the river's mouth.

In his letter to the soldiers of Coroticus, one of those half-tolerated petty tyrants who crowed loudest when the legions were farthest, Patrick writes as one who did not know the country as one would know one's home. The argument that Nemthur means " holy tower " erected in honour of St. Patrick at Strathclyde, cannot have held before the slave became saint. It is retrospective history, and the name crops up again, as we shall see. It shall have become a lighthouse, a " tower of the skies," when we meet it again, and the young man's father a lighthouse-keeper! Place not your trust in derivations. But look at the first lines of the Life in the Book of Armagh, lines which have no regard for orthography in the way they divide words, and wonder if Nemthur be anything more than a running together of the last syllable of bannanem and the first syllable of Thurburindæ. If this be so, it will explain why " Nemthur " is so puzzling to scholars and so hard to locate. The most obvious derivations are sometimes the most incorrect. It is as if one were to take it that his name defined and circumscribed himself and that he were christened at maturity, that you got your name only after you had begun to show your form, as it were. I am called Oliver, but I was called that before I had any chance of hawking olives, even if I could earn my name by that activity.

In spite of good opinion—and we have to go against eminent opinions when it comes to scholarship, though we have not to overcome such sound sense in some of our scholars as we should have to do were we dealing with a man of the calibre of Professor Hotson—in spite of good and, what makes it more difficult, eminent opinion, the Plain of the Tents by the River Mouth, the great plain occupied by the Roman camp at the junction of the Leven and the Clyde, won't do for Patrick's birthplace. Why? If we are not to fly in the face of the little history we have, because it was not far from " our sea." It was on the sea, and that estuary could hardly be called " our sea." Added to this, Strathclyde had a Patrician legend later on of its own, due no doubt to Vikings who had received their Christianity in Ireland. Even after their Ulster cousins were baptised the Picts were at the murder game, the raping, and the slave-trafficking. They had nothing to offer to civilisation. They darkened the face of the earth where they dwelt. They were not gentle men in any sense, and Patrick was well-bred. Strathclyde won't do it: it's too near the forests of the Black North. And who would have thought of building a villa there? It was no place for a Christian. Christianity connoted Rome. I abandon Dumbarton and its two-peaked hill.

In view of Patrick's own statement, it is a waste of time to explore the claim of Boulogne. The great Archbishop Healy describes the supporters of its claim as " giving loose reins to their speculations as to the birthplace of St. Patrick." An impression of confusion may be left on the mind of the reader by the perusal of one of these speculations ; nevertheless, I will offer this as a sample :

It seems generally agreed that the point of the coast which was signalised by the ridiculous bravado of Caligula, somewhat redeemed by the erection of a lighthouse, was Itium (Iccium), afterwards called Gessoriacum, and Bonia (Boulogne), a town belonging to the Gaulish tribe of the Morini, where Julius Cæsar embarked on his expedition, and which became the usual place of departure for visitors to Britain.

(The name " Iccium " (Itium) here recalls the " Sea of Icht " mentioned by the old writers.)

The high level of " Tour d'Ordre " was the one place in the neighbourhood suitable for a Roman encampment, " for the valley of the Liane and all the hills on either side were covered with extensive woods," whilst the sea and river united in submerging all the present lower town of Boulogne, flowing onward " into the Valley of Tintelleries and the Vale of St. Martin."

It is evident, therefore, that this town was one of the principal military and naval stations of the Romans, and might well be called " Tabernaculorum Campus," a military phrase indicating a place where the Roman legions were wont to camp. Consequently, those luminaries who have interpreted the word " Taberniæ " as " Campus Tabernaculorum," or field of tents, because it denotes a Roman encampment, are, if we limit them to the interpretation of the word, just as favourable to the Boulogne theory of Patrick's birthplace as Dr. Lanigan himself, who holds that the word " Taberniæ " denotes that Boulogne was included in the district of Tarvenna, Terouanne, which was the capital city of the Morini; but either interpretation of the word " Taberniæ " points to Boulogne as St. Patrick's native town.

Now, St. Fiacc tells us " Patrick was born in Nemthur." " Neam " and " Thur " are two Irish words which signify " a heavenly or high tower." The high level of the northeastern cliffs of Boulogne is called, even at the present day, " Tour d'Ordre," receiving its name from the " Turris Ordinis," a tower built on this lofty plateau by Caligula, but no longer existing. We are therefore free to interpret the words of Fiacc as referring to the district in which the tower once stood. Patrick was living at his father's villa (a country seat) in the suburban district of Boulogne, and Fiacc may be understood as giving us the very name of this district when he calls the place of Patrick's birth "Nemthur," or the district where the "high or heavenly tower" was situated—in other words, the district of "Tour d'Ordre" or "Turris Ordinis," on the north-eastern cliffs outside the town. We find, moreover, in this very same region, the modern Tournehm (Nemthur reversed). This place is a few miles from Boulogne. It was one of Cæsar's quarters-general when he was preparing to invade Britain, and in later centuries was a stronghold of the Dukes of Burgundy.

"Tournehm (Nemthur reversed)!"

Hitherto I have been trying to preserve myself and my readers from the ardours of scholarship, particularly that scholarship which overtakes and contradicts itself. But we must take notice of the claimant's claim. Dr. Healy has done it to some extent, by showing the discrepancy in the dates of the names. Let St. Patrick himself repudiate Boulogne and "all Gaul" as his birthplace by these words from his Testimony or Confession :

> Proceeding to the Britains—and glad and ready I was to do so—as to my fatherland and kindred, and not that only but to go as far as Gaul in order to visit the brethren and to behold the face of the saints of my Lord.

The distinction made here between his fatherland and Gaul is one of the most definite statements we can find in the only documents that matter, those which Patrick himself has written and which give us Patrick's own words. How we regret that he did not add a few words more, such as " proceeding to the Britains *to my home in* . . ."! We should have known then what place to venerate as the birthplace of one of the world's great figures. He did not; so we must for the present rest content with the knowledge that his home was *not* in Gaul.

I know Boulogne; but it knows nothing of Patrick, even though it is supposed that he may have landed there with those mysterious mariners who traded in wolfhounds. He must have recounted to his disciples many times that escape by sea, and told of where he landed. And they, after his glory had been established, must have named the harbour that was made after three days' voyaging from the Wicklow coast. Yet Boulogne has no trace left of any fame of this kind. Boulogne is as far out of all likelihood of being the birthplace of Patrick as it is of being the port of disembarkation of that mysterious and intriguing crew. But if Boulogne be improbable, what about Spain? And yet . . . Let me quote Archbishop Healy's words:

> Dr. O'Brien, emeritus professor of Maynooth College, goes all the way to Spain to find out where St. Patrick was born. Dr. O'Brien had stated that Patrick was a native of a Greek-speaking town, Emporium, in Spain. He has certainly the merit of discovering a new theory—but hardly anything else. We cannot admit that there is any ground for identifying the places mentioned in the *Confession* with the Spanish localities to which Dr. O'Brien has transferred them. No solid argument can be based on fanciful similarities between the names in question. And there is no other reason adduced to prove the thesis of the learned writer.

Emporium did not call me. In spite of all our

immemorial connections with Spain, we may take it for certain that it is not to that land we may look for one who led our nation out of bondage.

It was hardly in a Greek-speaking town that St. Patrick learned to read and speak that Latin of his which Stephen Gwynn (and it is to the Gwynn family that historians of the Saint must be for ever indebted) describes as being full of vigour and sap— a Latin which he spoke thickened with the Gaelic gutturals that turned "*gratias agamus*" into *grās agam*, and may to this day be heard in Cornwall in the expression *numinny duminny*, used as an exclamation for "*in nomine Domini.*"

Since I dismiss Dumbarton and its citadel from likelihood of being Patrick's home, let me buttress up my decision by one better qualified to express an opinion on the time and place than I. This is what Professor Bury wrote in 1905, when his standard work appeared. With it, simultaneously, the larger and more detailed work of Dr. Healy saw the light.

To the layman Bury may be recommended in the words of one who writes of him as a " great scholar bred in Ireland but standing aloof from all creeds and parties." In Ireland that is one way of calling a man an agnostic. But Bury was an atheist, as I discovered when I studied under him and found that he preferred Bacchylides to Pindar, the nightly guest-friend of the god! However, that is an aside. The suggestion in the statement of his aloofness from all creeds is that he had no axe to grind. The paradoxical idea that no one can hold a fair or detached view of another until he disbelieves in him and his creed, must be indigenous. On the understanding that I do not subscribe to this notion, I will give you our aloof scholar's reasons why Alcluith could not be the home of Patrick. Here are his words :

The glossator in the oldest (eleventh-century) MS. of the Hymn of Fiacc identified a misprint comparable to Nemthur with Ath Cluade, the Rock of Clyde at Dumbarton. We are ignorant of his authority for this statement, which does not appear in any earlier source. The fact, however, that it is not consistent with the direct statements of earlier sources has procured credence for it. But it is inconsistent with the probabilities of the case. Patrick's father was a *decurion* and he must have lived in civilised Britain. We have no evidence that there were Roman towns with municipal constitutions in Strathclyde. The truth is that North Britain was little more than a large military frontier. It is generally supposed that Theodosius, in A.D. 369, restored Roman rule which had fallen back in the north as far as the wall of Antonine, and that the district which he recovered (*recuperata provincia*, Ammianus, 28.3.7) and which was named Valentia (by Valentinian in compliment to his brother Valens) included the country between the walls of Hadrian and Antonine. The supposition that it was in the north and that Theodosius restored fortresses as far as the line of the northern wall is, however, not improbable. But there is no probability that it was colonised or became in the last half-century of Roman rule anything more than a military district. The Rock of Clyde at the extreme end of the northern wall is the last place we should expect to find the villula of a Roman *decurion*; and the opinion that the home of Calpurnius was in the remote spot cannot be accepted without better evidence than an anonymous statement which we cannot trace to any trustworthy source. Nevertheless, in the absence of any trace of a Bannaventa (or a Nemthur) in North British regions we must, I think, give decisive

weight to the general probabilities of the case and suppose
that Bannaventa was south of the wall of Hadrian, somewhere in western Britain not very far from the coast.

There is an additional reason, and it is this : the
relations between the men of Ulster and the men of
Alba were friendly in 405. Raids were things of the
past, as the fleet of eighty trading curraghs owned by
Breccan, Nial's grandson, testifies. It was not until
Coroticus, taking advantage of the toleration of
Rome by raiding the just-Christianised stronghold of
Dalaradia, that the friendly relations between Dalaradia
and Scotland were broken.

And that is why I, too, abandoned Dumbarton and
journeyed along the western coast of Britain, south of
the long Wall, until I took " Severn " for " Tabern,"
as Professor Windle did. But there will be time
enough to tell what I found there when we shall have
seen a raid in progress.

CHAPTER VI

"WE WERE MASTERS OF THE SEA"

ABOUT THE MIDDLE OF THE YEAR 405 A GREAT HOSTING of ships was ordered by King Nial. It was probably the strongest sea force that he had commanded since the year 395, when he is said to have destroyed five towns on the west coast of Britain. With him was his grudging ally, the King of Leinster. So great a force was it that we read of " hired " ships. All along I have imagined that native shipyards were not indispensable to sea-power in the fifth century. And this conjecture was confirmed when I read in Dr. Healy's great Life of " hired ships."

Tradition says that Nial advanced with his army along the banks of the Loire. This is more likely than that he should have coasted the Gallic coast to the narrows between what are now Dover and Boulogne. There was a Roman patrol posted here and visibility from the white cliffs might have brought all such available sea-power as was left, hurrying out from the British harbours along the south coast. Continuous was the transport traffic with the continent.

The hosting of the ships proceeded. Those coming south from Strangford joined the Leinster and other auxiliary kings along the coast before setting a course south-west. We shall never know the details of tha sailing, but we read that Nial was slain with an arrow in the Ictian Sea—that is, the English Channel—by the King of Leinster. It gives some notion of the strength of the respective forces if we imagine that the act was deliberate, or of the trust that the Leinster king put in what were probably his mercenary sailors and hired oarsmen, if he shot the High King and depended for safety on flight. But with the tendency to confuse Gaul with Britain, or more properly the Britains—for there were five divisions of Britain, and Patrick always writes of them in the plural, " when I went to the Britains "—it may well be that Nial fell, like another king long after him, from a glancing arrow, in the Ictian Sea south of what is now the New Forest. We must either regard the act as deliberate, in which case we must allow for the breaking up of the allied fleets, of which there is no evidence, or take the view that " a regrettable accident " occurred. This is more in character with Irish murders. There is no one immediately to be brought to book; yet, though all regret " this tragic " deed, nevertheless a person undesirable to one party or another is " removed."

This is what very likely occurred: Nial's death at the hands of one of his own countrymen was probably made to appear accidental enough to maintain the union of the fleets. But his son Leary, who succeeded him in 428 after the reign of his father's nephew and his own first cousin Dathi, gave as one of his reasons for not accepting Christianity that he desired to be buried as were his fathers before him, upright, armed, facing the Leinster-men. Evidently he did not like that aimless bowman, the King of Leinster.

But I am more concerned with the return of the fleet than with its sailing. Whoever took command could not escape from the problem of how on its return to soften the anger of the populace. Those left ashore are often over-critical of naval actions, whether from subconscious envy of the men who go down to the sea in ships and battle with the elements as well as with the enemy, or from ignorance of the vicissitudes to which those who manage warships are exposed. The fact remains that a leaderless fleet of empty-handed raiders is not likely to get a good welcome home.

The subjects of his fourteen royal sons will probably "demonstrate," and perhaps, seeing the times we are in, with force. "Why was Dathi brought to Cruch-aun? And what is wrong with Nial?" I am trying to recreate the picture of a fleet of sea-kings returning with their High King and Admiral dead, some two years before they wreaked revenge for their ill-luck in "the third devastation" of the Britains. "Nial is dead. We must distract attention by coming back loaded to the gunwales with booty and with slaves." That is the way I would commune with myself had I to return to Northern Ireland, where words are subordinated to results. A matter-of-fact people will bury sentiment in gain.

If I were "up against it," I would command the fleets to coast along some part of Western Britain, the inhabitants of which had been left alone long enough to gather confidence and to multiply without protection —though "protection" would have availed little against the breed that had razed "The Camp of the Legions" (Cearleon) itself and four other towns ten years before. But protection might at least have meant that look-outs would be posted and a watch

E

kept on the western and south-western horizon for a
sinister sail.   Therefore—for we are more or less in
a hurry back—let us raid some place which will not
deflect us too much or need a long inland excursion,
and will yet give good results—a place that may be
approached in daylight and yet be taken by surprise.
The Cornish coast is inhospitable, and it would be
hard to embark prisoners ; besides, they are neither
many nor prosperous folk along that line of fishing
villages.   And the worst part is its north-western coast.
We must stand off that coast on our way back.

What about the Bristol Channel ?   Well, we are
too well known there already, and that hunting-ground
has been spoiled by vagrant pirates, *Scoti per diversa
vagantes*, unauthorised expeditions—in fact, petty
raiders.   Besides, the only town worth raiding is far up
the river, and there is the Severn bore, which drags
the anchors of ships.   From two sides we can be kept
under strict observation for hours.   And hours could
give the civilians time to absent themselves from town
or from the coastwise villages.   That forest on the
north of the estuary would take months to scour, and
the marshes behind Bath (*Aquæ Sulis*)—no, let us
leave out an eastern diversion of the fleet up the Severn
against tide and stream, and think of some other place
more on our course.   And if possible one that has not
been skinned already by Irregulars.   It is hard to tell
where to go, but some place must be found a raid on
which may assuage the anger and vent the grumbling of
the men of war.   In that way, I imagine, I would
reason if I had the responsibility on my shoulders as

he had who steered home with his dead king on board
the archetypal flagship.   But there was much more
by him to be considered.   One of the difficulties—
nay, impossibilities—for one trying to get back to a
vanished century is fully to realise and to present to his
friends what the background was of the mind of a fifth-
century Ulster sea captain.   It would be bad enough
to come back defeated, or from an abortive foray,
but with a dead king!   He would have the Druids to
face, and, little as we know of them, we know enough
to rest assured that they were the makers of public
opinion: they were soothsayers, historians, poets
and publicity all in one.   They largely decided on
the successor to the throne and they officiated at all
coronations.   In a floating hearse it was more than
ever necessary not to return empty-handed.

I have an idea as to where the captain put in and
where the raids occurred.   I know where I would have
put in, for I did put in to the very spot, and learned
enough there to make me presume that it was the place
from whence Patrick was taken.   As I said, I came to
a decision in a preceding chapter about the birthplace,
but so many others have come to decisions, at all
events to their own satisfaction, that it is only fair to
give them a hearing and to examine localities they
indicate.   Daventry is much too far inland ; and Spain's
Greek-speaking port!   But I have still to explore
Bath, since the Rev. S. Malone has assured us that
" with the evidence before us we cannot avoid con-
necting the particular spot of his birth with Bath on
the banks of the middle Avon."   So I go to Bath, to

the *Aquæ Sulis* of the Romans, to the world's most famous medicinal spring. This is the *Udata Therma* of Ptolemy and the Akemanceaster of the Saxons. It was presided over by the goddess Sul. The remains of a large temple to Sul-Minerva still stand.

Don't let me appear to be unfair to Bath, but I knew before I went that I might just as well interrogate some of its steatopygnous lady visitors (Sul, the presiding deity of Bath was a goddess) or one of the overblown goldfish that float heavily, "taking the waters," as any-one else, concerning a boy called Patrick taken captive in a raid 1532 years ago that never took place in it. It remained for the Saxons to destroy it about 150 years after the sailing of King Nial. So his merry men never took the waters or anything else from Bath.

I was not disappointed, for I found what may well be the work of a Celtic artist—the head of the Gorgon, which is reputed to be the finest example of work in stone north of Rome. It represents the free work of an artist who carved in stone before Rome had suc-ceeded in Woolworthising all native Celtic art. This head is all the more frightfully efficient because it has the Wester Island sincerity and freedom of the Celt.

The legends of Bath concern not the saint, but the Bucks and Beaux. It may have been Bannavem, but I cannot imagine the clerical parents of Patrick living at such a salubrious and famous resort, only to be described cursorily by their pro-Roman son as a villa-dwellers who had a farm hard by. Besides, Bath, or for that matter Bristol, can hardly be described, nor the Severn itself, as " not far from our sea." Some-

where directly by or actually on St. George's Channel
is indicated. The joint editors of the Brehon laws,
Messrs. Handcock and O'Mahony, without any
argument to support it, make Bristol the scene of the
Saint's birth. Now, Bristol is a delightful town.
Even if it were never credited with being a saint's home
town, it is well worth a visit on other counts. Its
shipping seems to be in its streets, and it is the end of
England and the beginning of Wales : this turned
out luckily for me, as I shall presently record.

I did not make the mistake, when seeking traditions
of Patrick, of asking in the hotels. " Just try the
Inquiry Bureau "—that is what would be the result.
But down at the docks—that is where the coastwise
men are to be found.

It was already evening when I arrived from Bath.
That was no disadvantage, for the sailors would not be
free to go to the tabernæ until nearly the fall of night.

They were not inclined to be talkative—that is, at
first—but taciturnity is not irremediable in a pub.
Some suspicion seemed to be afloat. Was it my pince-
nez ? I took it off. And with that some of my
inquisitiveness appeared to be dissipated. After
mentioning the Saint's name three or four times and
having it bandied about in mutual inquiries, which I
could not stop, the awful thought began to dawn on
me that I was being considered as some kind of an
evangelist interested in a Revival or something of the
sort. I mentioned St. David, the Welsh patron, but
that was unconvincing. Was it the Salvation Army
to which they accredited me ? Hastily, to anticipate

their just resentment born of an unjust suspicion, I told them the story of Bluffer Duff who joined up. He was preaching one Sunday and repudiating his former life, though it had almost excused itself :

" And I who could run a hundred yards in ten seconds——"

An interrupter : " And be stiffened for half-a-crown."

"——was slowly but surely dragged down by DRINK. It dragged me down until I was down-and-out. Just as I was beginning to despair the Salvation Army opened its arms. That was two years ago ; and I haven't touched a drop of drink since."

And so confidence was restored. But for all that there was neither legend nor any trace of a tradition to be found in Bristol.

It may have been a pilot who followed me out :

" That saint's stuff has no interest for me, and if it had, it's not in a pub I would be talking about it. . . . But, listen. Go you up Milford Haven way and ask a few of your questions at Haverfordwest."

Milford Haven, Haverfordwest : Scandinavian names, I thought. And if Norsemen raided and settled there, they were only imitating those masters of piracy who preceded them by four hundred years or so.

" No ; it's not in a pub." He adjusted his bowler.

" Not in a pub." I stand rebuked ; yet, after all, it's not at the railway station or a petrol station that I could expect to find folk-lore. And was it not out of a pub this tip came to me ?

" Go you up."

" Listen," I begged.

But the square-cut figure in the reefer jacket stood set in disapprobation and I saw " a writing void of honour (to use one of Patrick's telling expressions) against my face." My hand was still tingling from his grasp. So we must have parted more or less friends.

It was perhaps just as well that I did not expose my ignorance of the etiquette of the Channel—that is, the Bristol Channel (not necessarily " our sea ")—by inviting him to take me as a coasting-passenger along the banks of the Severn. It meant that the " South Wales " theory would have to go by the board, if all I had was a disgruntled pilot who seemingly had more respect for tradition than I myself; " Saint's stuff " was very near to him. I had offended by my in-gratiating attempt at being all things to all men in an endeavour to find some local memory of far-off things and rapine long ago. " It's not in a pub I would be talking of it." Could this mean that the Bristol Methodists had as sensitive a jealousy about St. Patrick as we have in Ireland? If so, where was the place? " It's not in a pub." Bannavem Taberniæ! But can he help me? I always suspect the shallow-ness of those who express themselves by a certain amount of aggressiveness. Their squareness is hollow.

I will go to Haverfordwest. But not by Milford Haven. By the morning train. It would be easy to call on my friend Thomas, Director of the great Bristol Aeroplane Company, or on that—hero is the

word—Uwins, who broke his neck in a crash in the
Great War, and broke the world's record for altitude
twenty years afterwards, and ask them to flip me over
the Bristol Channel, as they have often done in days
gone by, so that I might get the lie of the land from
the air.

CHAPTER VII

SURELY IT WAS HERE?

WHAT IS IT CONSTITUTES THE *GENIUS LOCI*, AS THEY WHO had time to ponder reverently over words until they could make, as Patrick says, "their meaning plain in few words"—an excellent summation, by the way, of the classical style—and give to airy nothing a local habitation and a name, called the faint influence which emanates from the very soil of certain spots and affects the visitor according to his sensitiveness ? The gloom of a Druids' wood, or of a dark lake out of reach of the sun—this would affect even a rate-collector ; but there is a gentler genius—a power which breathes in the open fields in the broad noonday in lands where minds have dreamt and men have moved from time immemorial ; a soul that haunts the Celtic lands, older than the yew and ever-green as the ivy which never fades. I felt this gentle influence about me as I walked in Wales from Haverfordwest towards the sea, fifteen miles away. Warm valley after valley opened and closed, revealing their hedgerows and little streams. There are few places that can influence me like this. Sussex could not, nor Northumberland ; minds ancestral to mine dwelt here. How like Ireland it is ! I thought ; most like Wicklow of all our counties, with its warm, light soil pillared by Ogham stones.

I was on my way to Brawdy Church to see stones which for want of a museum are kept in its porch. Ogham stones in Wales ! Assuredly, for this part of Wales was Ireland in the fifth century, and represented

73

Ireland in any equilibrium it had with the Roman Empire. What is more, this country was Christian before Ireland : Christian, probably, for two hundred years before St. Patrick. And it feels like Ireland now in its atmosphere, which is mild and somewhat enervating to those who are not native to the place. Even the people have an Irish way about them, which comes out all the stronger when one has an opportunity of contrasting them with English visitors to their delightful bays. I must say that I like the Welsh. Their men and women are so charming that you never know what may happen. But you may be sure that it will.

One thing that is not present-day Irish about the Welsh is their contentment. When I met Tom John, or rather Moses John, his father—I met him in the boreen that led to his grand old farm-house called Tygwyn, with its great recessed fireplace and chimney opening straight up to the sky (young John was " scraping " at the time)—I met a Connemara farmer in all but poverty and discontent. The John household was prosperous, and, what is more, it was contented and happy. When young John appeared after his shaving, he came stripped to the waist (an oar had marked him under the left breast, for he had been rescuing the crew of a stranded ship some nights before), and he undertook with a smile to tell me all he knew about the traditions and legends of St. David's. I asked him, was the farm-land good ?

" It will raise anything."

I thought of the corn that this part of Britain used to send to the legions in Gaul.

" Will it fatten cattle ? "

" Indeed it will.   It will do anything."

It was then I realised that I was not, for all the similarity of the scene to more western sands and bays, talking to a Connemara man.   The emphasis in his sentences seemed to be unconnected with the meaning. And there was a certain lilt in his speech which was not harmonious.   But there was no disharmony about the pig which snored at his farmhouse door.

So this land could have supported many people, from its shores back eastward to the haven of Milford— " *tot milia hominum* "—in affluence.   Even the ten square miles around St. David's could contain them. But I was waiting for the local legends to appear; I would not lead with any questions.

" Have you seen the place yet ? "

" A little," I said.

" You should climb up to the Head and see the view. If it wasn't for the heat mist you might see Ireland. You should see the Druids' circles and St. Patrick's Chair——"

" St. Patrick's Chair ? "

"Aye—where he sat looking out to sea and was shown the promised land, Ireland, and was told that someone would come after him to take his place—St. David."

I dared not interrupt the narration to ask, " Told by whom ? "

" And there is St. Patrick's Chapel and St. Patrick's Well; it never ran dry.   It is above the harbour at Porthclais, but they bricked it over.   It's where he was baptised."

Porthclais, a narrow, winding creek into which the river Alan flows (thus making a " bun," *i.e.* an estuary as in Bun Owen) and which could shelter ten or twelve coasting vessels with its very ancient pier.

" Where is the Chapel ? "

" Just here by the sands.   Come along."

On the edge of the land, the nearest place of all that was Roman to Ireland, I saw the buried remains of a chapel, some thirty feet by twelve.   Four stones marked its corners and the walls were about three feet high.   It had been unearthed and was found to be built of unmortared stones.   This site was visited regularly by visitors of many denominations.   Clergymen held services within its ruins.   To preserve it, it was earthed up again.

I stood on the site of that ancient chapel thinking that, though it was retrospective history, this Chapel, Chair and Well made local legend deeply rooted. How came it that a chapel was dedicated to the saintly apostle to another land ?   I must get the ideas clear in my mind.   First of all, Wales, as I have said, was not so very different from Ireland ; secondly, the fame of St. Patrick's success, spreading at a time when there was a cessation of raids, may have been increased by the attribution of that peace to his teaching ; thirdly, many of the survivors of the frightful foray must have remembered the very spot whence the Saint was taken as a boy, and the tradition held until it was consecrated by this little shrine.   At any rate, I had found what I had come to find : local legend in the mouths of the

people and sermons in stones.   Legend enough there
was in books :

> It will be interesting to consider the evidence for and
> against the attribution of the chapel to St. Patrick.   So far
> as has been ascertained, the earliest evidence in favour of the
> claim is contained in Brown Willis's survey, printed in 1717,
> in which he says, " Not far off (from Capel Stinan) is Capel
> Patric full west of St. David's and placed as near his country,
> namely Ireland, as it could well be.   It is now decayed."
> He was quoting from a manuscript written in the latter end
> of Queen Elizabeth's reign, probably by George Owen.
> " It seems clear that the dedication of the chapel to St.
> Patrick rests solely on tradition."   According to George
> Owen, St. Patrick founded a monastery at St. David's, out
> of which was afterwards founded the cathedral church there.

Of course it was from tradition that all this history
came.   And here was the tradition in the living mouth
—a tradition that threw a new light on history.   It
accounted for some of the unrecorded activities of St.
Patrick when he went to Wales to visit his relatives,
who tried in vain to persuade him, filled as he was then
with the ardour of his mission, never again to leave them
after all his trials.   May he not have founded or found an
early church in the land of his birth before returning to
Auxerre ? Whence came the oldest diocese in Great
Britain but from a chapel which grew into the great
cathedral in the year 1000 ?   A cathedral presupposes
a congregation, and a congregation presupposes a road.
If I could find traditions of Roman occupation !

" There was a camp of the Romans."   Tom John
pointed up the hillside.   But it was a circular foundation I saw.   Not Roman surely, but Celtic.   I knew
that the Roman road skirted Cardigan Bay as it came

from the north.   It must have led somewhere.   And if
it led to Demetia, which was what the Romans called
St. David's, it must have come out here.   I passed the
circular camp, telling myself that after the gigantic
raid, reinforcements, or rather forces, were rushed up
from Castel Flemming in the true manner of Empire,
to lock the stable door after the steed was stolen, and
they availed themselves of the strongest ready-made
place.   But had I found on the very shore of the bay
beside the site of St. Patrick's Chapel, about a hundred
yards to the south, the traditional site of Menapia, a
Roman station, which may have held little more than
the garrison of a Martello tower, or have been an
outpost of Maridunum (Carmarthen), over thirty
miles away ?   If so, there must be a Roman road.   I
found one marked on a local map.

Now, if tradition is of any worth where history is
faint or deficient, the tradition of a Roman camp and
road leads me to expect that the population which
could support a monastery, and afterwards build a
cathedral, may have formed (even if we insist upon it,
as does Bury) a *municipium*, or at any rate a village large
enough for a few councillors (*decurions*).   It is unnecessary to postulate a village, because Bury has
already taught me that the taking of Orders exempted
a *decurion* presumably from the site of his business in
favour of his sanctuary.   And sanctuary we have, and
it still flourishes mightily at St. David's.

But I postulated the possibility of surprise as indispensable to the capture of so many people dwelling
near the pirate-infested coast.   Even if there were no

ocular evidence that there was a wood in front of the
building by the shore—a wood the remains of which
are visible at low water—and a tradition that Cardigan
Bay was submerged as late as the middle of the sixth
century, another feature of the place which would
enable raiders secretly to approach exists at Solva Bay.

Were it not for the fact that historically the birthplace of St. Patrick is a No-man's Land, I would not
allow conjecture rein enough to outrun the scholars who
favour " the South Wales theory " to the extent of
giving a " local habitation and a name " to the region
of his birth, or, at least, of his capture. Let me confess the premises I have begged. I put forward the
suggestion that it was a fleet of Nial of the Nine
Hostages which captured Patrick in the year of that King's
death at sea, 405, and presumed it to be possible that the
raid took place on the return journey of the fleet rather
than on its outgoing. I do not think that, consciously or
unconsciously, I have asked the reader to concede more
than that. Many scholars agree in naming Nial as
the raider, and many, too, agree with the conjecture
that the scene was " in the region of the lower
Severn." Having tramped these regions with the
results set out, I came to rest in the one place in the
neighbourhood where there is not only a living tradition
but also witnesses in stone to testify to the Saint's
having dwelt in and been venerated in St. David's.
And from this he was taken in a raid. That is the
reason why, deliberately yet tentatively, the first line of
this book links St. Patrick with St. David and couples
both their names with St. George.

CHAPTER VIII

THE ROAD TO SLEMISH

EVEN SO THEN THICK AND FAST FROM THE SHIPS WERE borne the helms bright-gleaming and the bossed shields, the corslets with massive plates, and the ashen spears. And the gleam thereof went up to heaven, and all the earth round about laughed by reason of the flashing bronze ; and there went up a din from beneath the feet of men.

That was how the Greeks sallied from their beached ships. It is all very well for Homer in retrospect to describe, and to take delight in describing, the glory of warriors landing on the laughing earth. Even long after Homer, Sappho's fairest and most favoured sight is a troop of Lydian horsemen. These old poets verily loved the colour and the pageantry and chivalry of war. There is always something happy about the battles in Homer. But a landing of fifth-century Irish pirates on the coast of Britain was a grimmer and unchivalrous thing.

As the young braves were wading ashore, or jumping overboard if the ship was run in " all standing," the captains warned them to go easy with the killing : only to kill the old men and women and such as were useless for servitude. They told them that the sight of the massacre of their parents would cure hysteria in the young women destined for slavery or for sale " *quasi in lupanar* " on the Continent, and make them docile with despair.

And now the horns roar to the different bands, telling them to close for the great sweep of territory. The braying horns strike terror into the inhabitants of the

DALRIADA

Dun Seburgi
(Dunseverick)

R. Buas
(Bush)

ULIDIA

R. Bann

DALARADIA

Scirit
(Skerry)

R. Braid

Latharna
(Larne)

Cross

Sliabh Miss
(Slemish)

Loch
m Eachach
(Neagh)

Lathrach Patraic
(Glenavy)

Oen-druim

Loch Cuan
(Strangford)

Brecna Strait

ORIEL

AIRTHIR
(ORIOR)

R. Quoile

Rathcolpa

Emain
(Navan)

Ardd Mache
(Armagh)

Dun Lethglasse

Saul
Sabhall

MAGINIS

Brechtan

SLEMISH AND SAUL IN ULIDIA

seaside town. From the highlands to the east they see wildly accoutred men with helmets and spears such as no Roman company uses. Retreat is cut off inland. Even far inland behind the woods the black smoke tells of burning villas. A crowd of screaming women rushes down to the sea. Long boats are cruising round the head filled with spears.

The wild warriors come nearer, and it is seen that before them they drive a crowd of men, some wounded, some with hands bound backwards. These are the first captives, loaded like beasts of burden with their own furniture become now their captors' loot. Young women follow them voluntarily into slavery or whatever fate awaits.

Now the houses are searched and guards lie in wait for the hidden when they shall have broken cover before the flames.

Shouts in a hoarse language that was heard on the Welsh hills for a thousand years before the first word of English, give orders for the bestowal of the captives. They are made to wade out to the rocking ships. Soon they are lost to view, thrown down as they are into the hold for the long voyage to the west. Little children peep timidly from thicket or rocks as their elder brothers and parents are being borne away.

The sun, red as a conflagration, burns behind the blackening boats. In which ship was Patrick, destined to tame and to conquer his captors, or how many captives were with him in it, we shall never know.

Nor shall we know the horrors of the voyage, with men and women huddled together in deckless

F

or half-decked boats, to the slave-market, which was
probably held at the mouth of the Boyne, where the
little bronze statues of Hercules are found indicating
an international market; or inland at Taillteann. Who
can tell of the despair of the journey to the dun of
Milchu? St. Patrick observes a martyr's silence on
his own sufferings and anxieties for his parents and
sisters. How much more poignant were these if the
tale be true that his sisters were taken with him!
He speaks only of his servants' capture, and it is a
relief to hope, after all the centuries, that some woe
was spared to an heroic heart. But that his parents
perished I infer from what would otherwise be an
unfilial act—his delay in returning to Britain after his
escape.

There is no longer need to pinion the captives to
prevent them from casting themselves overboard, for
they have arrived in an open-air prison at the ultimate
lands from which there is no escape. Perhaps I
should let my conjectures rest for a while, but it is
tempting to wonder whether or not his servants were
sold in the same group or lot as himself. Were this
the case, the task of giving them an example of fortitude would have enabled him to lose sight of his own
grievous position. But his statement " *devastaverunt
servos et ancillas domus patris mei* " leaves little ground
on which to build a notion that they were left un-
separated. It causes instead ominous forebodings :
" ruined the servants of my father's house." They
were not with Patrick for comfort, such as it was, or
companionship. He was given by the ferocious man,

his master, the hardest duties to perform. No room in the dun of Milchu for an amanuensis or an architect, nor even for a tutor to his children. These were probably somewhat older than their newly-acquired slave. Sheep on the hill of Slemish and swine in the woods were his care.

To reach this famous hill, which was called Slieve Mis and is now contracted to Slemish, one goes to Ballymena. I went on the 12th July, because I wished to get as near as possible to the mentality of the fifth century. I was in the country of the Picts or Cruithne. Now, these were the people who colonised West Scotland and gave trouble to the garrisons of the Great Wall, for they were terrific fighters. The double and treble redoubts of the Roman forts are witnesses to their prowess. When Rome fell back from the shorter and more northern wall to Hadrian's Wall, the condition of things in the intervening country, though unknown to the historian, may safely be said not to have been civilised. The Picts were pushed into the south-eastern corner of Ulster, but broke from the Highlands into the Lowlands across the north channel of the Irish Sea. These were the strangely tattooed warriors whose dead the Roman general Stilicho paused to examine in the pursuit. They were sent back to Dalaradia from Scotland when Ulster was being planted in the reign of Charles and under the Republic of Cromwell and during the plantation of James. Illiberal notions, and perhaps a change of climate, have made it no longer fashionable to go nakedly depicted, so they wear their colours now outside their clothes; and very beautiful and striking, if somewhat unvaried, I found them: sashes shaped like the stole of a bishop, but coloured a deep yellow, not exactly of the tone of that yellow which Friar John acclaimed as " By St. Pawtrick, the true Irish saffron! " to the discomfiture of Panurge; but an orange dye. Purple stoles or " sashes," as they are called in Dalaradia, provide a sacerdotal note and relieve any monotony which might otherwise arise from the sameness of the more primitive hue.

The Picts were in full war panoply on July 12th, to commemorate a royal legate who, like St. Patrick before him, was confirmed in his mission by the Pope. I saw 80,000 of them in Belfast, including 12,000 who had come from the Lowlands of Scotland, walking interminably, four deep, behind waggonettes in which sat silver-fringed chieftains with bowler hats. These were the Druids. At intervals of sixty yards or so large pictures were borne aloft on poles fitted to a yard-arm, to which the picture was attached. These were pictures of departed chieftains, some who died in their youth or early middle age. However, all looked mature. Here and there banners depicted a warrior with immense greaves or boots of a dark colour, who sat on a white or unpainted horse which was represented as if in motion. But motion was imparted, even to the picture of the gravest and most ancient of these chieftains painted on the banners, by the standard-bearers, who at intervals indulged in a kind of dance or rhythmic motion which invested

what might otherwise have been taken for a grave
ceremonial procession with a Bacchanalian character
in keeping with that of the musicians, who played on
fifes, tin whistles and other wind instruments; some,
too short in the breath, used a wind instrument of a
different kind—a concertina. All these instruments
accompanied the drums, which seemed to be the chief
musical factor of the festival: large drums beaten by
drum-sticks with a ball-like head covered in chamois
hide. One or two of the marchers who had not the
good fortune to possess a drum twirled drum-sticks
with amazing dexterity.

But these were as nothing to the great drums,
which, when they first appeared, struck the beholder
with wonder at the stretch of the sheep-skins with
which they were covered; hides which could only
have come from some enormous sheep. There may
be a breed of sacred sheep somewhere in Dalaradia,
but being a visitor, I forbore to evince curiosity. I
learned, however, that there is a difficult and elaborate
ceremony connected with the preparation of a drum.
The skin has to be treated with whisky over a considerable period before it can give the best results
and enable its imprisoned wind to drown the freer
airs of the fifes.

The great drums were shallow—about a foot in
depth—but in diameter they exceeded three feet.
These were the drums from Lambeg. Lambeg came
to mean these great drums or " Lambegs." They
were lashed with a cane or headless wand by men in
shirt-sleeves, who were seemingly of a lower caste

than the other processionists, for they wore no bowler
hats.   Yet they were the envy of the onlookers, for
theirs, as it were, was the King drum.   They held
sway over the circular dun of their drums, and they
beat the imprisoned wind until it roared and retched
in thunder and bellowed back in rage like Typhon
under Aetna, or as if the old demons of the land had
been caught up, impounded, and battered in the great
circular cell.   Whack!   The Flagellants scourged the
drums and they punished themselves in their frenzy.
Blood flowed and splashed from bleeding wrists and
stained a hand's breadth of the drum where the tendons
of the adept came in contact with the rim.   Boom!
And the jailed giants roared and erupted sound like a
volcano.   Outside, the careless notes of the fifes and
flutes led on.   But the Typhonic thunder of the
drums drowned all.   The fifes wailed like panic-
stricken furies from all this Congo of the drums.
Boom!   Boom!   Blood.   Boom!   The   crowd
cheers.   The waggonettes respond with Druidical
dignity.   No hats are raised.   A halt.   Time marked.
A whistle.   Silence.   The kilted pipers come into
view, cheeks distended, eyes bulging.   Boom!   On
it moves.   For two hours the procession passes.
" No surrender."   It is written on the drum.   " The
Ballymena Boys' Brigade."   Boom!   " The Protestants of Portadown," a particular stronghold.   Boom!
Portadown!   Doon!   Boom!

" Where are they going ? " timidly I venture to
ask a returned Canadian Orangeman.   His silence
was more disconcerting than the battle in the drums.

The great procession again comes to a halt. Under my window are the drums. I am in luck; I can see the faces of the drummers at close range. With heads thrown back and eyes closed they wait, tranced in silence, for the signal to begin. Slowly the great sound is re-awakened. " Wul! Wul! " Drum-taps no more. But the Lambegs are muttering " WUL! WUL! WU! WUL! " then, when the self-mesmerism has worked, challenging, triumphant, bang go the drums!

WULLUM PRINCE OF ORANGE! It is all so very marvellous. They are exalting William and the Battle of the Boyne. Aye, but the sounds of battles long ago are here roaring in the wind, magically caught up, treated by the Water of Life, *usquebagh*, and by incantation and pious memories of the im-memorial past, when the Picts fell on Roman Britain and extinguished the *Lux Æterna* and broke her world-wide Peace. The battle-noises of all time are here: the groans of the dying and the screams of the flying hags that scour the dark, the Choosers of the Slain. Wul! Blood! Boom!

And the winds will return to Cave Hill, the Cave of the Winds, above Belfast, there to be stored up against another Twelfth, another day when the Picts shall threaten Rome.

" Daddy," a little child beside me asked her father as he leant out, rapt, from the window-sill, " what are the men in the big pram doing? " But before he turned, the last waggonette had rolled away.

Well, I knew where they were going or, rather,

where the processionists would be found when the
last speeches in the field of assembly were over.   My
spirit had been mesmerised by the drum.   I yearned
to know more about that wonderful instrument for con-
juring up passion and enthusiasm.   And I was in luck.
As I entered a likely place two Picts were disputing :
    " If a mon is doon, isn't he beat ? "
    " But why should he be doon ? "
    " Because he can't play any more."
    " Why can't he play any more ?   I could drum as
long as I liked."
    " Could ye now ?   Suppose I was playing for
Lambeg and ye were playing for Ballymaccarrit. . . ."
    " How could I be playing for Ballymaccarrit ?
I'm from Darry."
    " Only supposing, only supposing for the sake of
argument."
    " There's no argument about it !   A tell ye I'm
from Darry ! "
    " Well, we'll suppose that I'm playing for Lambeg
and you for Hillsborough—I'll give ye Hillsborough,
where the Prince of Wales drummed, if that will satisfy
ye—and after eight hours or so I had ye down under
yer drum and I played on for half-an-hour, wouldn't
ye be bet ! "

    (" In yonder field, A knight lies slain under his shield.")

    " Why should ye play on for half-an-hour ! "
    " Because I have ye doon and there's not a sound
out of ye, neither stump nor tip, and yer cane's
listless. . . ."

" I'd like to see ye drumming over me . . . ! "

They were kept apart, for it would never do to break the peace of the Twelfth.

Since our speech became articulate, I mused, we have lost, with its deep nuances, the music of the growl, which lost in turn great sonorousness by being divided into words. These men are endeavouring to reach back to those days of innocence and by drumming restore the diapason of Cave Hill.

I had learned something. There were evidently inter-town drumming competitions. And eight hours was about the time the town's hope could go on drumming. They drummed until they fell. Lambeg was the home of the drum, with Ballinmecad an Olympian rival. And the Prince of Wales had been caught just as I had been caught, just as I had been caught by this allure, and he had drummed at Hills-borough—Hillsborough Regis from that on ! He was lucky. I had not his chance. Nor would I be for-given if I had, for I realised that the advantage of the great drums over those which were struck by a drum-stick lay in the variety of the sounds a cane could evoke. There is only one note in a drum-stick, but the cane stump and tip can lend variety to the sounds before they enter the whorled ears. What melodious melodies ! To enter this preserve requires preparation : not suddenly or without hard work, devotion, and a vocation can one play on the big drum. And a vocation to Orangeism is pre-eminently the prerogative of Lambeg or Portadown.

But even these enthusiasts may not have realised

that curative properties are attributed to the drums.
The day before, as I passed through Carrickfergus,
two Picts, one dressed in black, were seated on a
bench.   The sober-suited one had a long, thin, red
neck, on the front of which a prominent Adam's apple
ran up and down at regular intervals as if in sympathy
with his elbow.   He was wrapped in profound gloom,
which his companion tried to dissipate with : " Cheer
up, Geordie.   To-morrow's the Twalfth.   All ye want
is a swish of the auld drum ! "

As I went back through the littered streets there
was not a man to be seen.   The Picts had passed.
The first Catholics in the land were gone.

So went the annual procession of the only civilians
in Ireland who colour themselves on their anniversary.
The Picts had passed.   I thought of that obdurate
man, Milchu, who shut himself up in his dun and
burned it rather than yield to the faith of his one-time
slave.   The first case of " No Surrender " in Dalaradia.
The champion of imperviousness to new ideas.

But what is coming over me ?   As I drew away
from the window and prepared to catch my train, I
felt a strange envy of these Orangemen of the Twelfth.
I envied them their unanimity—even though I thought
of the poet's line :

> Hearts with one purpose alone
>   Through Summer and Winter seem
> Transmuted to a stone,
>   To trouble the living stream.

True, they were obstinate as stones, and they troubled
the living stream of progress, but with what enthusiasm

and zest! It is something to have one purpose, even though it lead nowhere. At least it maintains a *status quo*. And the status these men were maintaining was that of the mentality of Milchu; of the fifth century. One thing at any rate was apparent: these men were not to be caught up by new-fangled and disrupting ideas. They were not to be caught up by ideas of any kind. Their decisions were made before they were born; before they came to the use of reason. They had not to think for themselves: they accepted the authority and the infallibility of the Boyne. All their minds were drums.

Yes, I envied them their unanimity and singleness of purpose, and their view of the world from a synoptic perspective. They had three sources of enthusiasm: patriotism, prejudice, and mass panic predilections. In a dull and tepid age it is a great thing to get beyond one's self and to be capable of exultation. It is a great thing to believe that you alone are right and that everyone else is wrong. It is a great thing to forget the self in a great cause, no matter what cause. The Polish philosopher said, " A good battle justifies any cause." And here was, if not a good battle, the glorious and immortal memory of one. A man could be a hero—aye, even braver than the men who fought at the Boyne—with no risk to himself. He could participate vicariously in battles long ago, within the sound but out of range of the guns. If I could get a drum!

I had just time to catch my train. Who was in it but Fr. Paddy?

" The angel Victoricus ! " I exclaimed.

" Now what are you doing up north ? "

I told him of the reasons for my journey and I described the Procession of the Picts.

" There is a metaphysical question I want to discuss with you," I added.

" ' Utrum' what ? " he asked, for he was thinking of a famous volume about a problem which began with " Utrum " in the Library of St. Victor which had most of its books in the press.   It was a problem, strange to say, which was closely allied to the problem which was giving me seriously to think.   I stated it.

" Whether it would be more reverent and meritorious if Orangemen were to kick their wind in a spherical container—say a football—instead of be-labouring it in a drum ? "

He scrutinised me merrily.

" Are you thinking of becoming an Orangeman ? "

Crestfallen I admitted it.   " I have leanings."

" ' Even his failings . . .' But this question involves an article of their faith as well as a ritualistic observance. We must approach it sympathetically and give it the most patient consideration : ' Whether their wind would be better kicked in a football or beaten in a drum.' "

" Now, that is hardly a fair presentation of the problem : you are excluding the consideration of merit. ' Would it be more meritorious were the Orangemen to kick rather than to wallop wind.' "

" Well, now," said Fr. Paddy.   " We must consider, in the first place, what is gained by Orangemen from drumming. Here a consideration of the Concept of Expression arises. Every man has in his mind ideas which find expression in conventual sounds called words, which each who hears understands in his own way. Allowing for the idiosyncrasy of the individual, confusion should arise from this; and instead of understanding being the primal social phenomenon, misunderstanding should result. The drum relieves them from this difficulty which is inherent in human speech. Instead of having to transmit ideas by articulate words, they transmit them by inarticulate noises. As a result the primal social condition is understanding."

"You are not telling me that Orangemen cannot transmit ideas by human speech and that their hearers are too dense for anything but a drum?"

"I was beginning to demonstrate the place of noise in their polity before going on to deal with the question of merit. Through the drum Orangemen reach to and achieve a spiritual communion which is too deep for words, too primitive or too sacred. You must remember the antiquity of their ideas. They may reach back to times before the lips of man moulded speech as we know it."

"Yes!" I interjected, beginning to see light.

"It is in achieving this unity that their merit lies, and this is sustained by wind. Were this wind to be impounded, as you suggest, in a football, it would not boom with the same diapason, nor would it have the same appeal. They could not achieve identity with the Big Noise. Urban competition might result. And instead of unity, towns might compete with each other, instead of marching shoulder to shoulder behind the Lambegs. The flat round of the drum symbolises unity on a plane surface, whereas the orb of the ball. . . ." He broke off laughing.

" ' *Urbi et orbi !* ' It would never do," said Fr. Paddy. " The Pope has anticipated them."

I felt a little depressed. I usually do from metaphysics. Why had I started an argument with Fr. Paddy? There you go! I said to myself. You are the greatest martyr to words and phrases since Abelard the Nominalist. The drum would have saved me from all this : Arguments, words, ideas. And yet, and yet. . . . Perhaps it is as well. I have often blown my own trumpet, but to have my identity depending on a drum. . . . It would be a bit awkward in Dublin. Who or what would I be when it was silent? I would have no soul. And if it burst just as I was dying? No. It is somewhat too late for me to change my religion. I could never muster up enthusiasm for or belief on another, not at my time of life. That is why I thought of a drum.

And then the fate of my friend George Moore crowded in on me. He became a Protestant at sixty, when one's faculties are not improving. All he got was a blanket and a sack of coal, and that at Christmas ; for the members of the Representative Church Body, being gentlemen, never imagined for a moment that a gentleman could repudiate his tradition and turn from the faith of his fathers. So they took him for a poor creature and sent him a sack of coal.

I excused myself for a moment.

In the toilet of the first-class carriage I read three words in pencil suggesting the exemption of Portadown from the sanitary precautions which the Railway Company recommended while the train was standing at a station.

It was more devastating than any argument. I found my way back unaided.

" Will I press the bell and get you something ? You look rather depressed ? What ails you ? "

" My vocation is gone with the wind."

Thus it came about that I was shut out forever from the greatest middle-class organisation in my country, shut out from the society of men whose ancestors were the first choice of St. Patrick, the oldest Catholics in the land. Thus it comes that I am compelled still to think impersonally and dispassionately, still to regard the world with a detached and Hellenic look, still to " see Life steadily," etc., with no outlet for my emotions, no catharsis for the honesty and taciturnity of the year.

" *Sero te amavi Guilleamum, sero te amavi.*"

And now I shall never live in a row of those symmetrical little houses built of black basalt in the Black North, nor have a woman to sweep out the hall every morning when I point my cap at the shipyard, thus saving my bowler hat for the " Twalfth," when I can confirm my inherited convictions 80,000-fold with fife and drum ; which things show how one is being continually flouted by symbols of peace. Yet, for all that, my heart goes out in an undercurrent to the poor Orangemen, curt, monosyllabic, honest, reliable and free from humbug, who have for their portion not the joys, but the noise of Life.   May they never be merged with the South, or driven drumming up the Capitol in Rome. Athens might as well attempt to bring in Sparta—leave them alone.   We want no drums in Dreamland.

CHAPTER IX

THE HERDSMAN'S HILL

SLEMISH RISES MAGNIFICENTLY FROM THE MOOR. YOU come upon it suddenly as you advance over the long, mounded ridge of country between the road to Larne and the Valley of the Braid. This river is not very obvious, but a gleam of its water may be seen to the west under the trees in the valley, as you stand beside the Hill. About five miles away, a less-defined, much lower and more rounded hill ends in a steeple-like projection. This is Skerry, where Patrick's master Milchu dwelt. He was a Pictish king and one of the Magi or Druids. In the year 406 only the summit of Skerry could be seen, for those remaining trees surely are descendants of the woods which intervened of old and sheltered Milchu's herds of swine.

I took counsel with a wayfarer with a bicycle who had dismounted, for the incline was steep.

" Is that Slemish ? "

" Yus. That's where St. Patrick was."

" St. Patrick ? "

" And there's the priest's chair near the top."

" A priest's chair ? " I inquired, interested ; for of this I had not heard.

His dark eyes looked with steady suspicion :

" Are ye from the South ? "

" I am."

" Well, let me tell you we are a law-abiding people up here." It was the Twelfth.

I changed the subject, and inquired concerning the grazing of the hill.

" Sheep ?   Sure that's all that's fut to pit on it."

Suspicious of my courtesy, he went on his way.

Sheep are all that it's fit for.   And as I looked at one of the green places on a shelf high up, a flock of sheep appeared in strange formation : they went along the mountain-side four deep, in an extended column, and disappeared in the broken ground.   So it was sheep that St. Patrick herded.   I had read that it was swine, but swine were evidently not herded now-adays on the hill.   From a gateway I photographed this historic natural monument over two bushes of wild roses, which seemed to bloom with a pink deeper than the roses of the South, deep as the Burnet roses in the Welsh Valley of the Roses out of reach oversea.

And I turned towards Skerry, with some idea of the type (found nowhere else) of men the little lad Patrick " was up against " fifteen hundred and thirty years ago.

The road to Skerry is not direct, so I sat by a little bridge listening to the rippling water and recalling that it made one of the sounds that gladdened the heart of Finn in the days before Patrick was heard of, when there was an extraordinary feeling for natural sights and sounds, a sympathy that has never been expressed with all its sensitiveness since Ossian sang of Finn.   Wordsworth, with his flogged-up feeling for Nature and his pathetic fallacies, never approached the poet Finn in the sincerity and simplicity of his love of the world of life.

The dread voice which stilled my possible lawlessness was passed, and now it was time that I broke into song to cheer myself with Ossian's Lay.

The music Finn loved was that which filled the heart with joy and gave light to the countenance, the music of the blackbird of Letter Lee, and the melody of the Dord Fian, the sound of the wind in Droum-derg, the thunderstorm of Asseroe, the cry of the hounds let loose through Glen Rah with their faces outwards from the Suir, the Wave of Rury lashing the shore, the wash of water against the sides of ships, the cry of Bran at Knock-an-Awr, the murmur of the streams at Slemish, and—Oh, the blackbird of the Derry Carn. I never heard, by my soul, sounds sweeter than that. Were I only beneath his nest!

And here was I listening to the very streams that had sounded deliciously in the hero's ears two thousand years ago, and wondering, where could anyone find a list of braver sounds in all the world?

It is a great thing to belong to a land that has a past like this, where the farther you go back the more strong are the messages of delight in the beauty of external Nature and in the good cheer of sport. And the slight nostalgia for the oak-wood which held the blackbird! Nowhere in literature, until we come to the balladists of Robin Hood, is there so good a conscience—nowhere is the world so sound:

> The wood wele sang and would not cease,
> Sitting upon a spray.

But how small the note compared to the blackbird's! The difference might be taken for a measure of the heroes' statures and capacity for joy. And refreshed by the thought of old times, and by the sound of the very stream that Patrick heard long after Finn, I went along light-hearted on my journey to explore Skerry and to find the site of the dun of Milchu who was Patrick's master.

Milk-cans were cooling in a stone fountain fed by another little stream as I went up the path by the farmhouse which leads up the hill to Skerry's summit. Wild strawberries hidden in the hedgerows cheered me in the climb. Two little children were gathering flowers though the day was misty and overcast. " What is the name of this hill ? " And the little Picts chorussed, " Skirit," with accents which must have come down unaltered from the day that Milchu sent his stronghold up in flames.

The hill is steep and was evidently a strong place. It must have been on its summits that the dun was planted, for a site lower down could not be so well seen from Slemish Cross—though this place is 750 feet above sea level—and we are told that it was from the Cross beside Slemish that Patrick witnessed his old master's Die-hard act. " He groaned in spirit, and for the space of two hours stood on the spot watching the flames consume the house where he had served."

Slemish looked grey through the mist from Skerry. As I stood on its summit, up from some seventy feet below me came the grunting sounds of a pig in the local farm. This too was a thing little changed since the wooded slopes carried many droves of swine and Patrick heard their grunts. I photographed the old church on the top of Skerry and inspected the stone which the Angel's footstep marked. I leaped a wall and twisted my ankle. As I limped down I met a lad about sixteen years of age, a joyful lad who smiled readily, and we had a little talk. I thought that he well might pass for the Saint in his youth when he first came to the very spot. He made me think of the Saint, and besides he gave me an object lesson in the interpretation of tradition.

" Why do visitors come up here ? " I inquired.

" Have ye ever heard of St. Patrick ? "

" Yes."

" Well, he jumped from Skerry to Slemish."

" But—— ! "

" It might be the other way."

" But it's a long way ? "

" He could lep all right."

This nonsense became significant to me the moment I realised that it was a version confused with the Saint's vision of the angel Victoricus. And well might it be confused, for Muirchu the biographer himself is not explicit. Dr. Gwynn says :

Muirchu's two accounts of St. Patrick's vision (Book i c 11. IIc 13—pp. 5a; 16b) neither of which is distinctly expressed, taken together appear to describe the angel as mounting first from Skerry across the valley to Slemish, leaving his footprint on the former, and then from the latter upward. " *De quo monte* " is to be read with " *ascendisse*," not with " *vidit*."

So I can hardly blame the lad who said, " It might have been the other way." It matters very little, but it is a rather remarkable account of oral tradition which assumes sense the moment one realises that it refers to a vision and to no earthly man.

Milchu is said to have had two daughters and a son. One was the mother of Mochæ, and the other may have been the wife of the neighbouring chief forty miles away at Saul. This very interesting theory was advanced to me by the Most Rev. Dr. Fogarty, Bishop of Killaloe. " It may account," he said, " for the decision of St. Patrick to come to Ulster when his mission began. He may have known that he had a friend at Court." And he goes on to suggest the most interesting and very plausible theory that it was the children of Milchu whom Patrick saw in another of his visions and who called to him saying, " Come, holy youth, and walk with us again." " For who," asked the Bishop, " amongst all the savages would have known that here was a holy youth but they with whom he had played during his captivity ? "

I am delighted with this theory. It makes many difficulties clear. And if we are to take the Wood of Focluth as being a symbol of Beyond the Beyonds, the children of Milchu are they who walked beside it at the edge of the ultimate lands.

In spite of his reticence in speaking of himself, there is evidence of Patrick's homesickness, and almost of despair, in the years of his captivity. He was saved from despair by turning to God, and if any-where there seems to me to be evidence of a miraculous intervention of Providence whereby a half-instructed youth, alone in a foreign and savage land, grew to religious perfection, it is during his years of adolescence when he served as a slave.

There are an old burial-ground and the remains of an ancient chapel on the summit of Skerry now. The chapel contains the vault where the family of O'Neill is buried. It was this wall that twisted my ankle. A vindictive and enduring spirit must be that of Milchu, thought I. He has caused me bad luck. I always associate good or evil happenings with the locality where they occur. Thus I maintain the mystery of places, for I feel places have their genii, and one should cherish the mystery of things in these days, and more than anywhere in the Black North. It is lacking in magic. The spirit of Milchu was at work. Patrick was beyond his power, but he had luckless me within range. As I limped down the hill, I repeated the malediction of St. Patrick, as he groaned in spirit over Milchu while that man's self-homicide was going on.

> I know not, God knows. Yonder, Milchu's house is on fire. He is burning himself lest he should believe in the eternal God at the end of his life. Upon him lies a curse: of him shall be neither king or Tanist; his seed and offspring shall be in bondage after him; and he shall not come out of hell forever.

I felt that I had been walking on the very site of his cremation.

CHAPTER X

THE ESCAPE

AND AGAIN AFTER A LITTLE TIME I HEARD THE DIVINE Voice saying to me, " Lo, thy ship is ready." And it was near at hand but distant about two hundred miles. And I had never been there nor had I knowledge of any person there. And thereupon, after a little I betook myself to flight, and left the man with whom I had been for six years, and I came in the courage of God who prospered my way for good ; and I had no cause to fear anything until I came to that ship. And on the very day on which I arrived, the ship had been drawn down from its place; and I told them that I had the wherewithal to sail with them. And it displeased the captain and he answered sharply, " Try not by any means to come with us." When I heard this I left them in order to go to the hut where I lodged. And on the way I began to pray; and before I had ended my prayer I heard one of them and he was calling loudly after me, " Come quickly, for these men are calling you." And immediately I returned to them. And they began to say to me, " Come, we take you in good faith. Make a pact of friendship with us in any way you wish." And on that day I refused to suck their breasts for fear of God.

Hitherto I have had to use, as I said, conjecture to furbish out the gaps in the account of Patrick's movements. And conjecture, according to Professor Jebb, " is a question on which a writer must be prepared to meet with large differences of opinion, and must be content if the credit is conceded to him of having steadily acted to the best of his judgment." This is very well expressed and very true. Why is it that one who makes use of conjecture will meet with a large difference of opinion ? Simply because there is in it an implied challenge : if it comes to guessing, every man thinks he can do as well as the next. There is nothing conjectural about this simple and unmistakable statement of Patrick that he heard a divine Voice telling him of a ship two hundred Roman miles away.

I have employed conjecture almost to the point of invention; but here is no subject for conjecture. Here we are on firm ground, the firmest which we can hope to meet: we have the only things that matter— the very words of St. Patrick. In the last summation it will appear that the only sure statement we have is that to which he set his hand. And we have him here distinctly writing that he heard a divine Voice. Do you believe it? I most certainly do, and for this reason: that the soul is divine and subject to no limitations of inspiration. We have only to turn to poets to whom most people are willing to concede inspiration. Tennyson prophesied wars in the air years before they were credible; and the inspiration of Shakespeare on a plane far higher than the mere foretelling of fact or fortune—a plane high enough to be creative almost, that is, capable of bringing things to pass— is unquestioned. This faculty is more likely to be developed, turning back now to saints, in men of one purpose, men undistracted by things mundane. Therefore I believe in the unequivocal statement of Patrick, even of the days before he had reached the full maturity of his spiritual stature. Surely it will be conceded to me that the least I must do is to believe in the authenticity of my subject. The sceptical may concede this all the more readily when I assure them that my conclusion was reached not from any pretensions of mine to

theological knowledge, but from the knowledge open
to any medical practitioner who takes an interest in
psychology.   To disabuse their minds of the suspicion
of any pretensions of mine to being an adept in things
spiritual, let me hasten to say that there is room for
only one saint at a time in this book, and he is not the
author !

One of two prevailing conditions was required to
enable Patrick to escape.   Either the ancient chieftains
were so harsh and cruel to their slaves that they caused
them to form secret societies for helping one another,
or Christianity had already made headway to a considerable extent in the country.   The Irish are not
cruel for cruelty's sake ; but of all the Irish tribes
Patrick had fallen in with the most ferocious.   They
are careless of the condition of their animals, such as
draught horses and asses, and they pluck geese alive
and dishorn living cattle, but these things are due to
ignorance and to the want of imaginative sympathy.
But when they give a thought to it, they can be most
humane.   A farmer will sit up all night with a calving
or sick cow ; and a race-horse or a running-dog will
get almost more than human consideration.   So it
must have been with the slaves, for they were valuable
chattels.   It was in the system of the traffic in human
life that cruelty lay.   So cruel was this that we find
an assembly of the hierarchy of the Church declaring,
at a synod held in Armagh in 1171, that the Norman
invasion was a curse from heaven as a punishment for
the inhuman traffic in slaves ; they anathematised the
whole system and declared that all English slaves

should be free to return to their own country. And this in spite of the fact that it was a common custom, according to Geraldus Cambrensis, for the English to sell their children to the Irish for slaves.

But these conditions need not be regarded as alternatives. They may have co-existed; they did exist together, and both helped to enable Patrick to escape in the courage of God Who prospered his way for good and left him no cause to fear anything until he came to that ship.

To anyone who has been through the late war in Ireland it will be apparent that it requires but slight organisation to enable a man who is on the run to hide, provided that there exists a sympathy for his condition and ideals which is widespread enough to further his movements. Collins walked, by virtue of this sympathy, under the noses of that unconstitutional and irregular force of gunmen which received the name of "Black and Tans." He walked through the principal streets in broad daylight. Had Dr. Healy been through a successful rebellion and a civil war, he might not have postulated that Patrick had to avoid the frequented road to Tara and go by less beaten tracks to Ballina. "Neither would the Saint be likely to come to Wicklow, for that route would bring him along the eastern coast through the most fertile and populous parts of the country, where a runaway slave would almost certainly be captured." Obviously so, if he had no friends, or if he were likely to appear in the state Patrick tells us he was often in—that is, half naked. But no. He had friends and funds. His relatives were well off, and

they may have found means of getting into touch with
their son, or have contributed to some fund of the
British Church similar to the funds which the Gallic
Church used to spend on the work of rescuing (their
members or the baptised) Christians who had been
carried into slavery. Did we not know that such
organisations actually did exist, and if we were unaware
that there was a strong Christian leavening among the
oppressed population of the island, we might have
deduced these facts from the argument that no youth
who had been remiss in his religious duties, as Patrick
confesses he was, could have found grace unaided to
achieve religious zeal enough to inspire him to fast and
to pray a hundred times a night and, what is more
wonderful, to refuse to fraternise with the sailors who
were his only hope of escape to civilisation and of seeing
his parents again. The youth must have been in
touch with devout and secret Christians. One of
these may have been Victor (for there are times when
Victor appears to become identical with Victoricus
the angel). He would have nothing to do with the
strange pagan sailors—pirates they may have been—
though they said in all kindness, " Come, we take thee
in good faith ; make friendship with us as thou pleas-
est "—thereby maybe referring to some rite of friendship such as is found to this day among outlandish tribes.
But Patrick assures us, using a strange metaphor :

> I refused to suck their breasts through the fear of God ;
> but I still hoped that some of them would come to the faith of
> Christ, for they were heathen, and on that account I stayed
> with them and forthwith we set sail."

Among these, if they were Irishmen, as they probably were, he may have found his first converts; for during the march of twenty-eight days *per deserta*—that is, through devastated and desolate Gaul, which had been harried by the Suedes and Vandals and was still held by Teutonic barbarians, highwaymen, and other barbarous tribes who burned strong castles and walled towns and left not even a hut in the wilds or shelter in the caves of the hills—he impressed them by the efficacy of his prayer to God, which saved them and their wolfhounds from starvation.

What makes it probable that Patrick was helped by sympathising friends is the fact that he had money. Dr. Healy takes the Cottonian version of the *Confessio*, and not that of the Book of Armagh, when he is dealing with the escape and recording the parley with the sailors before Patrick is taken aboard. " And I asked that I might have leave to sail with them—*Et locutus sum ut haberem unde navigarem cum illis.*" The Bishop says, " The language is dubious. The above seems the most natural meaning." But if the sentence is an ellipsis, thus : " I spoke (to others) that I might have the wherewithal, etc.," as the Rev. Dr. Browne suggests, we might deduce from it that he spoke to those from whom he might expect sympathy, and such people were likely to be, if anywhere, at the nearest approach to an international port in the island, viz. Arklow, the port through which the gold of Wicklow was shipped to the continent. They were certainly a needy crew; and the offer of money may have caused the captain, a slow-thinking man, to change his mind, and to send one of the ship's company running after Patrick to invite him to come on board. " I heard one of them shouting strongly after me, ' Come quickly, the men are calling you.' "

Let us pause here to consider this change of mind. Patrick has told us, modified and softened as a saint would soften the language of a seaman, of a rebuff which never left his memory after fifty years : " And it displeased the captain and he answered sharply and with indignation, ' Try not by any means to come with us.' " This is a meiosis if ever there was one ! But let us get the picture. Let us try to re-create this all-important scene on which so much depended for us all. Do not let us be deceived by History with that old trick of hers by which we are led to isolate important characters to the exclusion of contemporary nonentities, the Much-Too-Many, who are always with us and present at every annoying incident that befalls. Rest assured they were not absent in the past. In this lethargical island of ours hangers-on have always been numerous. Any little event brings them out in their hundreds ; an accident particularly appeals to them and, we may be sure, so did in Patrick's time the launching of a ship. Louts young and old, longshore-men and land-lubbers of every kind, were sure to be in the way at the critical moment, while the captain, after directing the launching, was attending to the ship. We may be sure that he had refused, often enough, frequent and exasperating offers of unskilled help. The captain's temper was on edge ; what with the dogs which had been wild at having been taken from their masters and, now about to be put on shipboard by strange hands, were wilder still, a wildness which was increased every minute by the whistles and cat-calls of the youths whom he had ordered out of the way " with indignation," youths whose " Eh, Mister, take us on board " I can hear clearly even now ; and what with the prospect, for which he had made no provision, of having to put the dogs separately into crates to keep them from tearing each other to pieces—not to mention water and food supplies to be checked and the tide to catch on the turn—it was a harsh mood the captain was in, and one which was made no better by the sudden arrival of a youth who, as if he hadn't heard the young blackguards' shouts, came forward in all seriousness and asked to be taken on board !   " By no means seek to come with us " would have burst a blood-vessel without an expletive from the old sea-dog, which now we shall never hear.

But when he had a moment to himself and the men pointed out to him the calming effect of the young stranger on the dogs, by virtue of that sympathy for all creatures which emanates from persons destined to be blessed ; and when he remembered that the youth had not the slightest intention of fooling him, but was all in earnest and intent to come aboard ; and when he considered that the youth was evidently a Roman Briton, and therefore spoke a language known all over the civilised world—he sent a sailor " shouting strongly, ' Come aboard ! ' "

This, I think, is a fair rendering of what must have happened to cause such a change in the attitude of the captain and turn a harsh rebuke into relations so friendly with the crew that Patrick was embarrassed and was minded to keep his distance. Howbeit, the reader may agree that that strange ship and ship's company did not set out for the continent unseen and alone, from a port of embarkation with no one present but Patrick, the captain and the crew. It would, had it done so, have been a ghostly ship indeed, and ghostly ships do not carry cargoes of infuriated dogs. And a ghostly ship it very nearly came to being, a ship that sailed only the waves of memory uncharted beyond all human shores ; for so far is self-pity from the un-relenting asceticism of the Saint that, to our exasperation, he gives us only the events, and these merely in outline, which led to his spiritual development. I am sure that half Wicklow was gathered round the island's chief port on the look-out for Gallic ships and " foreign faces," and " How are things in Rome ? ", and their curiosity was nothing less than the curiosity of the dwellers in Dun Laoghaire, farther up the coast, for the arrival and departure of the Mail boat is at the present day.

Nothing can happen in Ireland without being over-looked. The only way to obtain privacy is to run out of petrol, a method too modern to concern us here.

With his deep study and great learning, Dr. Healy makes a case for a crew of hunting folk sailing from Ballina for the forests of Scotland. But there is no doubt—we have the Saint's own words for it—that they reached Gaul. So to go there *via* Scotland would be like going to Brighton pier by way of Bannockburn.

And what poor hunters they must have been, and what unattractive game preserve it must have been, and how much bigger than the present-day Scotland, if they found themselves within twenty-eight days (during which they saw no habitation) in a state of starvation, only to be saved by their passenger! Besides, where is there a desert in Scotland which could be called " arid " ?

Let us trace and follow Patrick's line of escape from Slemish to Wicklow. His ship was two hundred Roman miles away, waiting at Inver Dea, the mouth of the Vartry River at Newrathbridge. That would be about one hundred and eighty English miles from Ballymena or Slemish to Wicklow, where there is a tradition, strong to the present day, that a point north of the town was a point of departure for the continent in Patrick's era. " A well-known and opportune port." This is now called the Broad Lough. Patrick himself tells us that he touched at it on his return journey from Gaul many years later, when he came as a bishop.

Likely enough he may have spent the first night of his escape on the shores of Antrim bay on Lough Neagh. But this is a theory which may be misleading, because it depends on too much furtiveness and the necessity of avoiding beaten paths. Most little towns and villages are about ten miles apart in Ireland, and if he did not choose the Antrim route, or have it chosen for him by those who were in charge of his escape, he may have gone on to Carrickfergus and have been ferried across Belfast Lough to Newtown-

H

ards. A curragh coasting amid the numerous islands
of Strangford Lough would be unsuspected and hard
to find, and easy to escape from in taking to the woods
in case of alarm. But there was no alarm. All was
well planned. He may have had to wait until Milchu
was absent on a foray. " Thereupon after a little "
might mean so much. He, as he says, " had no cause
to fear anything." He was not pursued.

He may have, he must have, travelled through
Leinster in disguise. It may have been that there was
some very influential person at the back of this escape,
for though inured to fasting, and gifted with an iron
constitution as he undoubtedly was, unaided he could
not have subsisted undetected, and have trekked
unguided from Slemish through five counties or two
provinces. And this with the accent of a Briton
and the bearing and manners of a freeborn Roman
youth. It is an historical fallacy into which it is easy
to fall to imagine that Ireland was utterly impossible
for and unvisited by travellers. " In all ages every
human heart is human." There must have been
considerable going and coming between the nobles of
Ireland and Britain. Otherwise it is hard to explain
how the Ard Righ or High King, Leary and his son,
had British wives. And if one man in high position
were a Christian and had knowledge of Patrick's plight
in slavery, or were acquainted with his parents, he could
have sent him openly on a journey through Leinster
with a servant of his own. But this theory is rebutted
by the action of the captain of the ship, who warned
Patrick off in no uncertain terms. It could not be

that he thought that he was asked to take the son of a nobleman to sea on an escapade. I am afraid that the youth Patrick must have appeared in a sorry plight, as sorry as a slave's, after his journey of one hundred and eighty miles. I think, then, that those who helped and handed him on were slaves like himself, united in a common woe. Be this the truth, his was a most adventurous journey. The crossing of four rivers at night: groping through the woods to the hut of the next friendly slave, and the avoidance of the great mastiffs as he passed each dun and of what was worse wolves, and the wild madmen who lived at large. Maybe the dogs were the least troublesome if there be anything in the conjecture that it was his way with the great unruly dogs that was a consideration in his being accepted in an afterthought by the captain. It was one of the most hair-breadth escapes that ever occurred in our country, and the duration of the parley, during which his fate hung on that old sea-dog's decision, was the most momentous in our history.

When you look south from Slemish you see the Mountains of Mourne like pale amethysts, rising in four increasing summits to be crowned by Slieve Donard beyond the shores of Strangford Lough. It is to the west of these hills that the traveller must keep, for the mountains fall sheer into Dundrum Bay and forbid passage by its shores. Farther to the west the hills rise again, so the road must have run, as it runs to-day, through the Gap of the North. This would have been one of the Five Roads of Tara—the great northern road, a road hard to leave even now without entering marshy land and bog. But when the country was heavily forested the land must have been less in need of drainage, because a tree is capable of pumping up from the soil to its leaves thirty tons of moisture in a season. And Ireland was well-wooded we know. This came about not from any superior knowledge of the farmers to that of the farmers of our day, but from the fact that weapons were too valuable to direct against hard timber and woodmen's axes were unknown. Also, a forest was valued not by its trees but by the amount of swine its masts and acorns could carry. So Patrick could have left the high road, which I found I could not leave, to escape pursuit or to elude any strangers who might apprehend him. How much vicissitude and danger does the fact that he escaped alone suggest!

What a country he must have passed! What scenes strange to our eyes would appear, could we unroll and reel back the film of time and see on that greatest screen of all, the surface of the earth, glimpses of the generations of centuries until we came to Patrick's day! A land of waving woods, hidden rivers and palisaded mounds. For on the top of not very high ground, but ground easily accessible for man and beast, the ancient chiefs built their palisaded houses or duns. This was the way they were built: a double containing-wall of earth encircled a raised mound, on which was built a round house of poles interwoven with clay-plastered wattles. They were thatched just as the huts of Zulus are. It is remarkable that these duns were round.   The genius of the country runs in circles, as one may realise who connects the ground-plan of the great fortified houses with the design of the Tara brooch or the ornaments in the Book of Kells.   Annular design all through. To maintain the great earthen embankments in a condition steep enough to keep out wolves or fiercer foes, it may have been necessary to buttress them with wood, but as there is no evidence of this at first on the Aurelian Wall, or even in the later walls between Scotland and Britain, the sodded earth may have been in itself enough of a protection.   The height of the circular ramparts is not easy to estimate to-day.   That they were double is evident from the numerous remains, and that their entrance was recurved we can see from following their outline.   This was the practice so that the enemy, if he did succeed in forcing an entry, would have to expose his flank on each side as he forced himself in.   The greatest of all Keltic forts, Mai Dun in Dorset, shows this more clearly than any of ours because of the cement-like nature of the chalk of which it is constructed.   At night herds and horses were driven and probably kept between the two walls of the enclosure ; the open space within may have been used for dairy purposes and as a farmyard.   What I am sure would have caught the traveller's eye in the year of Our Lord 411, as he passed the dun of a chief, was the bright red door.   That the walls were whitewashed, as the tradition is for all native-built houses now to be so treated, I am not sure.   I would be more inclined to think that the dwelling-houses that crowned the duns were whitewashed, were it not for the fact that the Picts of south of the Grampians, according to Bede, writing of St. Ninian's mission in 360, "called the White House because he built there a church of stone which was not usual among the Britons." Maybe we had our own customs distinct from the Britons, and I would like to think that the duns were white, just as the cottages that climb the Irish hills are white and neighbour well to the sun as they catch its rising or setting rays. But a red door they surely had. Strong is the tradition of the red door, and it makes a pleasant picture set in a whitewashed wall.

Patrick passed many duns. These were residences of nobles, and there were many nobles holding territory under the kings. But he had to pass many huts like that hut which he tells us he sought after the refusal of the sailors at first to take him aboard. He calls it a tuguriolum. There must have been many of these, made of sods and thatch, in the neighbourhood of the duns, to house the serfs and slaves of which the land was full, a land without towns or villages. He may have lived in one on Slemish on nights when the ewes were lambing. The protection even of one so low that he could not rest his spear against its wall was reassuring. He could tell by them if he were too near a stronghold, and he could count on the sympathy of the occupier were he a shepherd or a slave. The woods were dry and gave him shelter and afforded comparatively easy going. But there were five or six rivers in the way. The Bann is a slow and a deep river even where it is not so very far from its source. This was crossed probably in one of those most extraordinary coracles which are found only on the Boyne and the Wye. Their antiquity probably surpasses all craft in Ireland and their utility is exceptional. They are circular wicker baskets covered with one hide, with the hairy part turned in. They are worked with one paddle. This would be an impossible feat were the paddle used to paddle; instead of that, it is used to pull the little craft. The paddler kneels and pulls in what thereby becomes the bow, and the passenger or the nets balance him behind. Very serviceable these boats are for fishing in rivers whose banks are over-arched or under-cut. There is evidence that they were used on one or two rivers in Ulster in Patrick's day, so I think it may be safe to say that they would be found in the rivers in Ulster which are nearest to their place of origin on the Boyne.

With the river at Ardee, which he would have to encounter next, things were different. This river is so shallow in many places, that it caused me to rack my brains to decide how it came that Cuchullin, the Hound of Culann the Smith, defended its ford (if indeed the ford were here and not on the Boyne) by Dowth when the river was nearly all a ford and an army could cross beside him and outflank him. I had forgotten the Black Pig's Dyke, a great wall (far longer than both Roman walls) which guarded Ulster from sea to sea four hundred years before Patrick, from the forces of Queen Maeve. If

this crossed the stream, there must have been an opening
in the Dyke to let it out, and if in this way it was that
Cuchullin stood, no army could reach his flank which
would be protected by the wall and, standing in the
ford, it would have been possible for Leag his charioteer
to float down to him from upstream and supply him with
the Gae Bolga (Belly Dart) (that floating harpoon-
like weapon of the Esquimaux) with which he slew
Ferdiad. This stream did not delay Patrick, however he may have had to overcome what remained of
the great wall. The Boyne was perhaps his most
serious obstacle. It would have been unnecessarily
risky to seek it where it could be forded, for although
it was not kept deep by weirs as it is now, it was
unfordable east of Slane and he could hardly have
gone to the Ford of the Alder, which is remembered
to this day in the name Trim, up to which town we
hear of one of his companions rowing forty years on.
The Boyne running as it does through the richest land
on earth—that is, rich for the purposes of feeding
human beings with the highest form of proteid—is
muddy-banked and tidal for miles. Without a detour
inland as far maybe as Bective, there was nothing for
it but to get a fisherman at its mouth, or near its
mouth, Inver Boinde, to ferry him across. This is
where certainly a coracle would come in usefully.
This is where they are on the Boyne to the present
day. They were saved in the nick of time just before
their last builder died. He lived to hand on the
tradition of the method of their making. And if
Patrick was helped by one of the most generous class

of people, fishermen, it is certain that he was given a
meal of fish ; for down to our own times, ever since
its blessing, has the Boyne estuary been famous, and
all the river for that matter, for its sea-fresh salmon.

He tells us that he was never anxious, and this, as
I said, makes me sure that he was efficiently helped.
His flight becomes easier for he has reached half-
way. The southern bank is steep unless you cross
immediately at the estuary, but this for the foot
traveller is impracticable on account of the mud-flats
which are edged in marsh at high tide. There is no
knowing now where the fishermen of old found a dry
spot on the south bank without going a little upstream
where the bank is steeper, between the mouth and
Rosnaree. Once across the Boyne, it is only thirty
miles to the Hurdle Ford by the Ridge of the Hazels
on the Liffey. And between these rivers lies the
loveliest of champaigns. Possibly it looked then
much as it does now, for things change slowly in a
country the parts of which were, and still are, largely
pastoral and suited without waste to little else. If he
travelled in the late spring the hedges would be all
afoam with the blossoms of the May, for nowhere out
of Meath is such hawthorn to be found.

And soon the faint blue Dublin mountains would
cheer him, even though they were distant, with their
lovely lines. But it matters little at what time of the
year you go south, towards the Liffey from the Boyne.
Provided that the day is clear and that visibility is
good, the eye is filled with seeing the long undulations
of the grey-green fields flung far as it can reach,

transformers of grass into horseflesh or beef, with the hidden limestone under it all. And when you come to Ballymun and the ground begins to fall, then across the wide margined Liffey within its shallow valley, the hills that nursed that granite-born stream seem to rise higher than they are, and to wall in that fair green garden of the West, the Hesperides of Wicklow. Unless he went through Naas—and there was no reason for such a detour—the way was smooth towards the Ford of the Hurdles, and from that along the coast by Booterstown to where his ship was to be found. There is much unprovable argument as to whether the fugitive ever visited the hamlet which has grown into Dublin. A runaway slave does not usually give his name to a place unless he has become crowned with glory and the benediction of men. So some of the three wells of Dublin which are called after St. Patrick may have got their names from a visitation after his second coming, when he came to re-visit Wicklow as a bishop of the Church of Rome.

Many of the wells called after the Saint, as that at Elphin, got their names from his having stopped by them, as Our Lord rested at the Well of Jacob where he met the Samaritan woman; and thus they each became holy wells. Of the wells in my own city I am entitled to speak, having visited them and taken their depth and sampled their waters. The one " to the south of the city," which was laxative, has disappeared since before 1757. That it never supplied Dublin in time of siege we know from the record that the Danes of that city were driven to drinking

brackish river-water when Mæl Shechlainn II be-
leagured it in 980. There is a St. Patrick's Well
at the end of Dawson Street, just under the stairs
which lead from that street through an iron gate in
the wall of Trinity College into the Provost's garden.
This is a carefully preserved well, not artesian but a
surface well, a still well with no visible flow, and it
may only mark the site of a larger well before the
town spread out in paved streets. But the well in
Nassau Place which is used to make that excellent
native product, the invention of Dublin, mineral water,
is very different. It is a deep and gushing well. I
had to send a bottle down sixteen feet before reaching
its dark surface, and it is eighty feet deeper than that.
Its daily output runs into thousands of gallons. This
is a well in the meaning of the word when a well was
all the water-works a people had. It is a well in the
same sense that the Fountain Arethuse at Syracuse in
Sicily is a well, and that, as the traveller knows, is as
big as a pond. This is the only St. Patrick's Well of
the three in Dublin which is springing as fresh as ever
to-day. It is in the premises of the Mineral Water
Distributors who make Thwaites soda-water and
Cantrell and Cochrane's table waters. This company
acquired the well about eighty years ago, and built it
up with stone sides about five feet in diameter. The
water comes to about sixteen feet from the top. Of this
water Dr. John Rutty, writing in the rather quaint
English of Dublin in 1757, said :

> These waters being purer than rain-water, and most to be
> esteemed for the preservation of health, and for the cure of

many chronical diseases, as hath been found by experience, such waters passing quickly through the minutest canals, diluting and sweetening the salt, acid and tartareous dyscrasy of the juices in the Gouty; and, indeed, whoever rightly understood the various uses and virtues of pure water, whether cold or hot, externally or internally administered, would undoubtedly be possessed of a medicine which would better maintain its claim to the title of *Panacea*, than any of the boasted productions of Chymistry.

But notwithstanding the faithful representation of the state of Mineral waters of this Country, I am well aware of the great strength and prevalence of the prejudices of the people against these native productions of their own soil, and that there is too little prospect of success in an attempt to introduce our own waters in opposition to the Fashion, established with the growing luxury of the times, of preferring all foreign productions to our own.

The old doctor was right. It is more suitable to the citizen to use his native wells than to import stale salines and effervescent waters from overseas.

If, as I think was the case, this well, a few yards off the present Nassau Street, got its name from the refreshment it gave to the little runaway slave who after his long trek from Slemish sat and revived himself at its brink, it behoves us to support it with the added consideration of the testimony to it written by a man who knew all the wells of our city 180 years ago. It is significant that it is directly in the old road to Booterstown. But, of course, it may have got its name, like so many St. Patrick's wells throughout the country, from the use made of it for baptism by the Saint.

What better can we do than revive our spirits in St. Patrick's Well?

If St. Patrick fled by way of the Ridge of the Hazels

which is Dublin now he must, according to tradition,
which is topical enough for my liking, have crossed
the Hurdle Ford under the Ridge of the Hazels and
then turned south by way of Booterstown, and so on
by Shanganagh to the valley of the Dargle, and
passed through Delgany and Kilcool to his ship at
Inver Dea. It is hardly practicable even now to go
on foot by Naas and Ballymore Eustace—such highlands are to be crossed before you come to Wicklow
Gap—to pass by way of Glendalough to Wicklow
through Rathnew. It would have required a guide
who could have left him, to steer him through these
wilds where natives even now get lost and tourists
fall to their death; whereas by skirting the sea, he
would have the shore for his guide—and his destination
was by the shore.

The feeling for natural scenery comes to us Irish
from Ossian and from Finn, as I have indicated above.
To Englishmen, who have not a language of their
own but a mixture of Low German, French, Latin
and the rest, it came in all its sweetness and sincerity
from Chaucer and Shakespeare, only to become a
matter of conscience in Wordsworth. The long
descent of our Irish love for natural beauty is so
innate in me that I will spare the reader a description
of that loveliest of rivers that St. Patrick crossed, which
is my own Anna Liffey, that dark, bright, black
perennial water, unsoilable, which is cradled in golden
sand and led through flowering irises and broad
meadows, verdant always, through the plain of Kildare: never does it fail the land nor leave its fishes

to die from want of freshets. Fortunately for the reader I am on a compass course, uncertain enough but still a course from Slemish to Wicklow, and I must not sit down by the waters of Liffey to rejoice and to enrich my spirit or to praise them over all. But where are the better known Peneus and Illissus, when it comes to the Dog Days and the summer heat beats down ?

I know the many cups in the light Wicklow hills that are brimmed half way up with the distant sea. And so by the sea-shore of Wicklow, where the winds are gentle with the level tides, after perhaps a fortnight spent in escaping, St. Patrick reached the strange men's plank-built ship in the Broad Lough which crossed the 500 miles to ruined Gaul in three days compass-less, guided only by the heavenly signs.

CHAPTER XI

AS FROM A GALLERY, YOU LOOK ACROSS A LEVEL WHERE
there is traffic from the streets, towards a panel framed
in light.　A dusty olive tree, tall and well rooted,
stands in an enormous tub which the embankment
makes where it takes the left-hand turn in a short
circle, of the walled, precipitous road.　The olive
grove, from which it is conspicuous, is hidden, but
suggested from the crowns of light green.　With the
declivity of the land here, which is but a foothill of
the Alps where they fall short of the sea, the eye is led
to a smooth expanse of turquoise blue on which float
two islands under a cobalt sky.　The nearer and the
larger one is St. Marguerite, which is called after a
sister of St. Honoratus, who reclaimed Lerins and
made it famous and holy.　Over all, a full and solitary
cloud lies like a canopy between heaven and the
Mediterranean.

This is the isle wherein " wells were dug and sweet
water flowed in the midst of the bitterness of the sea."
To this haven of peace came those whom the times had
broken or who were shipwrecked after the fervour
of their worldly ambitions had been dissipated ; and
thoughtful and pious men who wished to seek identity
with the Godhead " in Whose will is our peace."　This
island, St. Honorat, Patrick reached ; and here we
are for the first time treading on ground where we have
reason to think that he lived for a considerable time

(Bury), but Muller of Tubingen sees no reason to believe he ever reached Lerins. Strong indeed must have been his vocation to a religious life if he interrupted his homeward journey to spend years with a community which enrolled men such as Hilary, afterwards bishop of Arlate, Maximus, its second abbot, Lupus who was bishop of Trecasses, and Eucherius, who was probably one of the lordly rhetoricians to whom the Saint was to refer later on in his career. It was this Eucherius who wrote a treatise on the hermit's life, " as well he might," a witty if irreverent Frenchman remarked : " Madame Galla, his wife, lived on the larger island here, which is nearer the *plage* ; is it not so ? " I had not sufficient French to know whether he referred to the historical fact of the situation of husband and wife, or to the geographical and apparent situation of St. Marguerite, the larger and nearer island.

My business was to reach the outlying island " withdrawn into the sea." How beautiful a simple statement becomes in the Latin, and how it gains dignity from the great style ! The cells and vineyards of the monks in their peaceful island were " *in mare magnum recedentia* "—withdrawn into the great sea.

I can understand what an attraction the little, snake-infested, desert island, as it was then, had for Honoratus, who in the spirit must have felt that the world was about to crumble, as indeed it did crumble under the hooves of barbarian hordes. The ruin of Rome ! There was never such a catastrophe since the Fall of Man.

It had taken an hour to descend from the balconied

height whence the sea, with its misty islands, filled the eye. A greyness like smoke pervaded the panorama. The air was olive grey. But now on the Place des Anglais I can understand why men would be glad to seek an island and to escape from the most fatuous of all civilisations—that of the international pleasure-seekers of the Côte d'Azur. Addicted to self-indulgence as I happily am, yet I would prefer a cell any day to a casino. I began to examine the reasons for that, as I had some hours to wait for the motor-boat. What is it that makes life about a casino so repulsive? Its vapidity, of course. It has no meaning, or any meaning that it could have in such surroundings has been filleted out of it, and its purpose reduced to nothing but a game of chance. I saw the festoons of pink roses falling in little Niagaras, recalling that awful-coloured Horse-Shoe Fall near Buffalo, when the searchlights paint it pink at night. And they came from the Canadian shore! Here in Cannes there was an equal if less obvious and obtrusive vulgarity and display of bad taste. First of all, vulgarity in its strict sense reigned. Argentinos, Mexicans, Americans, under-dressed and over-dressed, met to look at and to vie with people whom they did not know. If they were intent on making an impression, it was all too transient, and as ineffective as tipping a waiter lavishly in a strange land. As I gazed at the glistening cars, I felt myself becoming dazed and unable to think, because I was at a loss to fix a meaning—any meaning—to the endless procession of aggressive wealth. Pleasure-seeking? Awful

I

women with the calves that betray old age more surely and more relentlessly than their face, stepped, showing silken shrinkage, in and out of limousines, disgusting rather than delighting the searching eyes of the Valuers, the sleek, black-haired and blue-jowled Levantines : The Watchers : The White-Slavers : The Invariably Amiable : The Uninsultable Cosmopolitans.

The Alps could not be seen.

The launch would be ready at 2.30.   Was I going to the Monastery ?   Ah, twenty minutes !   The outboard motor roared ; we were about to turn from the jetty when a strange figure presented himself apparently without hurry, but nevertheless with promptitude, at the little quay.   Without a word of explanation he was accepted or rather suffered aboard.   We got under way. The boatman, who was an Italian, had an ancestor who had perished in the convulsion that split the Island of Ischia, in the Bay of Naples, the isle that sheltered her whom Michael Angelo loved.   This ancestral accident apparently gave him and his boat-load some kind of immunity from the dangers of island ferryings.   He was full of news.   But it was so topical and up-to-date that I despaired of getting any legendary information about the island's history.   And why should I ?   If the Abbot was not to be outdone by a boatman, I must give him a chance and abide in patience until the twenty minutes—about as long as it takes from Rush to Lambay, though the distance is greater—were over. " Was Monsieur ever a sufferer from asthma ? " the strange man with the suitcase inquired.   Very re-

luctantly I exempt myself from any of the ills which
flesh is heir to, for fear of tempting the Fates to hand
me out a genuine disease. I did not repudiate asthma,
therefore, for fear that, if I hadn't got it, at some time
or other when I was not noticing it might be visited
on me, when I would have to take it seriously.
" Asthma ? It is quite possible," I said.

I found myself thinking of two things at the same
time, or wondering about one and remembering
another. What I remembered was this :

" And the worst of it is that trumpery diseases which
we never knew we had lift their heads and obtrude
themselves the moment you go on the water-wagon."

So Dr. Tyrrell spoke authoritatively. And who
can dare to contradict him ? What I was wondering
about was who was the passenger to St. Honorat. He
looked so disappointed that I found myself assuming
the airs of an invalid. Asthma ? Does one cough or
choke ? Can it be possible that on the island is one
of those countless sanatoria for those who conceal their
premature loss of interest in life under the name of
tuberculosis ?

" I have plucked of the ripest," I replied.

Don't let me deceive anyone. It was a phrase that
I had committed to memory from the mighty book of
the great Franciscan.

The intonation and balance of his sentences made
me think that he was an American.

" Asthma ? "

" Yea."

" Let me see, now. I may have had it. It means

' a panting ' in the Greek ?   I remember one evening
I was going down, no, up . . ."

" Now, look here.   There's no mistaking it when
it gets you.   I'm not trying to cure you, so you need
not be alarmed.   I am going to that island there for
six months.   I want to get away from things.   I have
been doing too much.   I should just say I have, I'll
tell the world.   They take people over there in that
monastery and make no charge.   That just suits me,
I should say it does."

I remembered that before the expulsion of the Orders
from France the monastery of St. Honorat was Cister-
cian.   It is so still.   They were never suppressed.   I
hope that the practice of freely entertaining visitors for
as long as they care to remain, which obtains in Mount
Mellary and Mount St. Joseph's in Ireland, is not
continued in St. Honorat, if only for the sake of this
American (and of the monks).

And now we are landed.

I had been careful not to look back at the coast of
the Var, so that my first sight of the snowy, sunlit
Alps should be from the island as St. Patrick saw them.
And here we are.

Pulchrior in toto non est locus orbe Lerina.

" No isle in all the world is lovelier than Lerina."

So sang the poet who could build a lofty rhyme, but
who had apparently never been to Ireland.   However !

The land rises so that it comes between the sight-
seer who stands on the south of the island and his view
of the Alps.   On this side is the long, three-storied

monastery. Far off, at a corner of a curving bay, stands an old fortified monastery like a castle, square and strong. This is no longer a monastery. It stands in the very sea, and so must have been distractingly shaken and noisy when the sandy hurricanes blew from Africa over the way.

I could not shake off my panting acquaintance who had attached himself to me in the motor-boat. Even if I pressed hard against the rising path, he would get me again at the side gate of the monastery. He cost me half an hour's delay before he had his wishes granted by a monk. The latter by this time was prepared curtly to dismiss a merely curious visitor. And though he listened with all courtesy to my some-what involved preamble, at last he exclaimed, with an emphatic nodding of the head which was meant perhaps to close the tale, " *St. Patrice. Mais oui !* " And there it was.

I felt as one who had sought for an artist in Chelsea without mentioning Augustus John.

For, after all, was it not the man of consular family, Honoratus, who had cleared, planted and founded the island, and made it one of the most famous places in Gaul seven or eight years before the refugee from outlandish Scotia came to it.

Without mentioning Napoleon I was touring Waterloo! Were I to ask for the Abbot, it would only make things worse. I climbed up from the richly cultivated market-gardens round the monastery, up from its olives and vines and from the clearance which these made among the pine trees, through winding paths under these wind-contorted and fantastic trees which waded down to the rocky and shingly beach as if to cool their roots in the clear water. As the ground rose, the shape of the island could be seen. It is longer than it is broad, and seems as if it could be walked around in less than an hour. Did Patrick walk barefooted with Honoratus and the Saints of God daily round this most peaceful and attractive island?

I must have reached the ridge for, on a sudden . . . lo! Summits ablaze in light. The mighty Alps rose out of the sapphire sea, their planes curved as if by the brushwork of a painter. But what painter ever held that white? It was light itself, the whitest of all earthly things : the snow on mountains standing in the sun. The long line of the palm-shaded Places of Cannes stretched in from the headland. Over the town which climbed up the steep foothills was the winding road by which I had come. I could see the grey mist which lay on its side ; but now I knew it for olive gardens about Grasse. This was the sight which made the poet exclaim, " May I be hanged if here I would not live for ever! " I began to wonder if . . . ? But knowing myself as far as scenery goes, I think that I have in mind an isle that can excel it.

If I could not see the Abbot, could I not see the spring of fresh water? That was sure to be enclosed and conduited into the buildings. There was nothing left for me to see. But just a moment. . . . " The island was afterwards purchased by an actress who loved its natural beauty, but made its sacred rites the scene of unholy revels." It is possible that these were counteracted and cancelled by the subsequent residency of an Anglican minister. But where was the villa of the actress? It would date from about 1850. What kind of orgies had they eighty-eight years ago? Was there a place in a sense something like Mag Slecht? And what was the minister doing? I learnt that her name was Mlle. Sainval and that she dwelt in the XIth century citadel which of old used to shelter the monks from Saracenic raiders.

The motor-boat mechanic blew a whistle—a signal calling all visitors. And it was just as well. My mind was beginning to wander. " From the spells of women Smiths and Druids. . . ."

I will go back to Ulster with the Saint, who in his self-appointed exile shall look back to Lerins, longing " To behold once more the faces of the Saints of God in Gaul."

CHAPTER XII

PATRICK'S SECOND COMING. HE COMES OF HIS OWN FREE WILL

"A help to Ireland was Patrick's coming, which was expected."
Fiacc's Hymn, " Genair Patrick."

IT WAS EXPECTED, AFTER THE DEATH OF PALLADIUS, BY the Christian communities in Legain, which is now Leinster, as well as those in Dalaradia, the scene of his captivity. He had been absent from Ireland for twenty-one years.

Now, from this on, when recording the journeys of the Bishop Patrick on his mission, it may be more acceptable to call him St. Patrick, and to call the places he visited by the names they now have, putting their older names—names contemporary with the Saint—beside them. This will be in accordance with the reverence in which he is held and with the continuity of that " help " which is benefiting our island—and never more strongly than at the present day. That he was expected, or a great Christian leader who would organise Christianity in Ireland was expected, appears from the interesting prophecy of the Druids.

> Adzehead will come
> Over the mad-crested sea,
> His cloak hole-headed,
> His staff crooked-headed,
> His table in the east of his house ;
> He will chant impiety
> From his table ;
> And all his household will respond :
> " Amen, Amen."

This is the Irish version from the glosses on the Hymn

(*Liber Hymnorum*, page 100), but, as the Latin version picturesquely says, " his head through a hole in his house." To explain that line : His head through a hole in his house refers to the robe everybody wore who was anybody—that is the *casula* or chasuble which they say is derived from *casa*, the Latin for house. The second mention of house in the prophecy is, of course, his chapel, and the table is the altar—they call it " table " still in Brawdy Chapel in Pembrokeshire— and the response is, Amen. " Adzehead " refers to the Saint's mitre, which was a band round the head bearing on the forehead a disc like the blade of an axe.

It was a prophecy which requires little foresight and less magic for its making. Were a proof wanting, the presence of Christianity widespread in the island might be deduced from this warning cry, but the Druids were well aware of what progress Christianity had made beyond the narrow seas, and they knew that it would not be long before the Irish Church would be welded with all the great organising power of Rome. Rome, whose secular arm, the arm of her Emperors and Generals, had never reached Ireland in the days of her glory, now in the day of her tribulation reached out more strongly than ever and spread her spiritual dominion beyond her former frontiers. She won over the invincible Picts in their fastnesses, those " haunts of the Britons inaccessible to the Romans but subjugated to Christ " (Tertullian in his " Answer to the Jews," Ante-Nicene Library, Vol. XVIII, page 218), and now she was about to win Ireland from Druidism and to introduce, by the nature of her organisation, another authority besides that of the tribal system, with its degrees of ascending autonomous kings.

And now Adzehead was in sight on the mad-crested sea with his dark sail making for Inver Dea, the port that traded in Wicklow gold with Britain, Spain and Gaul. Long, low, buff-coloured sand dunes undulated to the west beyond the sea. Another hour and they would see the roofs of the harbour huts and the ships beached beside them on the sands; and the crowd—the news-loving Irish crowd—would be coming down to the beach for tidings from oversea. The trees that marked the little harbour were distinct. " The well-known and opportune port " lay ahead. The crew were talking freely, now that all was well and soon they would haul ashore. The sweeps were going out, for it was advisable to strike the little river mouth and to ascend as far as possible while there was tide. And they had yet to find the passage through the bar. But now they touched the sand! St. Patrick had come to the port by which he had left in that mysterious ship which saved him over twenty years ago.

His Gallic and British companions gazed with apprehension at the Saint, and gained but little comfort from his eagerness. But he knew the country and the language; and the Christian emissaries from Tibroney had assured them, while on the continent, that all would be well. Yet the outlandish costumes and wild beards of the men around them were not reassuring, nor was the sudden taciturnity with which, after a rude scrutiny, they were received. They were at Inver Dea, which is called after Degaid, the

founder of the tribe of wild men whose numbers were
increasing. How would its present representative
behave? They must buy provisions from the local
fishermen, and wash themselves from the salt
spray after all that sailing. But the local fishermen
growled and would sell them nothing. St. Patrick
directed them to follow him to Anat-Cailtrin, to the
strong place where Nathi Macgarrchon lived. The
Saint would confront him and shame him for the
inhospitality of his underlings. The Saint had a
great presence and the majesty of a strong and righteous
character. He was a man whom no one could treat
with contumely or pretend to ignore. But before he
ascended half Kilmantan hill, called after Mantan, one
of the companions of St. Patrick, as we call it from that
day, out came the King in person with a guard, and
turned him and his companions back. This was the
same man who had refused rights to Palladius the year
before. For all he cared the sect might help themselves, but they would get no help from him, much less
be encouraged to introduce foreigners to his domain.
He was held in little respect by his father-in-law,
Leary, the High King, as it was, for the settlement of
Christians in his district. Did they think that they
had a hold on him? Did they think that he was a
weakling? The one thing of which he had been
warned was not to have any truck with these people
or their Druids unless he wanted to find himself with
his head shaved and his beard off, a laughing stock
for all the under chiefs. His wife's disdain was bad
enough, but she was right when she said that his

kingdom depended on his strength of mind.   Out they
all must go !   Wasn't the harbour his ?   And there was
not a flask of Burdigalam among the lot of them !

So the Saint was turned back.   And now the
common men began, being a multitude compared to
St. Patrick's gentle comrades, to show their courage as
common men will do by hitting behind the back.
Stones began to fly.   Mantan, one of his companions,
turned round and immediately a stone struck him in
the mouth, splitting his lip and smashing his teeth so
badly that he was spoken of as The Toothless from
that injury ever afterwards.

St. Patrick raised his left hand and, moving it
slowly, spoke a solemn malediction against the King.
They had time to take to their ship, which providentially
was unmolested.   After all, the port was a source of
revenue to the inhospitable tribe.

And now the voyage becomes interesting to us, for
it is instructive in that it throws light on the way they
navigated in the fifth century : they coasted wherever
they could and put in to the beach at nightfall.   That the
ship this time belonged to the Saint and his companions
appears from the obedience of the sailors, who were prepared to go farther along the shores of a land where for
all they knew they would receive no better treatment
than that they had just experienced from the King of
Wicklow.   It is likely that the ship was equipped by
friends and relatives of St. Patrick and that its pilot was
Lugnaedon, his sister's son, who, though a deacon, yet
had a mundane task, as had St. Paul in days before public
reverence exempted sacerdotalism from manual work.

They must have arrived early at Inver Degaid, for they seem to have gone out on the outgoing tide.

From Wicklow strand, where they were, to Mala-hide is forty sea miles.   The coast with its dangerous sand bars could not have been known to Lugnaedon, but that man, with all his experience of the sea, sought safety upon it, for although his ship was shallow-draughted, he stood well out from the shore.   This brought him beyond the reach of the changing currents which three times a day sweep round Bray Head. He left the coast alone, although he must have guessed from the coast's formation that there was another petty stream about as far north from Bray Head as the Vartry river is from Wicklow Head.   There was no need to put in there.   They were leaving Wicklow. So they set sail for Ben Adair, the greatest Head of all, which was to be called Hoved by the Danes, who built Baile Atha Cliath, our Dublin, four hundred years later. Directly ahead it lay, its rocks coloured like a mountain of wild rose.   Across one of the world's loveliest bays the boat went on and Howth (Ben Adair) was rounded. The Island of Ireland they kept to port, Ireland's Eye we call it ; and now they are somewhat sheltered by Lambay, for even in the twelfth century, the story goes, this island could be reached by wading at low tide : to-day it is twenty minutes' sail over many fathoms in a converted lifeboat.   The long Silver Strand lay on their left as they searched for another estuary.   The stream that enters the sea north of the Silver Strand enters it amid limestone rocks, and a

man can step across it if it is yet to be found amid all
the present-day " development."

Malahide has an estuary almost too swift and tidal
for the beaching of a boat.   This is where the Swords
river takes the sea amid steep sands, treacherous for
swimmers.   This was Inver Domnann, for " Inver "
always indicates a river mouth.   But for all its antiquity
and wealth of traditions there is no local legend about
the Saint at Malahide.   It may be that the boat only
touched there, leaving the Saint to rest while a few
went ashore in search of food.   And while the Saint
is resting let us all rest, because, if he is tired, it may
well be that those who are following my account of his
voyage may be tired too.   So we will step ashore and
look at an estuary which, save for the ever-shifting
sands, is unchanged since the days the Saint sought
refreshment by its shores.

As you pass along its southern bank you come to a
walled house with a great shuttered window in the
wall.   This dark red, door-like window opens side-
ways like a sliding gate.   This was the window which
the greatest landscape-painter Ireland ever produced
used to open from his studio in order to paint, over
and over again, tirelessly for fifty years, the ever-
changing lights and colours of the Swords estuary.
Nathaniel Hone was too rich and too regardless of
money ever to trouble to sell his pictures, or even to
put a price on them.   Thus it came about that, in a
time when most things are judged by their price,
his worth as a supreme artist was unappreciated.
It was undiscovered.   To my friend Æ, that com-

panion spirit to Hone, I owe the little knowledge I possess of Hone's great merit. Hone was a colleague of Corot, and they dwelt at Barbizon together. Hone may be called the Corot of Ireland. If his work lacks the silvern light of the great Frenchman, it is because the same tenuous light is not to be found in our misty, sea-girt island. True, the morning light out over Malahide Bay can entrance the eye with brilliance beyond all silver : it is too bright to be paintable when the sun comes through two floating clouds riding far out to sea. But from one of these clouds and a long crescent of warm sand he could make a greater picture, because more simple, than any composition of Corot's. His was an Æschylean outlook ; majestic, elemental and full of power. He was the most native of all painters, for he rarely left his land, rarely indeed his studio by the estuary, knowing well the infinite and inexhaustible variety of God's creation of light on sea and sky and the rain that slants on dark trees over lush grass udder deep, where the cattle are grazing. He gave his works to the Nation. Let us hope that it will not take the Nation fifty years to have its retina endowed and informed by the greatest genius who ever interpreted in paint the landscape of the earth and heaven of Ireland.

If this be a trifle rhetorical, how can you be re-created ? Come up the street where the joy-bells are ringing in gay Malahide (on Sundays from the church tower) and look for its poet and novelist Lynn Doyle, another of Ireland's great artists in another medium. He lives in Malahide in Leinster, in order to get the full enchantment of his native Ulster and the North. He will tell us a story or, better still—if we can talk like this about the incomparable—sing us a song he made lately about the North.   He has many poems; and they have the humanity, sweetness and appeal of Burns.

He is tall and straight-backed, like the McNeills. His wide eyes gleam over his broad cheeks—there is the mark of a sword-cut on the left.   Straight in every way.   Break into song, Lynn!

> Long since in Ballydugan mill
>   Two youthful lovers played
> I was the gay adventuring knight
>   My cousin Ruth, the maid.
>
> Slender her grace as any reed's
>   By Ballydugan side,
> Pale the dear lips so sweetly given
>   So tenderly denied.
>
> If I had known that gentle child
>   Had filled her span of years
> I might have changed my answering mirth
>   For vain beseeching tears.

You're a good fellow!   I like " tenderly denied." You have a sweet note.   I always said so.   Do you remember, to change the reed, that one you made about the Orangeman who had a Catholic pal for approximately 360 days of the year?   But about the Twelfth . . . " Is this what you mean ? "

An Ulster Man

> I do not like the other sort;
>   They're tricky and they're sly,
> And could not look you in the face
>   Whenever they pass by.

Still I'll give in that here and there,
　　You'll meet a decent man;
I would make an exception now
　　About wee Michael Dan.

But then he's from about the doors,
　　And lived here all his days,
And mixin' with us in and out,
　　He's fell into our ways.
He pays his debts and keeps his word
　　And does the best he can.
If only all the Papishes
　　Were like wee Michael Dan !

A better neighbour couldn't be :
　　He borrows and he lends ;
And bar a while about the Twelfth
　　When him and me's not friends—
He'll never wait until he's asked
　　To lend a helpin' han'.
There's quite a wheen of Protestants
　　I'd swop for Michael Dan."

"That's the stuff, Lynn!" I said in admiration.
And Lynn's grave face relaxed.

"If you are following St. Patrick, you had better
go easy in Skerries."

"Skerries? The mainland off Holmpatrick?"

"Precisely. Did you never hear the legend about
the Skerry men and St. Patrick's goat?"

I was silent with expectation. At length I asked,
having undergone a quizzical torture, "Is there a
legend?"

"You may be sure there is. Don't ask a man in
Skerries, 'Who eat the goat?'"

"Eat the goat?"

"St. Patrick was ordered goat's milk and rum for
his stomach's sake. And he sent his goat ashore at

K

Skerries for a rest and a bit of refreshment.   But the men of Skerries skinned and ate it.   I heard only the other day that some of the men of Rush, from the next parish, who were in a regiment stationed as far East as Shanghai, were having a bit of light refreshment in a bar with divisions or partitions in it, and they heard the sound of Skerry voices from the other side of the partitions.   One of them put his head over and shouted, ' Who ate the goat ? '   Pandemonium was let loose at once, and it took a week to quell it.   Even China joined in."

" So St. Patrick may be said to ' hold the gorgeous East in fee ? ' " I ventured.

" He got the Skerry men's goat, anyway."

It is always great to meet Lynn.   He will not have to wait to come into his own.   Even in Ireland he is famous in his own day.   We all know him and we all regard him with an admiration equalled only by our affection.

It must have been late September when St. Patrick touched at Malahide.   Or else the coasting boat was able to tack without a keel and to make six or seven knots, which is unlikely unless the wind was due south. And this would have meant rain.   There would have been no point in going on ten miles farther north to the largest island of the group of small islands known as the Isles of the Children of Cor, if darkness had overtaken his company at Malahide.   Undoubtedly he drew ashore on the largest of these islands ; if there ever is anything in tradition, here it is most definite— and they call it Inis Patrick to this day.   All these Isles of the Children of Cor are rocky—so rocky that

the Norsemen who held the opposite coast for four
hundred years called them the Skerries, which is the
Rocks ; and the town on the adjoining shore is called
Skerries after them.

You can reach Red Island, the nearest, without a
boat, but the second is half a mile farther out, Colt
Island, with its Martello tower, and another half-mile
into the sea is St. Patrick's Island. This is rich in
grass and, like all grassy islands in Ireland, is sweet
pasturage.   It stands well out of the sea, but there
is a little level, hardly a strand, on which a boat could
be beached.   It looks, though, as if the Saint's boat
rode at anchor.   Like Ireland's Eye, it has a ruined
church.   It was an important place in mediæval times.
St. Malachy and Gelasius the Primate attended a
synod on it in 1148, together with fifteen bishops
and two hundred priests.   So seven centuries after
St. Patrick we find it lending security to the Irish
Church.   Lord Holmpatrick takes his titular name
from it, and sometimes it is called by his name.

Here on Holmpatrick St. Patrick stayed overnight,
and next morning, we learn from the Tripartite Life,
again his mariners were seeking another estuary.
This attraction of the estuaries of streams, all about
the same size, is full of interest.   To those qualified
to interpret it, it ought to throw some light on the
probable size of the boats and the practices of the
sailors.   One reason—and I think a very good one,
one which would occur to the simple-thinking and direct
mind of a child—was given me by my daughter, who
suggested that if they wished to run aground in a wider

river—the Liffey or the Boyne, for instance—they would have to penetrate farther into possibly unfriendly country, with little chance of escape or protection from showers of stones from the banks. All the streams selected by the sailors are about twenty to thirty feet across where the tide ends, and a ship can be grounded on the bottom level and men can step almost dry-shod ashore. Whatever the cause may be, we find St. Patrick sending messengers to Inver Ainge, which, corrupted, is now called Nanny Water, just as the root word for water, Awni, becomes Anna in Anna Liffey.* This little river must have been known to the Saint, for he had to cross it in his flight. It is a thin stream widening into oval pools, which hold white trout and sometimes salmon. Of course it is overfished. But there are fish enough to give the lie to the author of the Tripartite Life, who is too prone to make the Saint inflict the innocent waters here and in Wicklow and Malahide with barrenness by his maledictions. It would have been more to the point had he directed those maledictions to the inhospitable inhabitants of the districts. He is not satisfied with dealing out curses, but he sometimes makes the subject of his Life a false prophet, as we shall presently see.

It was weary going for the French prelates and clerics from England ; not that they were accustomed to good cheer, for they were acquainted with the fare of monasteries such as Lerins and Auxerre, and there were ascetics in the ship : but to get no cheer at all

* Anna Liffey = Amha na Life. Amha = River Misge = Water. Rivers are always feminine in Irish, called after goddesses.—Donel O'Sullivan.

on their first visit to an isle to whose service many must have dedicated themselves for life, was beyond human endurance. Thanks be to St. Patrick, we have since gained some title to a better reputation for the more hospitable and Christian entreatment of visitors.

If his ship made forty miles in a day from Wicklow to Holmpatrick, leaving time enough to send messengers ashore for food, it may be expected to have reached its destination, which is about fifty miles distant, in a day from dawn to dark. But on such a journey it was impossible to set sail without food. And that it was attempted is unlikely for another reason, which is that Patrick, who must have heard of the tide race, knew well where he was going, for his seeking the Lough of Strangford was neither fortuitous nor an alternative to happy-go-lucky hospitality, so he must have heard, in his six years' captivity, when he went on errands near the great dun by the Quoile, of the force of the ocean river at the entrance to Strangford Lough. He could give no assurance, apart from a question of the uncertainty of the weather holding, that they could make the entry to the Lough before dark. Therefore it is more than probable that he went ashore in the Delvin valley on the coast of fertile Bregia, where a petty chieftain Sescnen dwelt. Here, it seems, he was met by the chieftain's son Benen, who led him to his father, who entertained the famishing company. Of this Benen a touching tale is told, which is true in all probability, save for what may be an error in the chronology of the Saint's journey, for if all the Tripartite Life tales were exact, it would imply that the first church the Saint founded in Ireland was founded in rich Meath—that is, Bregia in the Delvin valley—and this the overwhelming testimony of tradition denies.   But let the touching story be told : and let who will make allowance for its seemliness.   St. Patrick, weary with his seafaring and overweighed with responsibility, fell asleep in the grianān or sun-garden of the holt.   Then it was that the little boy Benen or Benignus, as he was in the Latin most happily called, took pity on the overwrought bishop and filled his bosom with flowers.   Being checked lest the Saint be wakened, the words awoke the Saint, who blessed him for his loving kindness and, as Tirechan his biographer states, "*Aedificavit ibi ecclesiam primam,*" he built there his first church.   But as many authorities hold this incident took place after his winter in Mag Inis, one tradition has as much authority as another.   But whatever tradition the men of Meath hand down is overwhelmed now by the insistence and tenacity characteristic of the North.

But before we follow the ship past the mouth of the river Boyne, which has been confused with the mouth of the Delvin river because some scribe wrote Inver Boinde instead of Inver Ailbine, and across the wide bays on each side of precipitous Slieve Donard (which, by the way, is much higher than the altitude given on the map)—from all the prominence given to the need for food and the way the Tripartite Life subordinates the journey to providing it—a viewpoint which is neither dignified nor worthy of the biographer—we are almost unconsciously left with the impression that the whole

mission of the Saint was simply a bow drawn at a
venture, a mission at the mercy of any surly fisherman
or inhospitable farmer on the coast.   The contrary
is the truth.   There was nothing peradventure about
the journey.   For long years the Saint had striven
to prepare himself for it ; he had been duly ordained
after tribulation of spirit, with full authority and
with at least twenty-four companions, some of whom
were priests, and he set out with sacred objects and
an artificer skilled in making ecclesiastical furniture,
to convert the hardiest pagans left in Europe as late
as the year 432.   It is incredible, as one not on his
guard might infer from the Tripartite Life, with all
its charming incidents, that the entire expedition
should be left to the hazard of a meal or two.   Ships
which could sail the open seas for three days, as one
did with Patrick twenty-one years before, were not to
be met every few leagues while coasting from Wicklow
to Loch Cuan unless indeed it had come directly
from France.   The quest for food and probably
fresh water would indicate this long journey, and
it is a point that may be of interest to the Saint's
biographers ; but to guard myself from holding an
opinion unworthy of the importance and magnitude
of the expedition (if that word can be used of a sea-
borne company), I must not let the Tripartite writer
distract me by leading me to under-estimate it or the
forethought and care with which the Saint must have
cherished what was dear to his heart and his life's
ambition as well as sacrifice.   St. Patrick was a sailor
with knowledge bought with grim experience of the sea.

His journey first to those Christians who had been visited the preceding year by Palladius and then to Ulidia, that part of Ulster where he had spent six years from about sixteen to twenty-one, was planned and decided first by the existence of these communities, and secondly by his knowledge of the district. There is another reason for selecting Ulidia for the commencement of his mission—a reason which is most interesting and very probable.   It was put forward by my friend and namesake, in the language of the Gael the Most Reverand Dr. Fogarty, the magnanimous Bishop of Killaloe, and it will be discussed in its appropriate place.

Lough Strangford is long and shallow, about nineteen miles in length from north to south.   The turmoil of the tides, as they go or come by the straight estuary of its ocean river which is called the Strait of Brene, presents a very serious obstacle to mariners. A lady, to whom I am indebted for great hospitality and much information about St. Patrick's legends, which abound on her property on the Lough's eastern side, believes, from her knowledge of yachting, that the feat of entering this race of waters was impossible to such a boat as was at the disposal of the Saint. She has an interesting theory that the missionaries put in south of the Lough's entrance at Ardglass and advanced inland about six miles on foot.   Only the assurance and enthusiasm which I found everywhere among all the inhabitants, from Saul through the lovely hanging village of Ratolp (Rathcolpa) down

to the mouth of the little Slan, cause me to adhere to
a tradition which is so lively and local to this day.
And then there was the line of the poet—and a poet,
no matter how halting, I can never ignore. The religion of the local people mattered not. In one thing
they were in agreement to a man. " Here he landed.
Of course the stream was a bit fuller in those days."
And so I photographed the streamlet's mouth, where
slowly from a bed of rushes it gathers current enough
to empty itself under the single arch of a long-overgrown
and broken viaduct of stone which led, before a road
was built, to a prosperous farm. As I stood on it a
child ran out and grasped my hand, until her anxious
mother overtook her, for the arch was overgrown,
and rank growth concealed a possible hole in its roof.
" That's where St. Patrick landed, sir ! There beside
the stream. You can't take your eyes off her but she
runs out. And there's his path to Saul." The
little bridle-path that skirts it, curving to the left under
the hazels that hedge the field of corn, is clearly to be
seen in the photograph, which would have been better
had it not been taken at low tide. As far as it would
go they forced their boat, which had been rowed
through the neck of the Lough (Brene Strait) when
the incoming tide was at the flood. And they hid
the vessel in the river-bed hard by, and went to put off
their weariness, as the poet to whom I referred has it :

In the fountain, in the region of Benna Boirche, which neither
drought nor flood affected.

The fountain Slan, the healer, is now called the Wells
of Struell near Saul. " He slept on a bare flagstone

there," to quote from the same writer, Fiacc, " with
a wet mantle round him. A pillar stone was his
bolster." This is quite an accurate description of the
cave and of what would happen to the clothes of anyone
who slept within reach of the Healer's spray.

They went ashore, we are told, " to put off their
weariness " on the bank of the stream. But first they
hid their boat. If they imagined when they were
resting that their movements had been unobserved,
they did not know Ireland and they would have been
wrong. Just as one could take for granted that
dozens of natives surrounded the boat of the captain
who carried Patrick to freedom, so here were observers;
not many, yet one was enough. A look shot out sharp
at the Saint and his companions, saw the furtive
concealment of their ship; and a swineherd ran off
to tell his master.

Now, his master is presumed to have dwelt in the
great fort of Down (Dun : hence, later, *Down*patrick),
that earthwork whose magnificent remains are so
imposing that the imagination fills with a sense of
pride and power seeing such unmistakable evidence
of the former grandeur of our land. Here is the
actual castle of a veritable Red Branch Knight, Celtar
of the Battles, who flourished about the beginning of
the first century. A right royal fortress it must have
been, when newly walled and manned. Even now
it stands sixty feet above the deep black tidal water
which may of old have flowed right up to its fosses.
It is little less than half a mile in circumference.
Truly reflected in " the waves beneath it shining,"

we " catch a glimpse of the days that are over, and sighing, look through the waves of Time, at the long-faded glories they cover." The swineherd's master, Dichu, was the son of Trichem, of the royal line of the Dal Fiatach. That he was a powerful prince is un-deniable, that he was an historical personage is un-deniable. Therefore, even to-day he can confound those who would make out that his friend the Saint never existed, or that he existed two hundred years before he was born, *vide* the Rev. John Roche Ardill, LL.D., from the Calry Rectory : " I have tried to prove that the facts of non-fabulous history dove-tail around St. Patrick at A.D. 180."

As I was saying, when Dichu was informed of the secret landing of a company of strange, bald, white-robed, sandalled men who spoke a strange language, which his swineherd was the first to hear—the language of an Empire, a spiritual Empire, the " tongue and tocsin of Eternity " which shall for ever sound in Ireland—he was at first minded to have them slain for robbers or pirates from overseas. But the de-scription must have aroused his curiosity. He came with his hound to look at the strangers. The story goes that he set his dog at them, whereupon St. Patrick chanted the Prophet's verse, " Leave not the souls that confess to Thee, O Lord, a prey to beasts." Whereupon the dogs became silent. At the same moment his master's heart was touched : " grief of heart seized him and he believed."

Full as the Tripartite Life is of dramatic moments and situations, it fails fundamentally through not having what may be called reverence for its subject. Here the movement is too rapid and the motives or causes of action are inconsequent, to say the least of them, or absent altogether. That version will not do. In all human likelihood, what actually happened was that curiosity, not apprehension, brought out Dichu, and that he recognised St. Patrick after he had made himself known to him in the Daladian dialect.

And it is here that the profoundly far-seeing conjecture of Dr. Fogarty comes in. He suggests, as I have already said, that the leading motive of the Saint's return to South Ulster (Mag Inis) was the fact that Dichu was married to one of the daughters of St. Patrick's old master Milchu, and that Patrick came, knowing that he would find a friend at Court. Of all the conjectures in a realm which is so largely conjectural, surely this is the best. Surely to the Bishop " the credit will be conceded of having acted steadily to the best of his judgment." To me it seems a superb instance of the exercise of imagination in explaining what required explanation along human lines and according to all probability.

So Dichu had something more to believe in than that which made his dog stop barking. He had the Saint before him to win him to Christianity—gradually, let us hope, for his sincerity's sake ; and perhaps the Saint had the influence of Dichu's wife, who, with her sister and brother, appeared as the children by the Wood of Focluth whom Patrick beheld in a vision, saying " Come, holy youth. Walk once more with us." They were described accurately as *by* the Wood of Focluth, which may to the youth Patrick have stood for the ends of the earth. Let me repeat, " For who," asks the Bishop, " among all those savages could have known that the young slave was a holy youth but the boy and girls he played with in Skerry during his servitude ? " In this context the statement of his biographer is significant: " Two maidens came to Patrick, and they received the pallium from his hand, and he blessed a place for them *at* the Wood of Focluth." But all the difficulties about the Wood of Focluth—difficulties which deceived the learned Bury —would disappear if scholars would accept, as Professor Muller of Tubingen has accepted it, McNeill's reading of Silva Focluti as Silva Uluti.

The results go to testify to the justice of these premises or theories, for the Saint is at once installed in Saul—that is, at the Barn which, being the only substantial building that was suitable, Patrick accepted, though it meant using an " alternate church," one that faced north and south and not east and west. His very silence on his relationship with Dichu and his gratitude speak of their being old acquaintances. How could St. Patrick, when defending himself from detractors, some of whom evidently accused him of accepting alms—though where the harm lay in that is hard to seek—acknowledge the great benefit he got in being accepted and himself and his companions given rights even where the High King, had he been so minded, could not have obtained them for him ? Dichu was absolute in his own domain.

Whatever way it was, the scene the Bishop conjures

up of an attitude of aggression turning into one of close scrutiny and slow recognition makes a far more dramatic and, at the same time, natural picture than the semi-miraculous and unconvincing episode of Patrick converting Dichu by quieting his dog with a line, which must have sounded outlandish to native ears.   Explain it how we will, Patrick got the grant of Saul and had no obstinate pagan to convert.

Thinking of Saul, the Barn, makes me suspect that Dichu's dun may not have been at Rath Celtair, but nearer to his Barn.   The remains of Rath Celtair are the grandest I have seen, and whoever ruled there was a holder of a house greater than the dun of the High King at Tara.   It may have been a combination of a fortified barracks and a house for hostages— that is, a prison somewhat like the Tower of London. Hostages were held, we all know, by every great king—witness the House of the Hostages at Tara and Nial's title " of the Nine Hostages."   And the name Dun Celtair came to have later, The Rath of the Two Broken Fetters, may be an allusion which would go to support the theory.

The greatest Welshman of all time had come, " the living coal of fire, bringing good for evil, to show goodly compassion towards that nation that once took him captive and harried the menservants and maid-servants of his father's house " (Letter to Coroticus). Adzehead had come, the son of Calpurn, " a help to Ireland."   And Dichu established him.   His first church was built; and even already the place of his landing was lovingly remembered.

CHAPTER XIII

"AND NOW LET US PRAISE FAMOUS MEN"

IT IS NOT EVERYONE, MUCH LESS A WRITER, WHO HAS the good fortune to be piloted by an ex-Air Minister of Great Britain, in a private aeroplane, over the most significant territory, in the tracks of St. Patrick. Nor is it every country that has an Air Minister who can fly. This suits me well, I said to myself. I have suffered many disappointments by adhering to my theory of the pre-eminence of the aristocratic type over every other form of humanity—a view which, if you are suspected of holding it, is liable to make you unpopular with your fellows and which, quite conceivably, though quite illogically, might lay you open to the suspicion of being a snob. I myself was once suspected, as this shows: " For all that," a chance acquaintance said to me, " many a good man was born in a slum. Take me, for instance. What's wrong with me? Eh, what? I'm as good as any of your swells, and I hadn't a castle over my head either. On the contrary, I was born in a room. What's wrong with that?" . . . "This," I said. " You are a specimen not quite unknown to social science. A very dangerous type, because you and your like make it almost impossible for corporations and other bodies to improve housing conditions. You are *amica luto sus*." . . . " What are you calling me?" he asked. . . . " I will come to that presently," I said. " You are one of those who revel in a sty. You are a Slum Snob." He did not answer, but looked as if his fate were in his slum, not in himself. From that I concluded that it is unwise to seek the concurrence of the unworthy. It is all so trying. So don't read further in this book if you regret that you were not born in a slum.

But a man must have some opinions of his own even in Ireland, if he is to retain his individuality, or any individuality at all. And my opinion is that a good aristocratic is the highest type that humanity or evolution has evolved. It is hard to defend it, because, up to this, I have been able to point out so few examples, which may be due either to my knowing so few or to the fact that the few I know are not quite the most outstanding specimens of the Pre-eminents. Let not a limitation such as this stand in the way of the principle which I have announced and which I maintain. But even if I knew dozens of the best people, there is another obstacle which must yet be overcome. And this is the heresy of Pelagius, which has been driven out of the realms of theology only to infect our social and political life. This heresy excluded the doctrine of original sin and held that a good pagan could be equal to a Christian. We see " patriotic " Pelagianism all around us at the present time. You have only to visit the National Museum, where you could have found until lately, right up against the gold ornaments and miracles of crafts-manship of our heroic age, large dolls of life-size grannies with red petticoats, washy but unwashed children and fishermen in *blue* bawneens or the *white* buttonless coats the fishermen of the Gaelic-speaking parts of the country are presumed to wear. You will notice no young women, because they have emigrated long ago. (Since this was written the dolls have been relegated to another part of the Museum.) Here you have Pelagianism at its worst, for here it is implied that the poorest and most illiterate and dole-debauched members of the nation are free from social and political original sin and equal to the best, to the heroes who colonised Wales and made it possible for that blend with the Britons to produce St. Patrick, to the artists who left us the only remains to which we can point as exempting us from barbarism, and to each and all of us who have had grace enough to enlighten our under-standing by study and true patriotic corporal works.

Meanwhile bullocks are herded on Tara, on the graves of Kings.

Progress and Pelagianism are opposed. We must get rid of our political Pelagians if we are once more to hold up our heads among the nations of the world. Bear with me if I maintain that " one man is not as good as another," our Pelagians' way of saying that our worst is equal to our best. As if there were nothing worthy of imitation or adulation remaining in Ireland. Let us leave this mental slum.

We took off from his flying-field one sunny, windy morning at 10.45, and circled twice over the great house, where the Red Hand of Ulster worked out in crimson begonias in one of the Italian gardens could be seen plainly from the air. The Red Hand of Ulster is the crest of the MacDonells, but it has been awarded, modified with all the punctiliousness of the College of

L

Heralds, to the Royal Ulster Air Force.   The Mac-
Donell hand is a left hand, the Airmen's a right.
However, as it depends which way the hand is turned
it does not make much difference from the air.   The
way the MacDonells got it, the legend tells, was as
follows : Two chieftains were contending for Ulster,
and it was agreed as they rowed to its shore that
he who reached it first should possess it.   As the rival
boat forged ahead, MacDonell drew his sword and,
severing his left hand, flung it across the waves to
grasp the land of Antrim and win her who held Antrim
as her dowry.   At best this was a left-handed way of
doing things.   But as I have often used my left hand
to take photographs of Ulster, I should be the last to
talk about taking places in that manner.

Out over the bright sea we swung.   The far coast,
low-lying, was barely visible, and the Mountains of
Mourne were hidden in silver light.   Soon many
islands appeared ; Island Magee or Nendrum, where
another little swineherd, Mochae, the grandson of
Patrick's master, founded a monastery and a school,
was clearly seen.   And now an archipelago of little,
brown-edged, green islands spread out, edged with
seaweed, for the tide was very low.   The bump-
ing ceased as we got well out over the Lough, and
this was opportune, for we had to make many sharp
turns and banks as the pilot manœuvred for position.
After fifteen minutes I could see the Church of Saul,
the Barn which was Patrick's first church, and I
knew by that landmark that the landing-place of the
Saint and his companions could soon be picked out.

I was looking for a rushy rivulet that fell down through the little village of Raholp, lost in flowers, and entered the south-western limit of the Lough through a single arch in a long, grass-topped bridge. In a moment I saw an arch and photographed it, but I realised almost as I did so that this was not the bridge, for there was a cluster of houses to the north, and not a substantial farmhouse standing alone, as there should be. I had not realised that at our height the considerable stream of the Quoile river would look but a few feet wide. But I had "got" the Quoile as it flows, making islands past the great dun, and merging with the salt sea beneath Downpatrick, thus verifying the description of Downpatrick as "very near to the sea." We dived down to eight hundred feet and banked about, and I tried again. This time I made no mistake. I photographed his landing-place, with the little path by the right bank of the stream which is flowing towards the inlet of Lough Strangford. Only its channel shows where it grooves the Lough, for the tide is farther out than I remember ever to have seen it. A stippled field on the left was a field of corn in stooks, and past the angle of this field the path curves between a pond and the rivulet, to climb the hill to Saul and probably to Dichu's dun, in the day when the white monks followed one, to whom this path was not unknown—fifteen hundred and six years ago, at this very season, when corn was high; but not so high as to-day, for the ancient people only cut the ears, and left what must have been shorter straw to lie. My eye had caught the great dun when we first dived down on

Inver Slan, and up again we zoomed, to get a broad perspective with the church where the Saint is laid. " He died at Saul.   But he awaits at Down his resurrection.   In the high place of Celtair, the son of Drach," like a High King, buried near his dun. You can visit the modern Church of Saul with its round tower, and see in the graveyard all that is left of the Barn—a gable of rough stones.   This structure shows the handiwork of one of the Saint's three masons, Caeman or Crinnlach or Luireach the Strong.   Beyond the embossed fields the arms of the Lough hold their islands, and as I looked back the ground brightened just a little at the cornfield which hides the mouth of the Slan.

The morning was growing late.   We were getting towards the time when some of the limit men who were competing for the King's Cup might be expected at the first control at Newtownards, that spacious aerodrome which my host and pilot, the Marquess of Londonderry, presented to Newtownards. We zigzagged up the Lough so that the position of rocks barely submerged at this extraordinarily low tide might be noted, for there was to be a yacht-race in the afternoon, and my pilot was a competitor.   It was remarkable that there was not more wrecks of old, from the way one of three great rocks beset the fairway.

The wind had abated somewhat, even over land the going was not bumpy.   Round Newtownards the Marquess circled, and we could see little knots of those who had gathered to look at the great air-racing planes. Our bi-plane showed that we were not competing !

In we came into a nor'-easter : a perfect landing on a
windy day !

After we had taxied in and bestowed the plane, I
met a friendly journalist.

" At first we thought you were in the King's Cup,
until we saw the two wings," he said. " And wasn't
that a fine landing ! "

" Yes. The Marquess of Londonderry is a good
pilot," I remarked.

" Good is it ? That man knows no fear. I saw
him take off for the first time in his life that he flew
an auto-gyro, and land it away over there at his place
in Mount Stewart. There's nothing to touch him."

" I believe," I ventured, " that he gave the town this
aerodrome."

" It wasn't he told you," he said.

" No."

" It looks very stormy. There was a fellow flung
out through the roof of his cabin yesterday, and
killed. Were you belted in ? "

" Now what do you think ? " I asked, " with the
father of a belted Earl ! " And I began to ponder
on what an advantage to any town it is to have a great
house beside it and great hearts within. And if it
be snobbery to worship mean things meanly, what
is it to worship great things whole-heartedly ? And I
thought of my great preceptor who lived in a grander
day. Now, it might possibly appear to us, addicted
to democracy as we are, that he was somewhat super-
cilious when it was revealed that he was in the habit
of judging places by their inhabitants :

" Your address ? " he asked an undergraduate.

" Belfast, sir."

" Belfast ?   Now let us see, what is that ? "

Incredulous, the student explained: " It is the capital of Ulster, sir."

" A town, of course.   I was unaware of its existence. You see, it has no gentlemen's houses."

No, it had no place where he could remember that he had " stayed "!   But I was as happy as Mahaffy. I was " staying " at a gentleman's house for the King's Cup Air race.   After a most interesting and exciting afternoon spent in scanning the sky, picking out the first glint of light on the spinners, that glanced like daylight stars, and hailing the pilots as they arrived, we returned.   One of the guests, a Commodore, asked me how I got on.   And I told him.

" You should have seen him at the Coronation," he remarked, " in his robes of the Garter.   There was no one else there to touch him.   No one that looked the part so well."

It was encouraging to find someone who was apparently a sharer in my theory and belief.   It made it all the more pleasant to have someone in agreement. And when that someone was a good sportsman, pleasanter still.   One's fame is safe when sportsmen praise a man, decry him who dare.

I was not at the Coronation, for I dislike crowds, but it was compensation to be where I was.   I would be no one in Westminster.   But to be a guest of the Lord of Mount Stewart !   A house so hospitable that after a few days you wouldn't know which of you owned the place.

CHAPTER XIV

IF A CHURCH AND A PRIESTHOOD ARE TO SUPPORT themselves in a country whose only wealth is lands and herds, it is obvious that it is necessary to obtain lands and herds. But land could only be obtained through the generosity of someone in a position to grant it, a chieftain or a man of kingly or noble rank. Dichu was a chieftain. He seems to have been, if not a powerful, at least an influential man. He took the Saint and his household under his protection. And the value of his friendship can be measured by the success of St. Patrick in the few months that remained of his first autumn in Mag Inis, the Island Plain. Dichu, as has been recorded, became a Christian, and this meant that all his followers took example by their chief. Working along the lines of the chieftain's family and connections, the Saint converted Dichu's older brother Ros. But Ros was a much older man than his brother Dichu, and one set in his ways and conservative and less amenable to persuasion or conversion than a younger and more liberal mind. That he was old and infirm appears from the following story, which tells us that when St. Patrick first went to visit him " he fought against the Saint," who said: " Why do you strive for this life which is failing you and neglect the life to come? All your senses are failing—your eyes are growing blind, your ears are growing deaf, your tongue stutters and your teeth are falling out; all your members are going. If anyone made you young again would you believe in him ? "

" Yes," replied the old chief.   " If anyone gave me back my youth, I would believe with my whole heart."

So this case of presbyopia, chronic adhesive auditory process, slight right-sided hemiplegia and pyorrhœa, by the prayers of St. Patrick received his youth at the ideal time, according to the late Lord Oxford, for receiving such an inestimable boon—that is, " later on in life."   And, true to his promise, Ros believed with his whole heart.   And small credit to him, as you might say, when you think of all the men of mature years who believe in quacks, rejuvenating operations and monkeys' glands.   But he did more, he proved that he had faith and that it was fervent ; for when the Saint asked him if he would prefer to live long on earth or to go to Heaven at once, " I prefer to go at once to the life eternal," the fearless old warrior answered.   He received Holy Communion and he went to his Lord.   However, a space of at least seven years must have elapsed before Patrick put the question to him, for—if indeed it be the same Ros—we find him among the Nine selected by St. Patrick to amend and codify the Brehon Laws.

Within an area of less than ten miles in Mag Inis the Saint established three churches in three months. His first was Saul, east of the great Dun on the banks of the Quoile, and less than three miles from the shore where he landed and took to the bridle-path.   Rath-colpa, through which the little river Slan flows, was

the next, and then the church of Bright (Brechan),
where Durlus lay, the stronghold of Ros.

It was about this time that the Saint found Mochae,
the grandson of his old master, herding swine.   This
was before the Saint's attempt to convert Milchu, so
that in the reign of a very powerful chieftain we find
the sister's son of that chieftain herding swine.   From
this it will be realised that the prejudice against swine
and, accordingly, the indignities which are attributed
to the duties of a swineherd, are of modern making
and proceed largely from the conditions under which
swine are kept now—conditions which may be good
for fat bacon, but are by no means good for the clean-
liness of the pigs.   In Patrick's days the swine ran
free in the woods of oak and beech, eating mast and
acorns.   They were as clean as sheep—cleaner, perhaps, than the little half-wild ancient sheep which
were hardly as large as an average-sized collie dog, a
meal for a great man.   Apparently they were bred to
run in herds and to fend for themselves.   So the task
of a keeper of " the fair-tusked swine " was no meaner
than that of a shepherd ; and the life of shepherds has
always been counted honourable.   I go this far out
of my way to explain how it came about that Mochae
could be attending to swine and yet not be so ignorant
as to make it impossible for the Saint to ordain him
and set him over the school of Nendrum which, later,
was widely famed for learning.   One of the greatest
gentlemen that Ireland ever produced, the late Earl of
Fingall, was a large farmer of pedigree swine, and he
took a personal interest in their welfare.   They were

as clean as if they had the range of the woods of
Uladh, the Silvae Uliti, which may have been mistaken
for the Wood of Focluth by the scribe.   He gave me
a fine bonham which grew to be an enormous boar, the
father of an hundred swine in the ultimate lands of
the West.   A swineherd's task was in itself about as
pleasant as a huntsman's, for there was much open-air
work, variety, and excitement when the herded wolves
fell on the scattered swine and the wolfhounds gave
tongue as they stretched themselves out to the rescue.

So St. Patrick rested and prospered through the
winter of 432.   As recounted before, his only dis-
appointment was the self-homicide of Milchu his old
master.

What the great and growing urge was against which
Milchu despaired of fighting we do not know.   But
the suicide of such a man, Die-hard though he was,
indicates that Christianity, at any rate in Lecale and
to some extent in Dalaradia, had grown beyond his
hope that it would be destroyed or scotched.

But Patrick had the supreme task of his life yet
before him.   If his mission were to embrace the
island, instead of being shut up in a small part of a
province, he had to face the High King, and face him
in his high place at Tara.   And if this were to be done
at all, the more thoroughly and finally it were done
the better.   The kings of Ireland would be assembled
in the spring, and with them the Druids, nobles,
ollaves and all the descending hierarchies down to the
smiths and leeches.

Nowhere in the life of the Saint is there evidence of

cunning or of calculation. That is one thing which entitles him to a place in Irish hearts in addition to his straightforwardness and his dauntless courage.

His determination to seek an audience of the High King arose not from any hope of preferment he might win, but rather in face of evidence to the contrary. Dichu must have told him how the High King had sent—as he had undoubtedly sent them to his son-in-law of Wicklow—messages warning him to beware of the missionaries. The Saint's visit to Tara was forced on him by the social organisation of the island. This will be only necessary to illustrate in a few lines. Each king and petty king was absolute in his own domain. The High King was over all. And though he might overlook the growth of the new faith in the territories of his subject kings—subject by virtue of a formal tributary gift and the giving of hostages—if he disapproved of the growth of the faith, he would have to act if and when it invaded his own immediate kingdom. Thus, by visiting Tara, the Saint put the question, as it were, directly to Leary the High King, " Will you believe and protect me, or will you persecute and destroy me and your subjects who believe and who are my brethren in Christ ? "

St. Patrick did not go wholly without support. Behind him was the mighty prestige of Rome, and about him was the discontent of the British slaves who had heard of the good tidings and who were filled with the hope of salvation through the new doctrine of good will. They might well mutter and murmur against their masters, since the official recognition of the new

faith by the Emperor Constantine had left the kings
of Ireland backward by a hundred years, and barbarous
still.

These considerations were far from being material
protection. The Saint took his life in his hands
when he set out for his conference with King
Leary, who, ignorant though he may have been that
Rome's secular arm was almost paralysed in the West,
could not regard Patrick's mission as anything less
than an attempt to subvert the entire social order of
his kingdom by encouraging slaves who were already
grumbling, and to depose him in the end from his
High Kingship in favour of a ghostly King. This the
Druids would have inculcated had he not seen for
himself how the new doctrine had put down the powerful from their seats and exalted men of low degree.
The moment for seeking an understanding with the
Saint could not be postponed.

A feast of Tara was at hand, and the sub-kings of
Ireland would be present. Dichu must have been a
noble or a minor chieftain only, for there is no mention
of his presence at Tara on Easter Day (or Easter Day
may not have been a general feast day at Tara). Yet
it was a favourable time to settle in solemn conclave
what place was to be accorded to the Christian communities in the country, and how the principles and
doctrines of the new religion could be brought into
harmony with the law of the land. The civilisation
of Rome was impinging on the culture of the tribes.
The problem before Leary was a problem similar to
that by which greater kings than he were confronted ;

how to harmonise two codes ; how Christ and Cæsar
could be served in the same dominion.   Obviously the
great Christian bishop and Roman citizen, the man
who more than any other man in the land represented
the ideas of Roman civilisation, could not be excluded
from the conference, unheard.

A peaceful meeting with the High King does not
satisfy legend or even the biographers of the Saint.
They, with their gift of drama, which is but a way of
emphasising, not the actual happenings but their
significance, tell us of marvellous exhibitions of magic
on both sides : Druid mists and snowfalls which could
be conjured up by the Magi but not removed.   On
the Saint's side there was manslaughter.   But this
the ingenious biographer seems to consider a private
affair ; an introduction of personalities, as it were, in
an argument.

The probabilities are as I have endeavoured to
reason : that there was a peaceful meeting and a
discussion.   As " my Pompeian friend " Livy says :
" In affairs so ancient, I shall be contented if what
looks like true is taken as true."   Thus far my
conjecture goes.   But what am I to do with that
other form of truth, the imagined truth, whereby the
significance of an event is magnified at the expense of
the matters of fact ? This form can rise to a revela-
tion.   I should be the last to discount it ; I will not.
I cannot, because—I must confess it—like a rather
wayward fellow, not " quite one of the nicest Emperors I know "—as Provost Mahaffy called the
Kaiser—who made history, instead of going in search

of it, I am " enamoured of things incredible." Therefore let the mind's eye see again that ancient heroic
era of ours, with its strange, shadowy wonderland
about it all.

It is fifty miles from Inver Slan to Inver Colptha,
the mouth of the river Boyne. St. Patrick, with a
dozen of his companions, may have sailed there in
ten hours between tides. We are told that the voyage
was prosperous. He left his ship in the care of his
nephew, Lomman, and advanced upstream by the
left or north bank of the Boyne to the Hill of Slane or,
as it was called in those days, Ferta fer Fiacc—The
Graves of Fiacc's Men. This Hill of Slane is about
twelve miles from the river's mouth, and unless the
Saint meant to ford the river at Slane, he would have
gone on by the river's left or northern bank until he
could begin to climb the hill. Slane is on the left bank
of the river, which rises above the dangerous ford
rather steeply : even to-day few of our mechanical cars
can take it on top gear, and its hill looms green and
stoneless above the richest meadows in the world.
The company, had they followed the lower road, would
have passed between the river and two monuments
which were immemorial even then, and long regarded
with awe by the magicians of the King : Dowth, the
great green tumulus, and Brugh, that sepulchral
final hosting of warriors, inviolable and august,
for it belonged to a race of immortal heroes who
had long ago become divine. This was the Brugh
of the Boyne, a cemetery, older than our history,
which the minds of men peopled with gods. It was

Brugh na Boinne, the Brugh of Angus the Long-
Handed, the Gaelic Apollo, the Master of all Arts.
It is the only megalithic monument in Europe associated with a name. It shone white as the evening
gathered, for the twilight does not last long so early
in April; and its dome of white stones stood ghostly
within the twelve tall pillars standing about it in a
ring, wardens of the spirits of ancestral gods.

The Hill of Slane is the grandest hill in Meath.
As they ascended it by the path which comes off the
road to Ardee, about a mile from the river, the great
Plain of Hills spread more and more widely behind
them. Away to the south-west, in the white evening
brightness, the roofs of Tara could be seen breaking
the long, level line like a crown. The mighty Hall of
Mead Circling, built of old by Cormac, stood loftiest,
with its great gables rising thirty-five cubits high.
The rounded tops of the entrenched palaces were
defined in dark shadows as the sun went down. There
was Tara, that was a temple before it was a palace,
Tara the seat of gods and kings. And now the river
could be seen no longer. The great, rich, loamy
mount had still to be scaled. It is no hard climb for
the middle-aged, even after the long walk from the
mouth of the Boyne, for the air is refreshing and
invigorating.

When I visited this hill, of " The Graves of Fiacc's
Men," the sun was going down. I tried to time the
ascent to the end of the day. The view is magnificent, and even now the earthworks, that are all
that remain of Tara, can be distinctly seen throwing

the skyline into irregular patterns that tell, far off though they are, of the mighty work of men's hands. The great beeches beyond the graveyard were coloured with the season—there are still a graveyard and ecclesiastical remains on the summit.   As I went down, the light coming from the west through the great trees that lined the path caught the dewy air, and made it visible in a mist of silver.   It was as if there still breathed round the hill incense from of old.   But a strange sense, from days long before St. Patrick, of memories pressing on the mind, messages ancestral, not to be comprehended by modern man, invaded my spirit, and I felt the weight of immemorial dreams.

On the hilltop the tent was pitched and some shelter used for the lighting of the Paschal fire.   The night was evidently mild and clear.   The Easter Light was not lit then as it is lit now in the church, in the morning, but at evening on Holy Saturday.   St. Patrick, as night fell, blessed the new flame born of flint, and lit the Paschal fire at the door of his house. The High King had his guests to feast on Tara, which is about nine miles to the south-west.   And by solemn ordinance it was forbidden to kindle light before the lamps were lit in Tara's royal house.

But soon a sentry sees a light blazing beyond the river in the opal twilight.   It is a stationary and solitary light, and one lit far earlier than the low beechwood fires which illuminate the Fords of Slane. Even these must wait for Tara's signal.   The sentry reports it to the keeper of the fire, who has not yet stirred its dousing-stones : consternation seizes the

magicians, who go with prophetic warnings to the
King. " Unless that fire which you see there to the
north-east where the Hill of Slane must be, and which
has been kindled before the royal fire was lighted here,
be quenched to-night, it will never be extinguished in
Ireland."

I stood with a Meath man on the Ridge of Tara
watching the light of the spring evening fade. To the
left, as we looked north, the sun fell in a broad ava-
lanche of fire, but the long orange of its glow could
never be mistaken for a flame kindled by human
hands. From the east, cerulean clouds lay low upon
the world. The Hill of Slane was lessened by the
rising ground dimly seen beyond, crowned by the
wood *en brousse* on the hill of Cullen and by an intervening hill. Earth loomed bluer than the sky, and
so blue was the land that a faint mist caused a lake-like
water to spread between the hill and Tara's height, as
if the submerged and invisible valley of the Boyne
were flooded as in the days when it first overflowed
from its uncovered source. Motor-lights coming
from Navan to the west gave out bright and inter-
mittent gleams. Their movement was not perceptible.
This contradicts my mental picture of the sentry.
" It is not a moving light." At a distance—and let us
get this accurately—at first sight, lamps without a
background do not show the progress of their speed.
Lights oncoming at thirty miles an hour are apparently
stationary. This shows how a plain sight or accurate
observation can " set us down."

Darker blue the land lies, heavy greyness looms

M

above it.   From the right, darkness closes all the view.
This is the moment when, if ever, the flame that is to
give its light to Tara's lamps must be awakened from
its smouldering wood and its incandescent stones
stirred.   Patrick's bonfire is leaping yellow far to the
right.   The sentry is not deceived by the great lake
that the land mist has welled into his view.   A
mirage.   Evening fall on Tara is one of the most
impressive sights in this legendary country.   Dim,
sea-blue, immense, immemorial.   And the spectator
is left with a sense of loss, of inadequacy and in-
feriority; why, God only knows.   My friend, whose
imagination has been lost for a colour filter, caught
me by the elbow.   " If only I had my infra-red! "
But I was seeing infra-red.   This is no stuff for an
instant in time, no matter how clearly the scene can
be made to show up after dark.   Why should darkness fall on Tara?   We spend millions on Woolworth
Irish—call the language Gaelic if you will—but where
is the knowledge of our terrific Past?   Where is its
message to us its heirs in the Present?   What has put
a caveat between us and Tara?   Here we are on our
own soil.   The thick grass trammels our feet, mutely
endeavouring to anchor us to our real estate, to halt
us from our vagaries and our aimless crusades.   Here
is a noble natal place which the many unreckonable
races of modern Europe would give their treasure to
possess.   But what man or nation can purchase a
past?   We have the most credible and accountable
past in the heroic period of any nation's glory.   What
have we done with it?   We have let it to legend and

to tradition to become a tale told by idiots.   While
even the dumb land heaves up in a mute appeal to us
not to be unmindful of the nobles who have gone.

*   *   *   *   *

A large brown hare, the loveliest of our wild things,
leaped and zigzagged before me.   Then over a wall
with him, as I went down the hill.

*   *   *   *   *

Nine chariots are yoked, and at first they are wheeled
circle-wise—a strong spell—to the left against the
course of the sun.   Thus was magic power obtained
over those who had dared to light the defiant fire on
the opprobrious hill.   The owner of the land beside
the ford was not remiss in his duty.   The pyre of
logs had been tended and was blazing well, and its
glare on the strong, black waters met the glare of its
companion on the river's farther bank.   The water
coiled in ruddy circles, but the horses felt the bottom
of the ford, and their foothold was secure, although
the rains of early spring had covered the guiding stones.
Up the steep bank the charioteers gave rein to the
steeds nervous from the river.   The light was invisible
now because they were under the Hill of Slane ; but
scouts ran up before the chariots and shouted back.
A mile, and the magicians gave the signal for a halt.
By no means must the King go within the influence of
the alien fire.   Let him summon the offender forth
into the presence at a safe distance.   So, out of range,
the company took their places, and the Saint was
brought before the King.   " No one must rise when
he comes in, for whoever rises now will worship him

forever more." Robed in but one colour, robed in
ghostly white, crowned with the golden fillet of his
mitre, from which a flat disc like an axe-blade rose
over his forehead, the solemn figure, greater than all
magicians, appeared. In his chasuble and mitre he
looked like a Roman Cæsar, crowned, divine, triumphant on the Capitoline Hill: and Tara heard the
mystic voice of Eternity, the everlasting words of
Rome, Latin, the strongest spell of all:

"*Hi in curribus, et hi in equis, nos autem in nomine
Domini nostri ambulabimus.* . . .

"Some in chariots and some on horseback, but
we in the name of the Lord!"

Adzehead had come! The Druids were face to
face with their destiny.

CHAPTER XV

THE SAINT CONTENDS WITH THE MAGI

THE TELESCOPE, THE MICROSCOPE AND THE TEST-TUBE
have made sceptics of us all. We have changed
wisdom for an exact knowledge of stains, precipitants,
reactions and refractions, and put it, for this generation
at least, beyond recall. Even when our calculations
are found to be deceptive, we go on by the same
narrow, exacting formulæ, correcting "calculations,"
but never correcting the preposterous hypothesis on
which they are founded, which is that everything that
cannot be reduced to one or other of our " sciences " is
ipso facto false. Therefore, when you object, in the
scientific twentieth century, to the magic of the fifth,
it is no use expecting me to share your incredulity.
You do not believe in angels because you cannot see
them ; but you believe in X-rays, which cannot see
the living flesh but reveal only the bones of the skeleton,
without asking yourselves how many magical beings
there could be between us, as we look at one another,
invisible to these eyes of ours, which can see only solid
flesh. Even the magic of your own science is lost on
you. The telescope and the oil-immersion lens have
immersed you in speculations which tell of many things
in heaven and earth, but nothing of man or of his mind.
And yet the mind is all-powerful, it has made your
test-tubes ; what you pin your faith to is but a suburb
of the mind. And who for a part would deny the
creator of the whole ? So come not to me, who am
" enamoured of things incredible," with the touch-

stones of scientific results—results which will be
" co-related " or corrected or repudiated before the
year is out. The magic of the ether, timeless and all-
containing, can teach some people nothing—at least,
it cannot reconcile them to its magic ; and yet matter
is but a node of its being, a change of etherial density
in its all-pervading substance, a substance in which
resides, undiminished, everything that has ever lived :
in it are the songs of Sappho and the tears of Andro-
mache ; all the hostings of Tara ; all thoughts and
feelings and all dreams, past, present or to be. It is a
metaphor of the immortal mind itself to which a
prophecy of the future is as easy as the foretelling of
an eclipse.

In studying the external universe we have neglected
the universe within ourselves.

It is not because I have the consensus of the belief
of all humanity behind me that I believe in miracles.
Even Arthur Balfour believed in miracles. Just before
his death, he wrote :

> Superstition may be negative as well as positive, and the
> excesses of unbelief may be as extravagant as those of belief.
> Doubtless the universe as conceived by men more primitive
> than ourselves was the obscure abode of strange deities.   But
> what are we to say to a universe reduced without remainder
> to collections of electric charges radiating energy through a
> hypothetical ether ?   Thus to set limits to reality must be the
> most hazardous of speculative adventures.   To do so by
> eliminating the spiritual is not only hazardous but absurd.
> For if we are directly aware of anything, it is of ourselves as
> personal agents; if anything can be proved by direct experi-
> ment, it is that we can, in however small a measure, vary the
> natural distribution of matter and energy.   We can certainly

act on our environment, and as certainly our action can never
be adequately explained in terms of entities which neither
think nor feel nor purpose nor know. It constitutes a
spiritual invasion of the physical world—it is a miracle!

I believe in miracles from a scientific or a rational
standpoint too—that is, from a consideration of our
" godlike Reason " and immortal mind ; and because,
in spite of science, I have retained my imagination.
Wonder which has gone out of the world remains in
me. I want more of it. I believe in miracles because
I am a miracle.

> Give me miraculous eyes to see mine eyes,
> Those rolling mirrors made alive in me,
> Terrible crystal, more incredible
> Than all the things they see.

Belief takes many forms. Some believe in God,
some in themselves, and some in science, which is
neither God nor man, but an idol worshipped in the
form of a pillar of stone with a column which is hollow
and transparent and is known as a test-tube. And
the worst of it is that it controls its idolaters with the
benevolence of a pillar of stone, and children are
offered to it as the men of old, before the coming of
St. Patrick, offered their first-born to the garnished
pillar of Moy Slecht.

As the pagan poet Erc acknowledged the super-
natural when he stood up, though forbidden, to do
reverence to St. Patrick, so do I.

At the King's command, the Saint " came out of
the place which was lit up." In the shadowy dark he
saw the King among his seated household. Around
him his warriors seated on the ground, their chins

resting on their hands, which held the rims of their shields. Behind these the guards, a semi-circle of spears. Their eyes and harness caught the torchlight. Only the chains of the chariot poles made a noise. So far behind him were his companions that it seemed that he stood alone, but this increased all the more his majesty and power. The light shone on the upright blade of gold which rose from the golden circle round his head to cover his forehead. This was the mitre proper to the fifth century. The flat disc was like a cooper's adze, hence the Druids called him " Adze-head." There was silence in the night. After a minute the spell was broken by Erc the young poet, whose mood was so deepened by the strain that his mind was suddenly flooded by prophetic light. In a moment of inspiration he rose to do honour to him who stood alone. Charmed words were pronounced by the Saint, and the Druids grew uneasy and afraid of the incomprehensible spell.

They began to " converse," and Patrick answered the charge of having ignored the royal edict governing the kindling of the fire. Why had he lighted up his house before the royal palace was lighted? The Saint explained the symbolism of the sacred fire, and dwelt on the mysteries of the Trinity, the Incarnation and the Resurrection. Seeing the effect of the words of the Roman bishop on those about the King, Lochru the Druid, to undo it, blasphemed. St. Patrick, wrathful, caused him to be raised up high into the night, from the darkness of which he fell and his brains were dashed out. " And his stone," the writer in the Book of Armagh, Ferdomach, adds, " is in the south-western edge of Tara down to the present day. I have seen it with my own eyes."

It was only when I began to visualise this scene and to call it up that I realised how dim the mind's eye of him who had written it must have been. Put another way, the scene, if it were given to an artist to picture or to illustrate, could hardly be illustrated without the absurdity of it becoming manifest. He would have had to draw the picture of a Druid falling upside down from an undivulged height, and to suggest that his brains were about to be dashed against a stone. He could not have avoided making the Saint look, if not murderous, at least vindictive. And anyone who has visited the Hill of Slane would know that to introduce a stone on that deep-sodded earth would be to strain his credulity. Few rocks break the surface anywhere in deep-clodded Mag Bregh, nurse of heroes.

To the guards Leary called, " Seize him who would by his enchantments destroy us all." But as they rushed, the Saint cried with a loud voice the " *Exurgat Deus* "—" Let God arise and let His enemies be scattered "—and they were confused within a cloud, and, panic seizing them, they fought with one another, the horses cut loose and went wild over the country, dashing the chariots to pieces and sending the presumptuous warriors, mad with terror, headlong to Mount Moduirn. The King, with his wife and two attendants, were all that were left of the occupants of the nine chariots that had set out from Tara a few hours before.

We are told that the Queen interceded with the Saint to spare her husband.   If she were a pagan, her prayer sounds strange : " O just and mighty man, do not kill the King ; he will bend his knee and adore thy God."   The silence of the narrator about the King at this juncture is masterly ; it leaves him full of dignity as not deigning to speak, silent in the fortitude that became a grandson of Nial the Great.   But the scribe hastens to undo his effect, because he makes the King, having pretended to worship, move off a little distance and call to the Saint in a treacherous attempt to decoy him to his death.   This crowding of events arises from the close way the incidents are gathered together and narrated in haste, as if the precious parchment were the first concern.   To a great extent this is true : so precious was parchment that many a history was never written ; and many a name that might have shaken the earth with deeds of heroism is unrecorded because the parchment was more precious than a hero's fame.   " *Vixerunt fortes ante Agamemnona multi.*"   This difficulty about the medium is not unknown even at the present day, but, like so much in the present day, the restriction on writing comes, not from the price or value of the paper, but from the calculating thoughts of publishers (the modern equivalents to the scribes), who must fit their author into the linotype at so much in wages per hour, per yard, per column, peradventure.   The only redeeming feature in this is that it tends to reduce the present-day spate of printed words.

So the Saint is hurried to Tara, whither the King

has summoned him to attend on the following day, which was Easter Sunday, March 26th, 433—a wonderful coincidence with the Vernal Equinox.

But before we follow him to Tara, it is necessary for me to remark that, however ready I may be to accept the miraculous, the contradictory gives me pause. And it is impossible to accept the attribution of the miracle which brought about the death of Leary's Druid at midnight on the Hill of Slane. It carries its own contradiction. The Saint would never have begun his exhortation to the milder ways of Christ with a murder to prove his point, particularly as we know that one of the principal difficulties which beset St. Patrick was the inculcation of horror for the crime of manslaughter and of a proper reverence for human life, carrying as it did the destiny of the human soul.

It is doubtful if the Saint ever succeeded in getting more than one year's penance for manslaughter generally accepted. He never mentions his miracles in his *Confession* or Testimony to the miracle which God wrought within him. Zeal turned his biographer prematurely into a crusader. God save all and sundry from their biographers, particularly to-day, when they wait till a man is dead and cannot defend himself, and then run a stake through his body at the cross roads in the form of a " Life " with all the envy and hostility of friends. Biographies as demonstrations of how much their authors are superior to their subjects were unknown in Patrick's day, but he suffered martyrdom to some extent at the hands of his admirers, and this miracle is one of his many trials.

Therefore let us, by delaying the visit of the Saint, stay the hand of the scribe who would hustle him to Tara without rest or refreshment, in his desire to get on with the miracles, a haste which St. Patrick's writings contradict.

I must not take it for granted that everybody knows the history of that historic place, supreme court and armed camp, seeing that though I have visited it many times, it was but lately—since the reorganisation of archæology in Ireland and a perusal of Coffey's and Macalister's works, with an examination of the raised map made to scale which is in the National Museum in Kildare Street—that I began to get an idea of its significance.

On an overcast day Tara is the most depressing hill in Ireland. It lies some nine miles south of the Fords of Slane, in the middle of the Mag Breg, The Plain of Hills, which is the translation of the Gaelic name for Meath, Magh Breg. Truly it is a disappointing hill. You approach it with a heart full of heroic memories, vague, noble and gigantic in the mists of Time, only to find a field heaved up into a long green mound full of bullocks and sheep, and crowned by a statue of St. Patrick with an anachronism for a mitre, and, hard by, a square-towered conventional Protestant church.

" They have herded bullocks on the graves of kings." And yet this desecrated hill was the nursery and the hearth of Ireland's heroic past. It dates from dateless neolithic ages. It is as old as the Tiber's Town of the Twins. And when I think of the little Greek

bronze of Hercules found in the Boyne's mouth, my
mind ponders on the strange, ancient cults of this im-
memorial hill.   Was Tara, like Rome, a Twin Town?
As far back as the fourth century B.C. Timæus tells
us, " The Celts who live on the shore of the ocean
chiefly honour the Dioscuri " :   the Boys of Zeus!
From Murrisk on the edge of the Western ocean to
Tara of the Kings there are twin stones in many a field.
Was Tara a Twin town like the Rome of Romulus and
Remus ?   Did the ancient Irish worship the Twins ?

For this, as for most of my information, I must go
to the works of Professor Macalister.   What does he
say about the Twins ?

> " The birth of twins is regarded as a supernatural
> portent among peoples *below* a certain moderately elevated
> degree of civilisation in all parts of the world."

And again :—

> " There can be no doubt whatever that the twin-cult
> crops up in all manner of unexpected places, and that
> it is associated with a number of other phenomena, chief
> among which is the thunder and lightning.   How are the
> twins to be recognised ?   There is a number of attributes,
> differing with different pairs of twins, different centres of
> civilisation and different forms of the traditions. . . . It
> is also surely significant that the closely cognate site [to
> Tara] where the kings of the Ulidians had their seat, bore
> the name Emain Macha which means, without disguise,
> the Twins of Macha."

Were the games of ancient Ireland presided over
by the Boys ?   I like to think that they were. Pollux
was immortal, but Castor, skilled in taming horses,
was subject to senile decay and death.   I like to think

that our bookmakers shout in the great tradition of the
horsey Castor before they go the way that great
sportsman Dan Leahy went. But the Heavenly
Twins were gone from the earth long before the
Greeks sailed for Troy, and they were gone from Tara
long before St. Patrick came. Yet the Irishman's
love for horses survives, and the soil of Ireland still
produces men fit to put up a good fight.

There are no antique bronzes of the Twins, and their
cult is over long ago and forgotten; yet there are men
who go about in pairs and are associated with horses,
and with whom you can back your fancy. Can it not
be that bookmakers and their clerks are in the great
tradition of the Heavenly Twins, Castor the horse-
fancier and pugilist Pollux? I like to think that this
is so, and that from the great green Twin Town in
horse-nurturing Meath the Twins came down and are
to be found at every race-meeting in the land to-day.
And their cult has been legalised by the Government
of our country. You will see the lightning in the
flashy ties or scarfs they wear, and hear the thunder
when they roar the odds in answer to the thunder of
the hooves on the turf. Twins, Tara, Thunder and
Turf! Brude Pant! Brude Urpant! Up Brude!
And the two Cregans!

Here all that gave us a claim to civilisation, from
the first century, when the harbours of our country
were better known than those of what now is England,
to the days of its sanctification as the scene of the
triumph of our Apostle. Did I say Tara is disappointing? But when you reach its heights, on a bright day,

what of the broad prospect that it commands? Five counties they say are to be seen from its immemorial mound. We sweep with the eye the grandest champaign in the world. When Leary reigned from his great dun farthest to the south of all the high places of Tara, to him the endless fields of the Leinstermen were extended. And our Saint had to pass and to pity the sinister "Mound of the Graves of the Hostages." "There was never a king in Ireland who had not Hostages." So ran the ominous and unChristian statement of the bards. And he saw the great dun of the magnanimous Cormac—who had anticipated him by a hundred years in intimations of Christianity—and the great seat of kings. What the intricate windings of these fortresses were, who can pretend to know? Mighty are the mounds of their foundations, though a thousand and a half years have passed since the earth stood up and the pillared house shone out kingly, far-seen over the richest home of heroes of the world. Tara is not disappointing when the light is clear and the Plain of the Hills extends on all sides. But you are on its summit now. Thousands of years are trammelled in the grass. The House of Cormac is no older now than the strong place of Leary in the timeless earth. But Leary's palace was nearer to his enemies than all the strongholds of his antecedent kings. This is what I heard of the Founding of Tara.

After the revolt of the plebeian races, the Attacotti who comprised the Bagmen or Firbolgs, the Fomorians and the Dedannans whom the Milesians had conquered, the Milesian nobles were all but exterminated or driven into exile.   The Attacotti chose a man called Carberry Cathead for their King.   Evidently government was beyond them.   The greed and chicanery of those born to be subjects brought about within a decade an appalling condition of national confusion and degradation.   For this—and sound was the view—the King was held responsible; for the ancient Irish believed that prosperity depended on their leader.   Thus when a good and just king ruled, the whole country was happy—the seasons were mild, the crops were abundant, the cattle multiplied, the waters abounded with fish and " the fruit trees had to be propped up, so heavy was their produce."   Let the Four Masters tell us what happened in the reign of the plebeian King Carberry Cathead :

> Evil was the state of Ireland; fruitless her corn, for there used to be only one grain on the stalk; fruitless her rivers, milkless her cattle; plentiless her fruit, for there used to be but one acorn on the stalk.   There are seven proofs which attest the falsehood of a king: to turn a church synod out of their lis (enclosure); to be without truth; without law; defeat in battle; dearth in his reign; dryness of cows; blight of fruit; scarcity of corn.

It is easy to imagine how the return of Toohal the Legitimate from exile was welcomed; the lesson that when the underdogs get up the whole place becomes a kennel, was not lost on the inhabitants of this country, who had suffered from slaves in office as long as nineteen hundred years ago.   The Milesian dynasty was restored; and the rejoicing people helped Toohal to consolidate his kingdom, which he had made into the supreme state of Ireland by including within it parts

cut off from each of the provinces. This new demesne
included what are now the counties of Meath, West-
meath and Longford, with parts of Monaghan, Cavan,
Offaly and Kildare. This was the Kingdom of Meath,
and Tara was its royal seat. In the ancient places of
hosting he built palace-forts: Tlachta in Munster,
Taillteann in Meath and in Connaught Ishnagh. Their
ramparts can be traced to-day on the earth into which
they subsided long ago. Thus was Tara founded;
and it was not long without a romantic tragedy which
affected the destiny of us all—a tragedy with which
that brought about by Tereus, King of Thrace, in a
parallel state of society, may aptly be compared.
Many already know how the King of Thrace, having
taken to wife one of the daughters of King Pandion of
Athens, seduced her sister and, to prevent her de-
nouncing him and revealing the crime, cut out her
tongue. But she wove her story into a tapestry and
told in

> The woven web that was clear to follow,
> The tongueless vigil and all the pain.

In his rage the King pursued her and her sister, but
the gods, in compassion, changed the one into a
nightingale, the other into a swallow. So that immemorial sadness survives in the bird's broken-hearted
song. But no divine bard or compassionate god has
softened the crime of Achy Ainkenn, King of Leinster,
who married one of the High King's daughters. But
desire of her sister filled him, and pretending that his
wife was dead, he prevailed upon the King to give
him his second daughter in marriage. Each girl was
ignorant of the other's lot, but when they met by

N

accident in the palace of Ainkenn, they were so overwhelmed with horror, grief and shame that they died
immediately—the old Irish stories are not lacking in
tributes to woman's modesty. The vengeance for
this awful crime was the beginning of the feud of the
Leinstermen against the High King, which lasted to
the days of Dermot, who brought the Normans in to
assist him against native enemies. He has been
blamed quite erroneously for bringing in the English
or the " British." Dermot brought in Scandinavians
(who had become Frenchmen in Normandy before
they settled in Wales) from Wales, whereas they
who actually brought the British in to be their
queens and princesses, or their serfs, servants or slaves,
were the ancient Irish kings, who ruled at Tara seven
hundred years before Dermot was born. Conn the
Hundred Fighter and his grandson Cormac mac Art,
that illustrious king, glorified Tara. Cormac insti-
tuted three colleges for military science, literature
and law; for even thus early in Irish history, law
was dissociated from literature. Cormac, after an
illustrious reign, abdicated because he lost an eye, for
no blemished or half-blind king was permitted to rule
at Tara. Elected by the votes of freemen, the chief
was required to be free from all personal deformities
which might impair his efficiency as a leader or lessen
the respect of the people for him. The more I read
of the laws and customs of the Gael, the more I admire
their soundness, yet the abdication of Cormac mac Art
was a great loss to the country. That he was a wise
and well-informed king, and one not unacquainted
with *real politik*, is apparent from the peace, prosperity

and enlightenment of his reign. The tradition is that he died a Christian, which shows that he was receptive to influences which were about to transform the world. And it is an additional evidence of the length of the period during which the Christian movement was felt in Ireland before St. Patrick's mission.

He was the first that ever believed in God in this Kingdom, and because he refused to adore the Golden Calfe which was then worshyped as God and for saying that he would sooner worship the artificer that made the Golden Calfe than the Golden Calfe itself, and that the Goldsmithe was a worthier Creature than it, and therefore Rather to be adored, for which the Priest of the Golden Calfe being heavily Displeased wrought such meanes by the King as he made a salmon bone stick fast in his throat untill it choked him, and soe Dyed in one of the King's mannor houses called the house of Cleiteagh near the River of Boyne.

Cormac mac Art was Ireland's first Christian king if the legend which inspired Sir Samuel Ferguson to write his fine poem be true. And connected as it is with Tara and the Fords of Slane, this may be a good place in which to quote it. No excuse should be required of one who quotes poetry when thinking of the great hill which housed all the inspiration of Ireland for half a thousand years.

The Burial of King Cormac

He was choked by Druid magic because he had discounted their god Crom Cruach and his sub-gods twelve. Dying, he gave orders that he was to be buried not in the ancestral cemetery of Brugh na Boyne but at Rosnaree.

> For all the kings who lie in Brugh
>   Put trust in gods of wood or stone;
> But 'twas at Ross that first I knew
>   One, Unseen Who is God alone.

His veteran captains urged otherwise, but the
Boyne rose when they tried to cross the Fords of
Slane to Brugh.

Dead Cormac on his bier they laid :—
    " He reigned a king for forty years,
And shame it were," his captains said,
    " He lay not with his royal peers.

" His grandsire, Hundred Battle, sleeps
    Serene in Brugh : and, all around,
Dead kings in stone sepulchral keeps
    Protect the sacred burial ground.

" What though a dying man should rave
    Of changes o'er the eastern sea ?
In Brugh of Boyne shall be his grave
    And not in noteless Rosnaree."

Then northward forth they bore the bier
    And down from Sletty side they drew,
With horseman and with charioteer,
    To cross the fords of Boyne to Brugh.

There came a breath of finer air
    That touched the Boyne with ruffling wings ;
It stirred him in his sedgy lair
    And in his mossy moorland springs.

And as the burial train came down
    With dirge and savage dolorous shows,
Across their pathway, broad and brown
    The deep, full-hearted river rose ;

From bank to bank through all his fords,
    'Neath blackening squalls he swelled and boiled ;
And thrice the wondering gentile lords
    Essayed to cross and thrice recoiled.

Then forth stepped grey-haired warriors four :
    They said, " Through angrier floods than these
On link'd shields once our king we bore
    From Dread-Spear and the hosts of Deece.

" And long as loyal will holds good,
    And limbs respond with helpful thews,
Nor flood, nor fiend within the flood,
    Shall bar him of his burial dues."

With slanted necks they stooped to lift;
    They heaved him up to neck and chin;
And pair and pair with foosteps swift,
    Lock'd arm and shoulder bore him in.

'Twas brave to see them leave the shore,
    To mark the deepening surges rise,
And fall subdued in foam before
    The tension of their striding thighs.

'Twas brave when now a spear-cast out,
    Breast-high the battling surges ran;
For weigh was great and limbs were stout,
    And loyal man put trust in man.

But ere they reached the middle deep,
    Nor steadying weight of clay they bore,
Nor strain of sinewy limbs could keep
    Their feet beneath the swerving four.

And now they slide, and now they swim,
    And now, amid the blackening squall,
Grey locks afloat with clutchings grim,
    They plunge around the floating pall.

    *   *   *   *   *

At morning, on the grassy marge
    Of Rosnaree, the corpse was found,
And shepherds at their early charge
    Entombed it in the peaceful ground.

Round Cormac Spring renews her buds :
    In March perpetual by his side,
Down come the earth-fresh April floods,
    And up the sea-fresh salmon glide.

But before the one-eyed monarch abdicated, the great police organisation or militia-men of Ireland, known as the Fianna, were getting out of hand. Their rebellious and turbulent conduct may have been winked at, if not condoned, by the monarch, who was not anxious to risk a civil war which might lead to irretrievable measures if an attempt were made to put down this great armed force which was under the command of his son-in-law, that historic and fabulous figure, the famous Fin mac Cool. He cajoled, placated and played for time. To others he left a bloody deluge. He left it to his son Carbery of the Liffey, his successor, to deal with the army of Finn. The greatest battle in Tara's ancient history ensued. This was the battle of Gavra, which was fought in 326, near the Hill of Skreen in Meath. Carbery the King slew the son of Ossian, Oscar, the Irish Hector. If Hector was the archetype of the first gentleman in Europe, Oscar, brave, honourable and generous, may readily be entitled the first gentleman in our land, if not in the heroic records of the world. It has been stated that, to the enlightened, Christianity was not unknown. Oscar lived after the time of Cormac, and his virtue lacks nothing of the gentler doctrines that caused the enmity of the Druids in King Cormac's reign. In Ossian's lament for Oscar, Ferguson reaches the summit of his song.

> No more, dispelling battle's gloom
>   Shall son for me from fight return ;
> The great green rath's ten-acred tomb
>   Lies heavy on his urn.

> A cup of bodkin-pencilled clay
>   Holds Oscar ; mighty heart and limb,
> One handful now of ashes grey . . .

But the battle of Gavra, in which Carbery slew Oscar in single combat, nearly ruined the victorious army. But it put an end to the pretensions of the Fianna to be an army in opposition to the High King.

The sea-kings and the colonisers of Scotland and west Wales, the greatest of whom was Nial of the Nine Hostages (" for he is not a king who has not hostages ") and his nephew Dathi, hand on an expanding kingdom to Leary of Tara, whom we find enthroned five years before the coming of the Saint. He broke his oath by the sun and wind to the Leinstermen who had taken him prisoner. He had little love for them, and he may not have considered it binding, seeing that by treachery a king of theirs had slain his father in their allied invasion of Gaul. That he kept faith with St. Patrick appears in the progress of the Saint, who could never have spread the Gospel without the protection of the High King; and this is indeed remarkable, and redounds greatly to the character and statesmanship of Leary, which enabled him to separate his own personal views from the policy of his State. Even in less barbarous times this is not always the case. But Leary, though he gave the Saint scope to speed up and regularise his doctrines with the social code, never adopted them. Like his fathers, he was to be buried upright in full armour, facing the Leinstermen. And on the rampart of his ruined stronghold his remains are to this day.

On Tara's desecrated grange may still be traced the outlines of the great banqueting-hall, which had seven doors on either side, the hospitable shelter for a thousand men. It was here that the Saint was to undergo the trials which his biographer, full of pious attributions and parallels from Holy Writ, describes. And though the miracle of St. Patrick's own life and mission may satisfy us as it satisfied him, the legend of a contest and a competition in miracles cannot well be omitted, in deference to tradition which holds us so much in its debt.

The great parallelogram of the banqueting-hall, seven hundred feet long, lies with its long axis north and south on the north-eastern aspect of the hill. It could be approached before the royal palace, and doubtless there were paths to it on all sides from the Slighe Midluachra, the great north road, which was one of the most important of those radiating from Tara. Owing to the rich, loamy character of the soil, which, unlike the chalky soil of southern England, does not show by deeper shadows the existence of ancient and forgotten tracks, the lines of these ways are not visible. They may be found yet by the spade. But the Saint took a more direct path. As the King was feasting with kings and nobles on the morrow after the Paschal fire had been on the Hill of Slane, the Saint with five companions suddenly appeared among them, though the doors were shut. Again the incident of a poet rising. This time it was Dubthach, the chief poet in the land, and after him his pupil Fiacc, who later wrote the Hymn. Assuredly these ancient poets of Ireland were men of vision. Patrick blessed them, and the King invited him to sit at meat. But the Druid Lucetmael, who had not forgotten his companion's fate over-night, put poison in his cup as the Saint said grace. The contents of the cup were frozen, but the venom in the draught remained liquid, and was easily poured out. The Saint blessed the cup and the drink melted. Then the magician said, " Let us work miracles. Let it snow upon the plain."

Bip Pares

St. Patrick answered, " I will not interfere with the elements against the will of God."

But the magician covered the earth with snow girdle deep in the presence of them all.

" Remove it now," said the Saint.

" That I may not do until this hour to-morrow."

" You are potent for evil, but not for good."

So he blessed the plain, and the snow disappeared without rain or mist or melting wind. Then the Druids brought down the Druid dark, called Feth Fiada—for the Druids, like some of our later wizards and tregetours in another sphere, could shroud everything in an envelope of vapour—but they could not dissipate it. And the darkness remained on the land. This is not hard to believe. I have *heard* darkness conjured down by our modern Druids, darkness which they are powerless to remove. We want a modern St. Patrick for these our times. St. Patrick dissipated the darkness and brought back the light of the sun. Then, proceeding to the south-eastern side of the hill, to the little stream that springs from the Well of Nemnach, called Nith, " on which was the first mill made in Ireland for Ciarnait the bondmaid of Cormac," the King proposed a contest.

" Hold your books in the water, and we will worship him whose books uninjured are."

St. Patrick was willing to abide by this test, but the Druid said, alluding to its use in baptism :

" No ; he hath water for a god."

Then the King proposed the same test with fire this time instead of water. But the Druid still declined. He said :

"He worships water and fire alternately."

But now it was the Saint who proposed an ordeal, to which the Druid agreed, shamed as he was before the High King and the assembly. St. Patrick said, "You and one of my youths shall go into a hut half built of green and half of dry wood. My garment shall cover you and yours him. Then let the building be set on fire."

His pupil Begnignus in the Druid's gown, and Lucetmael the Druid cloaked, entered the hut and its doors were closed, and it was set on fire in the presence of them all. And St. Patrick prayed.

"And the fire consumed the green wood and the Magus within, but not the cloak of St. Patrick; whereas Begnignus was unscathed, although the Druid's gown was burned off him."

In these legends are to be found traces of antecedent customs. Some are invalidated by results which are contradictory to Christian ethics. But these Magian miracles of the snow and the darkness are to me as readily acceptable as they were to Chaucer. Let Chaucer testify to the tregetours:

"Sometimes they will bring in the similitude of a grim lion, or make flowers spring up as in a meadow; sometimes they cause a vine to flourish bearing white and red grapes; or show a castle built with stone; and when they please they cause the whole to disappear." He tells of a learned clerk who for the amusement of a friend showed to him "forests full of wild deer where he saw an hundred of them slain, some with hounds, some with arrows; the hunting being finished, a company of falconers appeared upon the banks of a fair river, where the birds pursued the

herons and slew them. He saw knights jousting
upon a plain;" and by way of conclusion "the re-
semblance of his beloved lady dancing which caused
him to dance also." But when "the maister that this
magicke wrought thought fit, he clapped his hands
together and all was gone in an instant"

> There I saw Coll Tregetour
> Upon a table of sycamour,
> Play an uncouthe thynge to tell;
> I saw him carry a wynde-mell
> Under a walnote shale

Even at the present day the Hopi Indians in Cochiti
can conjure rain, as the poet Witter Bynner so marvellously sings. Not for nothing were the Druids
honoured in ancient Ireland.

Meanwhile Lomman, who had been left with the
boat from which St. Patrick and his companions dis-
embarked on the morning of April the First, had rowed
it to the Ford of the Alder, a word which is preserved
in the present-day name of Trim. In one of the
loveliest curves of the river, which reflects now in its
bright black waters the grey towers of King John's
castle, lay the ancient ford. At dawn, Fortchern the
High King's grandson, going down to the river, found
Lomman "with his gospel with him." This strange
and unprecedented sight aroused the curiosity of the
child. He asked questions and was instructed. And
the story goes that he was baptised in the open well
close at hand. His mother, Fortchern, wondering
what kept her son, came herself to the river. And she
found her son conversing with the clerics and receiving
instruction from Lomman, who, to her great delight,

spoke in her own British tongue.   This goes to show,
if the child understood Lomman, that the Brythionic
language must have been very much akin to the Gaelic,
or that his royal mother had taught her own language
to her son.   Going home, she told her husband what
she had seen and heard; and he too welcomed the
clerics from Britain, for his own mother, Scoth Noei,
The Fresh Flower, was the daughter of a British king.
Now, as everyone in Britain was understood to be a
Christian—and St. Patrick takes it for granted—it is
not to be doubted that Fortchern, this daughter-in-law
of the High King, was a Christian.   It is significant
that there is no mention that she was baptised at " the
open well."   She was baptised in Britain in her
infancy.   And it must have been a great delight to
meet her countrymen.   " And Fedilmid offered Trim
to God and to Patrick and to Lomman and to his own
son Fortchern, for ever."

After his morning in Tara with the High King, the
Saint set out in the afternoon for the hospitable house
on the banks of the Boyne beside the Ford of the Alder.
Trim is, by modern roads, about eleven miles due west
of Tara.   Doubtless while holding his momentous
conference with the High King, the Saint was aware
that the hospital house at Trim was ruled by a Christian
fellow-countrywoman.   It would give but a partial
and very inadequate idea of the Saint, were we to treat
him as one who had not devoted his life to preparing
for his mission, and who was likely to have knowledge
of every factor which might help him to bring it to a
successful ending.   One of the most important of
these factors was a knowledge of the whereabouts of

the scattered members of the Christian communities in the different parts of the country. One in such high estate as that which befitted the wife of the High King's son could not be unknown to St. Patrick and his British fellow-countrymen. And the contribution which they made to his prestige at a critical time bears out this contention. The Royal House was favourable to his mission and actively abetting it.

Prestige of this nature in a country where it counts for so much was of immense service to St. Patrick. After Mag Inis, his earliest foundations are in Royal Meath. It would be more accurate to say that the Saint enjoyed the favour of some of the members of the Royal House, for the King was at best not actively hostile. That he was a trickster we know : he broke his oath to the men of Leinster ; he tried to deceive the Saint and to lead him into an ambush, according to biographers, who sometimes, in spite of their inaccuracy, allow the character of a man to emerge from a list of wonders and impossibilities. It is significant that the nearest church to the palace at Tara was not founded by St. Patrick, but by Sechnall, his nephew, at Dunshaughlin, seven miles from Tara Hill. This church of Sechnall has given its name to Dunshaughlin. Sechnall was Secundinus. He may have gained favour with the King at the expense of his uncle. Who but a nephew would have been so daring ?

CHAPTER XVI

TO TELLTOWN

IF YOU WANT TO FIND YOUR WAY ABOUT MEATH YOU must go to Navan. I entered the tea-rooms of that prosperous town. Whom did I meet but an upstanding fellow—tall, grey, straight and young! I knew him well, but I had forgotten his name. Instead of feeling complimented for my preference for his personality:

" I hate the sight of you," he said with a slow, reassuring smile.

An old friend of mine was talking to the Sergeant of the Guard at a table. He saw me, jumped up to his full height, and caught me by the arm:

" Come along," he whispered tensely, pointing to a passage.

" I can't. It's too early. I am looking for Telltown."

" That will be all right. I have a farm at Donaghpatrick, on the way."

" Is Donaghpatrick on the way to Telltown? "

The Sergeant produced a map and pointed: " A few miles up the Kells road turn to the right."

I memorised the map.

" And what do you want at Telltown, anyway? " the big man asked, looking for his hat.

" I want to see the place where the old games were played."

" The ' old games ' ? " the tall man said. " They were not at Telltown at all. The real Telltown is Lough Crew. There were two Telltowns."

Two Telltowns! This was somewhat disconcerting, and all the more when I realised that that
well-read official was by all arguments right. The
ancient Irish celebrated their " games " or, as we
might call them, " races " or " fairs," hard by the
grave-mounds of the famous dead. And next to
Brugh na Boinne, Telltown was important.

Knowing that if I accompanied my friend I might
be tempted to linger over-long at his hospitable
thorpe, I prepared to go.
" No! no! Can't you hold on? " And they
grasped me by the shoulder.
" I can't. Go back to your tea, it will be cold."
" And what other way do we take it ? "
Escaping from these cataclysms of kindness I went
on my way thus directed by men of goodwill. And
going along I thought of the ancient games of
Telltown, for I had studied as much as I could read
about them when we were reviving them in 1924.
I wrote an Ode for the Taillteann Games as (*longo
intervallo*) did Pindar for the many games of Greece.
But it is gone with my lost verses, and I doubt if
I can remember half-a-dozen lines. They are not
much loss, for I have their fruit, a medal with a head
of Queen Taillte all in gold.
The games or assemblies of ancient Ireland were,
with the exception of little local practices, very much
the same. The *Dindshenchas*, in describing the Fair
of Carmen in Kildare, gives a picture that could be
painted of any one of them. The verses are so well

translated by Professor Macalister that I had to ask
his permission to transcribe them to save the reader
from my own versification.   And his masterly analysis
of the stanzas is so full of information that I besought
him to let me quote at length.

> But what noisy rabble's there
> On the border of the Fair ?—
> Vagabonds with drums and bones,
> Shrieking to their bagpipe drones.

Now, these are the people who would have interested
me.   Whenever I go or, rather, am brought to one
of the modern examples of an ancient Fair, a race-
meeting, it is not the horses that interest me, nor the
men in the outlandish costumes, nor the women
" smartly (why smartly ?) dressed," but the beggars
who are so natural, and the women with shawls and
babies who are so natural, and the good inveiglers and
the wild men.

What would I not give if that sound-restorer of
mine which I have invented (but not perfected) could
be got to work ?

Across the innumerable and unimaginable noises of
the whole world's past—battles, volcanoes, waterfalls,
mass-meetings and week-ends in Mexico—I would
tune it in first of all to ancient Ireland before switching
it on to ancient Greece.   The rumour of the rabble
at Taillteann would rise up from the gulphs of Time:
the shouting, the abusive cries of women, the mockery
of tinkers, the cheering and the general ructions.
Then stillness and the sound of an extraordinary and
compelling voice.

The road falls swiftly down to one of the loveliest rivers in Ireland, the Blackwater, bright and dark with its mild, deep stream. I leant over the side, gazing at the current and looking at the green-haired weeds that swayed half down to its depths as its surface coiled into half-circles making patterns of La Tene. Two water-hens met each other in mid-current, and far away, where its light as it turned whitened into that of the evening, four swans stayed themselves without motion. On one side rose a tall grey ruin from a mist of hazy willows ; on the other the green ridges faced a water-meadow full of reeds.

How wonderful it would be, I thought, if I could get rid of my body that is open to so many stimuli and distractions and at the mercy of external conditions, and turn myself, a mind only, into a river to flow forever, slowly and silently, luxuriating through the rich land hemmed by lush grasses and bordered with willows, aware of the deep wavering weeds and the grey-green budding trees, and capable of insinuating into the soft pores of the rushes, to rise with their sap and with the sap of the lilies that flower on the dark, untroubled pools, drop from the bent alembic of the willows in dædal and beneficent dew, and to hold reflected within me all that passed with the seasons of unending years ! If one could be only a mind and flow forever like a river that is perennially replenished by the same substance and conscious only of change without it, itself forever fresh, exempt from age, identified and made one with the Perpetual Flux !

So I who am touched by Eternity, a minion of That

o

Which is Ageless, mused. And with the waters I murmured παντα ρει.

But the last glow was on the decent church which topped the opposite hill. If I am to see it, I must hurry. This is that church repeated in cut stone which Conall, son of Nial, gave to Patrick, " whom he received with great joy." There it stood in the last glow of evening light.

" He measured out a church for God and Patrick with sixty of his own feet." That is, it was sixty feet long, Dr. Healy explains. But it is not. It is eighteen yards long not counting the porch, and this would show that Conall measured as many a man measures a length to-day, by his own feet. Thus we get the length of the chieftain's foot, which was not uncomely.

Now, we are told that Patrick's followers and servants were repulsed by Cairbre, who scourged some of them into the river because they would not reveal the whereabouts of their master. This makes it hardly likely that it was from Telltown immediately beside Donaghpatrick that the Saint was driven. Had it been so, it is hard to imagine his getting a grant of land and a site for a church next door, so to speak, to the surly Cairbre. There is a great dun at Telltown by Donaghpatrick ; evidently it was the palace of a considerable chieftain, and considerable chieftains, in this instance princes of the blood royal, did not dwell side by side. " Silver-hair is right," I thought. " There were two Telltowns." Owing to the corruption of Taillteann in English into Telltown, the

visitor is led to expect a town, or at least a hamlet.
When I had driven as far as I had been directed, I
knew that I had lost my way. A knot of men were
standing by the roadside.

" Can you tell me, where is Telltown ? " I enquired.

" You have passed it."

" But I haven't passed anything."

I wondered how I could have missed it, for I had
not passed anything except a well-kept farmhouse and
some beautiful trees. There was no sign of a village
or of a settlement. I was in old Ireland at any rate;
free from hamlets.

" I thought that there was an ancient fort about
here ? "

They looked at one another and then suspiciously
at me, but with a milder suspicion than that of the
man of the North whom I met on the side of Slemish.
I was to be humoured, particularly as it was Sunday
and time was on their hands. Besides, they were
being challenged for information on their own ground.
They looked at one another. No words. To relieve
the embarrassment :

" So I have passed it ? " I said.

" Give this man a lift and he'll show you."

What we call a " strong " farmer (that is, in herds
and acres), intelligent, neatly whiskered, stepped out.
I hoped that I was not bringing him out of his way.
There was no fear of that. It was on his way home.
A pleasant odour of peat smoke filled the car. I had
a man of the soil to be my guide.

" The first boreen on your right."

We wriggled down a little lane until we came to a cottage gate. We got out. My guide led the way for about two hundred yards through lush grass, until we came to an earthen embankment still devoid of grass in places, so steep was its wall. We climbed to a large green plateau. " An Irish Acre." He waved his arms to take in the great earthen platform.

"A stout man must have lived here ? " And I looked at how it commanded the river.

"Yes," he answered. " He must have loved horses. My brother and I came across a lot of their teeth when we were digging outside there below." He pointed to a field which lay below the rath or fort on the side opposite to the stream, and he said : " There were two lakes at one time over there, but they were drained. The people used to go there bathing from this fort. They were great people for bathing."

Now, how had that tradition and the memory of two long-vanished pools survived ? I asked him what the fort was called.

" Rath Dhu."

" The dark Rath ? "

He nodded.

This is Rath Airthir—it must be so, I thought. Thinking of a chieftain buried with the battle-steeds that drew his war-car, I asked if there were any bones with the horses' teeth. There were skull-bones. When I made myself clearer, he told me that there was a tumulus in the field beyond the lane ; I couldn't see it now with that tree in the way, but I could see it on my way back. A queen's grave. Very tentatively

he ventured : " Eithne." But I would not hold him
to it, for even the best of our archæologists agree to
differ on more important things. But he was not
done. " They were decent people in those days.
They made no display when they died. But they just
heaped the earth over them and let the grass grow.
There's many a ripe rascal lying with lettered stones
and stained glass over him that had better have nothing
said."

If Rath Dhu was the house of Conall who received
Patrick " with great joy," I could understand his
granting church lands in his immediate neighbourhood. But I could not understand those lands being
the gift of Cairbre, who in all likelihood may have had
his strong place, as his brother Laery had, hard by
ancestral tombs. Lough Crew, like Tara, contained
grave-mounds the antiquity of which was very great.
Next to Brugh na Bōinne, Lough Crew might be placed.

From the high place of Rath Dhu I gazed to the
west, to where the ridge against the skyline was
broken by a tower on the hill of Kells, and beyond by
the earthworks on the top of Lough Crew. Now, if
Patrick " turned aside " from Cairbre to Conall, he
must have retraced his steps, for the Telltown that
neighbours Donaghpatrick and holds Rath Dhu is
nearer Tara by four miles or more than Lough Crew.
And he must have passed at first without visiting
Conall. It was necessary to find out if possible from
local tradition to whom Rath Dhu belonged.

" Does no one know the name of the chieftain who
owned this fort ? "

" One of those writer men down from Dublin lately. You wouldn't have been him ? " I denied the soft impeachment and described Professor Macalister. " Aw! That was him and no mistake." Evidently I was " coming on " when I could paint an unmistakable portrait in words, and the same flattering!

The speed with which the old writers make the Saint move would do credit to a modern motorist. Even with the advantage of that vehicle and the fine cement road to Kells, the best part of a day would be taken up in going to Lough Crew, extricating your servants from an angry chieftain, shaking off pursuit and " turning aside " to be received with joy by Conall at Donaghpatrick. Once we allow the Saint the time it would take now to obtain a site for even a cottage, we will untangle the confusion to which ignorance of place and distance gave rise. And the best way to do that is to give the Saint a headquarters and time to do his evangelising work. As far as conjecture can be made plausible, Donaghpatrick was his headquarters. It was the nearest to the stronghold that could protect him. It was nearest to Tara of all the strongholds from which he could expect protection. It was the site of his largest church, the one wherein he placed his altar stone ; and it was the palace of the High King's brother who received him with joy.

So by the banks of the Blackwater, within call of Rath Dhu, on the dry ridge above the river, the Saint and his household rested to consolidate their gains like a general after the turmoil of a great engagement. It happened to be a lovely place, for in the early days of

the Church the choice of site was not always with the
founder. It depended, as we have seen, on the
propinquity to the fortress of a man of goodwill. How
is it that in Ireland the most important finds, the
famous places and the sites of important events
occurred as a rule out of the neighbourhood of what
are now the principal towns and villages? We will
search in vain in the descriptions of the golden-coloured
bronze spears, or the so-called Tara brooch which was
found on the beach at Laytown, or of the magnificent
golden ornaments, for the name of a place familiar to
us to-day. This fact alone should show how greatly the
social organisation of the country differed from that of
the present. It was a townless land with thirty thousand
great houses, around which the people gathered and
into which the households came for shelter in time of
raids or war. Tara is deserted to-day, and Donaghpatrick would have been nameless but for the Saint.
You may miss Telltown as I missed it; and even now
we are not sure where it was that the games were
held; nor can we contradict any man who says " There
were two Telltowns," and tell him he was seeing
double.

Have you noticed the way that, up to a little while
ago, the drivers of springless carts were wont to stand
upright with the knees slightly flexed as they drove
afield? This, I think, as I survey our coal-porters,
must be an age-old custom derived from the way men
used to drive in chariots. It is unthinkable how those
barrows on springless wheels, on roadless plains, ever
bore anybody. And yet the " ringing plain " was full

of them, two-horsed and pole-driven. Now, St.
Patrick, as I have realised all along, must have come in
a chariot to Tara, for it was incumbent on him, if he
were to impress the High King, that he come in a
manner not unworthy of Imperial Rome and of a
bishop. But what a drive—or, as the Americans call
it, a " ride "—it must have been ! Even though the
vehicle was of wicker and though the track was a grass
track, the bucketing and shaking must have been
awful.

And since this is not a guide-book, and since it is
impossible to separate St. Patrick wholly from any part
of Ireland, I shall not attempt to follow all his journeys
through the length and breadth of the land. I will
follow him (as I have already done) from his incoming
to Tara and now across the country to the lands
" beyond which there is no man," to Croagh Patrick
and Murrisk in Mayo, and furthest west and out to
Cahir Island ; and write of places he visited in his
twenty years of travel as an active missionary. A
glance at the map with its criss-crosses will show that
to go round to every village would only be to repeat
the visit to any one. And we don't want repetition.

So in his chariot he comes ; when he handed over
Donaghpatrick to Presbyter Cassan, he ordered
Buadmæl his charioteer to drive to Delvin, where he
founded five churches, and thence, after due residence,
to Mullingar.

CHAPTER XVII

THE VILLAINS OF THE WORLD AT MAG SLECHT

NOW, MAG SLECHT WAS THE CENTRE OF PAGAN WORSHIP in the land. Here were Crom Cruach and his " subgods twelve," whose priests for his mockery choked King Cormac with a salmon bone one hundred years before the coming of St. Patrick by turning the " maladictive stones." But of these cursing stones there was no trace.

There is a quarter of a mile of limestone rock about a quarter of its length in width rising above the plain for sixty feet. Here was the platform whereon was the great Firbolgian idol, " the King idol of Erin according to the Dindshencus "—namely, Crom Cruach—and around him twelve idols made of stone, but he was of gold. Until St. Patrick's advent, he was the god of every folk that colonised Erin. To him they used to offer the firstlings of every issue and the chief scions of every clan ! 'Tis to him that Erin's king, Tighermas son of Follach, repaired on Hallowtide, together with the men and women of Erin, in order to adore him, whence is Mag Slecht, " Plain of Prostration."

This limestone shelf is in Edentinny, and it is remarkable for the great gushing spring, evidently the issue of a subterranean river coming from the lakes of Fenagh some miles to the south. There is no doubt that, between the water-lovers and the builders of circles and pillar stones, it was a high seat of Druidism. All these things are here. I must be a bit of a Druid

217

myself, or someone who would seem pathological to Professor Freud, so fond am I of wells and waters in general. The marvellous monoliths are still on the top of the Plain of Prostration. One is prostrate now —a great " needle " like the so-called Cleopatra's, but rude and unengraved. It is about the length of a cricket pitch to the first white line, and about four feet broad. Beside this, one is leaning to the east, as if in acknowledgment of the influence which came therefrom—an influence stronger than that for which it stood. The third is sunken, as is the stone on Tara ridge. Another leans to the west, and this makes my fancy vain, for the stones cannot " seem " to do anything both ways. Two circular enclosures are clearly traceable. So this is Mag Slecht, a place of human sacrifice.

This was the place that St. Patrick attacked and where he put himself to the proof more dangerously than at Tara. The story of his attack on the idolatrous crowd gives us, in spite of his biographer, an idea of the fiery and zealous man. As he drew near, he protested against the idolatry with " a loud commanding voice." Then Patrick, drawing nigh, saw the idol from the water afterwards named Guth-ard— that is, the Loud Shout. He lifted up the staff of Jesus, but the idol fell prone. Patrick acted " with prowess " against the idol, and hence it came to pass that the broach which fastened his cloak fell off in the herbage, which he ordered to be pulled up till he found his broach.

I was stooping to drink at the side of the great

fountain when, looking up, I saw an " extensive " sheep-farmer who hailed me with a roar. " Hello, Luke," I said. I spoke to him of the Loud Shout. He was one of those gallus fellows not to be found outside Ireland, whose minds dated from days before St. Patrick and even now were like a continuous presentation of Macbeth, full of great ruffians, exulting in excursions and alarms. He was as obdurate a pagan, if he only knew it, as the ancient Ossian himself.

" Oh, you Villain of the World," he said. " It was you gave me the start when I saw you libelling your liver with that water." His glass eye actually twinkled.

" I only sampled it. I have a palate for water. I could almost tell its wellage, since it cannot have a vintage."

" It must be by way of contrast, then. Your palate has never become jaded, I bet—not with water, anyway."

I laid the flattering unction on the right spot.

" That rock and well was the centre of all the devilment in this part of the country and that was as bad a spot as any. And is still ! "

" I was surprised to learn that St. Patrick shouted at them. I suppose he tried to put a stop to it before he climbed the hill ? "

" There wouldn't have been a heathen converted but for the way he shouted at them and frightened them out of their wits."

" There was queer goings on," he said abruptly,

" if you are to believe them that should know.   Very queer goings on."

" Worse than at a Welsh Revival ? " I queried.

" Ah, for God's sake !   Mag Slecht would make a Welsh Revival look like as mild as a Magdalen Asylum or a meeting of the Dorcas Society.   The Plain of Prostration !   They were prostrating themselves before the idol, praying for more power to give each other hell.   I know the kind they are.   They're prostrating themselves—that's as far as taking their hats off goes—to me in the day-time, to blaze through my windows at night.   And all because I'm too gentle and easy-going.   I mind the time I could shoot the dudeen out of a tinker's mouth at ten yards.   There was peace in the district then.   But now you never know who it is putting dogs after your sheep or breaking the fences.   It would take two St. Patricks to be up to them."

Suddenly " Mudebrod !   By the Doom of God ! " he shouted.   He seemed transfigured.   He pointed his beard after imaginary enemies, shouted and waved his stick.

I could not expect the *genius loci* of Mag Slecht to be dissipated utterly in fifteen hundred years.   And I was at a loss to know in whom it resided most, my friend or his foes.

" But you have got your farm still."

" Farm ?   The Blackguards !   They left me the bog and the demesne round the house : but they took the best sheep-farm in the world."

" Was it very good ? "

" Good, is it ?   I declare to God I had to go round in the mornings and give the sheep a kick to remind them to go on grazing, it was that rich ! "

I looked at his pointed shoes and I thought of the welling limestone, the wool, the twitching tails and the goodly, satisfying grass.

He pulled me by the arm.

" It seems a long way off."

" Don't be talking," he said.

Like my Uncle Kevin, who told me that he had " humped Hannibal's elephants over the Alps with small Latin and a translation of Livy," I felt that, having followed the chariot and horses of Buadmæl half-way across Ireland, I deserved a little rest.   My trim-bearded friend was depending on me to be his audience for the dramas in his mind.   He talked in gusts, a bearded, thin, upstanding, abrupt little man, with a glass eye which recorded barometer-like, his minimum in popularity during the days of the Land League.

CHAPTER XVIII

ST. PATRICK CROSSES THE SHANNON

LIKE DEW ON THE FIELDS OF ERIN, THE NAME OF ST. Patrick has satured the very land. It would be vain to trace his footsteps everywhere, for the retracing and retracing again would confuse the reader. To follow him from his entry into the country, and in his journey to its ultimate coast in the west, is all that his devotee can do if his record is to be clear and routined. And now that he is crossing the Shannon, the ford may be described.

It is still a wonder to me how the ancient Irish crossed the rivers, for as we see them they are unfordable to-day at these places which were called " fords," *e.g.* Trim, Slane and Athlone. It well may be that the weiring and conservation of the waters have made the rivers too deep for fording at the present time. You have only to lean over the bridge of Slane to realise that a man could not ford the Boyne there now even on stilts. But I learned something at the ancient Bandea, or Snam-da-En, the Swimming Ford of the Two Birds. A name that brought back the picture of the moorhens on the Blackwater beneath Downpatrick near Telltown, far away in rich Meath.

From Mag Slecht, due west by the foothills of Slieve Erigna, by the foothills of the Iron Mountain to the head of Lough Allen, the road goes. It might be called the Road of the Little Lakes, as Alice Milligan called Cavan. But as he crossed the ford the

Saint suffered a loss, for by the waters of the Shannon on the edge of unexplored Connaught, on the right bank of the river, Buadmæl his charioteer lay down and died.   We are left to speculate if it were the harassing he got from the horse thieves in the vicinity of Boyle that hastened his death, or his struggle to bring his chariot safely through the swift current—both were predisposing factors.

To the north of Battle Bridge, about a mile and a half to the north of Drumboylan, the river is split by an island as it cuts through an eskar.   Here the stream is swift but shallow, and on the bank the ancient stepping-stones—those that remain of them—may be seen foot-worn by the sandals of two thousand years. But the stones that crossed the river-bed were removed by the Board of Works when a footbridge was built. This may explain the absence of the ancient stepping-stones from other fords : they were built into bridges which now cross the rivers at their sites.

The old people show you the field where Buadmæl died and the place where the little church stood on the rise that bears his name.   The flagstone on which he died is preserved in the house next the ford, and the wall of the house is partially over it.   This would look as if the house was built on the very spot.   Strong as the current of the river is, the tradition about St. Patrick and his charioteer at the ford is stronger still. What else does the name of the village mean—Drum-Buadmæl : Drumboylan ?   Here I am looking at the greatest river in Britain, foaming like beer in its bed. I think of my friend the engineer who, when the

Shannon Electric Scheme was first suggested, asked,
" What do you expect of a river that can hardly get
itself out of the country ? "   To look at it here, you
would think it had a full, fair flush.   Fast or slow, the
tradition is that no man was lost in its ford of all the
many who had slipped off its stepping-stones.   The
Saint had blessed the ford whereby Buadmæl laid
down his life.   But the Saint had to engage another
charioteer.   In a country so choleric, and amid
chieftains whose attitude to the new Faith had to be
put to the touch personally before it could be certainly
ascertained, neither the life of the Saint nor that of his
servants was safe.   He selected Odran to replace
Buadmæl, and Odran gave his life for his master long
afterwards in Offaly.   This was the way of it:

The ruling prince of Offaly boasted that he would
kill the Calpurn, *i.e.* St. Patrick in revenge for his
destruction of Mag Slecht if he entered his territory.
This was known to the Saint's charioteer, who concealed the boasting threat from St. Patrick.   And the
manner of the life-saving and the dialogue smacks too
much of the truth to be dismissed lightly as a mere
legend.

Odran said to Patrick, " It's a long time I have
been driving you."

" Fair enough," said the Saint.

" Give me a chance to take your place to-day only ;
and lead the horses yourself."

" Fair enough," said the Saint.

So north they went from Brittas to Bridam (which is
Killeigh under another form).   Here the prince ap-

SLEMISH

L. Neagh

ULSTER

L. Erne

Supposed Escape

SAUL

CONNAUGHT

L. Conn

MAG SLECHT

DRUMBOYLAN

CEARA

ELPHIN

SLANE

Cother Isle

CROAGH PATRICK

CROCHAN

GRANARD

TELLTOWN

Renvyle

L. Corrib

R. Shannon

L. Ree

TRIM

TARA

1st Landing

R. Liffey

LEINSTER

INVER DEA

Escape

MUNSTER

MAP OF VOYAGES AND
JOURNEYS DESCRIBED IN
THIS BOOK.

Bip. Pares

proached, and assaigied Odran, who was sitting where his master should have sat.

And Odran, in his great charity, diverted the Saint's curse from his slayer to the tree of Bridam.

Thus died his second charioteer.

" Thence from ' Cairraige Airtech ' St. Patrick went farther west," where he met Ernaisc and his son sitting under a tree. " And Patrick wrote an alphabet for the youth." The idyllic moment of " sitting under a tree " must not distract scholars from the significance of what is implied in " Patrick wrote an alphabet for the youth Loarnach." But to me, a journeyman, the few minutes I had with my friend Sweeney of Oughterard were more fruitful than the archaic names could ever be.

" His nephew is buried in Inchnagoill."

Now, Stephen Gwynn, the scholar poet, and son of the greatest scholar of Patrician lore, had told me that Inchnagoill meant not only the Isle of the servant or stranger, but the Isle of the Devout Stranger.

" His nephew is buried at Inchnagoill."

It was five miles out in the lake. Who had a motor-boat ? No one for hire. There was nothing for it but to hire a row-boat. This desire to get for a moment, be it never so short, from the beaten track of the Saint might be interpreted to mean that I was beginning to lose interest in my quest. Not so. I had come upon a subject that was full of the promise of an added interest. The boatman told me that Lugnaedon, the nephew of the Saint, was a pilot.

" That explains it," I said to myself. " Though his

P

lot was cast inland, he did his best to hold by the water, and so he is buried in the greatest of all our lakes. If he steered his uncle to Strangford Lough, and if he died far away to the west of the seas he knew, what better attempt could he have made at being true to his ruling passion than to wait his resurrection in a sea all his own ? ''

So I hired a boat for Inchnagoill. It would have behoved me more not to have forgotten the uncle for the nephew. But he was a pilot. How could I resist ?

This is no guide-book. If you want to go in search of any particular place in Europe there is always Baedeker. But to follow St. Patrick through Ireland requires a double or a treble compass, because one has to follow him first through the face of the country, secondly through the century in which he lived and wrought, and thirdly through the legends which began during his lifetime—legends which were engendered by the affection in which he was held by the peoples in the " outlying parts where still the tribesmen fight." And all the time we must be prepared to put a slow tempo on the movement and to reduce the compacted outlook of his biographers.

I cannot tell (who can ?) how long the Saint lingered in the vicinity of Telltown, or how long it took him to reach Elphin. What does it matter, anyway ? The long, washy plain, fenceless to this day, was far more of a marsh than it is now, when the road is raised dyke-wise ten feet above the surface. He passed by Ballinalee, which, fifteen hundred years later, was to become the birthplace of one of Ireland's heroes, second in the hearts of the Irish people only to St. Patrick himself: Sean McKeown the Chivalrous.

Very probably the Saint's journey was dependent on the time of year, in that rain-ruined land. But reach the ridge of Elphin he did, and thereabouts befell one of the most beautiful and dramatic incidents of all his wonderful career in a land of savage people.

About eight miles from Elphin, the Fountain of the White Stone, is the royal cemetery of Cruachan. Here, under his standing stone of red granite, lies all that was mortal of Dathi, who led his Irish champions, auxiliaries of the Roman General Ætius as far as the foothills of the Alps. This is the famous Cairrthe-dhearg, the pillar that stands up forever, immortalising the story of a " campion stiff in stour " who in battle ne'er gave back. This was a king who fought side by side with the legionaries of Rome, a valued ally and a commander of swift spearmen and roaring targeteers. I could give a list of the kings and queens and of " the warriors of Erin in their famous genera-tions who slumber there " beside the " fierce fair women " in the ever-beauteous Cruachan!

What a wonderful thing is a standing stone! The simplest and the grandest and the oldest of all monu-ments. It means that the uprightness during life of the dead hero is perpetuated by men who were his followers and who would not forget him even when he was futile and no more a man. There is something terrible and yet pathetic in the very primitiveness of such a monument. It was under one of these that

Fergus son of Roy, the last of the men to whom the great saga of the Tain was known, lay deep down; and over his head the Ogham spelt " Fergus son of Roy is here." And it was to one of these that the stricken and dying hero of Ulster, Cuchullin, looped himself by his shield-thongs, and his enemies had to wait until the ravens lighted on his head, so terrible was his fame. And around the Cairrthe-dhearg the turf covers many a blue eye and many a swan-white breast.

From Elphin the road leads to Shankhill, and thence a high ridge saves you from the marshes and many little lakes that come between you and Tulsk, and the great gush that comes out from the rocks below the road. And here were enacted the most tender and extraordinary scenes in the whole life of the Saint. I make it the central adventure of his life, and well I may, for literally it took place as near as the ancients could go in their computations as to what was the centre of the land. It is by things like these and by topography that the Saint is remembered for ever. And now he is midway on his journey in the middle of the land. It is enough to make you think that the whole narrative is a metaphor of his central and crowning success. But let his great biographer the Archbishop speak:

Patrick and his household camped during the night close to this well of Cliabach, or Clebach, intending next day to proceed to Cruachan. They rose early, before the sun, to chant their office, and prepare to celebrate the mystic Sacrifice. They were dressed in their long robes worn by the monks of the time; but their tonsured heads were bare, and their feet were sandalled. There is a green bank all round the well; and limestone crops up here and there, making natural seats just on the margin of the great limpid fountain. It was a quiet and beautiful spot; and so the clerics sat down on the rocks, with their books in their hands, to chant their Office, just as the sun was rising over the far-distant hills of Leitrim, through which they had traversed some days before.

But now they, too, see a strange sight at early morn—two maidens tripping down the green meadows; one of fair complexion, with her golden hair streaming in the wind; the other of ruddier features, crowned with auburn hair. They were attended by their maids and by two aged men, clearly Druids, who had charge of the maidens, as their fosterers. It was customary for these royal girls, according to the simple habits of the times, to come and wash in the fountain, as royal maidens did in ancient Greece. But now, when they came to the fountain and saw the clerics seated with the books in their hands, dressed in strange garments, and speaking strange words, they stood lost in amazement. But they were royal maidens, daughters of the High King of Erin, and they were not afraid. Their curiosity prompted them to speak, for, as the Book of Armagh tells us—they knew not who the strangers were; nor of what guise; nor of what race; nor of what country—they thought them fairy men, or gods of the earth, or, perhaps, ghosts.

Wherefore they said—" Who are you, or whence have you come ? " Whereupon Patrick, repressing their curiosity, said—" It were better for you to confess your faith in our true God than to ask about our race." The narrative is exact, but the questions are compressed in it.

" Then the elder girl, the fair-haired Eithne, said—" Who is your God ? Where is your God ? Of what is He God ? Where is His dwelling-place ? Has your God sons and daughters, gold and silver ? Is He ever-living ? Is He beautiful ? Have many chiefs fostered His Son ? Are His daughters beautiful and dear to the men of this world ? Dwelleth He in heaven or on earth—or in the sea, or in the rivers, or in the mountains, or in the valleys ? How is He to be loved ? Is He to be found ? and shall we find Him in youth or in old age ? Tell us this knowledge of God, and how He can be seen."

This flood of questions the curious maiden, with royal courage, addressed to Patrick, the leader of those strange beings. Then Patrick, full of the Holy Spirit, says the writer, replied to the royal maidens, answering all their questions, but beginning with the most important.

" Our God is the God of all men; the God of the heavens and of the earth, of the sea and of the rivers; the God of the sun and of the moon; the God of the lofty hills and of the deep valleys; a God who is over the heavens, in the heavens, under the heavens; Who hath for His dwelling-place heaven and earth and sea, and all things that are therein. He breathes in all things, gives life to all things, rules all things, sustains all things.

" He kindles the light of the sun, and the moon-light He keeps by night. He made the mountains in the dry land, and the dry islands in the sea; and the stars He has set to aid the greater lights. He has a Son alike and co-eternal with Himself. Neither is the Son younger than the Father, nor is the Father older than the Son, and the Holy Spirit breathes in them both; nor are the Father, the Son and the Holy Ghost divided.

" Now, as ye are the daughters of an earthly king, I wish to bring you nigh to this heavenly King. Believe ye, then."

And the maidens, as with one voice and one heart, said— " Teach us with all care how we may believe in this heavenly King; tell us how we may see Him face to face, and how we may do all that you have told us." Then Patrick, after instruction, no doubt, said, " Do you believe that by baptism the sin of your father and mother (original sin) is taken away? " They said, " We believe it." " Do you believe in penance after sin ? "—that is, as a remedy for sin. " We believe it." " Do you believe in a life after death, and a resurrection on the day of judgment ? " " We believe it." " Do you believe in the unity of the Church ? " " We believe it." Whereupon they were baptised, and Patrick blessed a white veil and placed it on their heads. This was, apparently, not the veil of the baptismal rite, but the white veil of their virginity, which they consecrated to God.

Then they " asked to see the face of Christ," but the Saint said to them, " You cannot see the face of Christ except you

taste of death and receive the sacrifice" (before death).
And they replied, "Give us the Sacrifice that we may see
our Spouse, the Son of God." So, by the well-side, under
God's open sky, the Sacrifice was offered, and they received
the Eucharist of God, and fell asleep in death. Then they
were placed in the same bed covered with one coverlet; and
their friends made great mourning for the maidens twain;
but all heaven rejoiced, for so far as we can judge they were
the first of the white-robed host of Irish maidens who passed
the gates of death to be with their Spouse for ever in heaven.

"Give us the Sacrifice." Each bright head
　　Bent towards it as sunflowers bend to the sun :
They ate ; and the blood from the warm cheek fled :
　　The exile was over ; the home was won :

A starry darkness o'erflowed their brain.
　　Far waters beat on some heavenly shore :
Like the dying away of a low, sweet strain
　　The young life ebbed, and they breathed no more :
In death they smiled, as though on the breast
　　Of the Mother Maid they had found their rest.

Aubrey De Vere.

We have here given the account of the Book of Armagh,
word for word. To add to it would be to spoil it. The
same account, in almost exactly the same words, is given in
the Irish of the Tripartite; so we may fairly assume it gives
us not only an exact, though brief, account of what happened
by Clebach Well, but also a fair summary of Patrick's
preaching to the people whom he was about to baptise there.
Then we are told of the two Druids who hitherto were
listeners only, if they were at all present at the earlier portion
of this beautiful scene. It is rather doubtful, for it is stated
when the maidens fell asleep in death, that Caplait, who
fostered one of them, came and wept; whereupon Patrick
consoled him, no doubt, and preached the Gospel to him
also, " and he believed, and was shorn as a cleric "—that is,
he received the tonsure by which he became a cleric destined
to the service of the Church.

But his brother Mael acted differently at first. He came
up in anger, and said, " My brother has become a Christian,

but it must not be so, nor shall it profit thee; I will bring
him back to heathenism; " and he spoke injurious words to
Patrick.   But Patrick here, in a patient spirit, made allowance
for the anger of the man.   He was long-suffering with Mael,
and continued to preach to him until he converted him also
to penance; then he tonsured him like his brother, changing
the *airbacc giunnæ*, or Druid's tonsure, into the frontal clerical
tonsure then used in Ireland, whence, we are told, arose the
celebrated Irish proverb, " Mael is like unto Caplait," which
seems to signify the hardened sinner has at last been converted.

So both the Druids believed in God, and when the time
of wailing for the maidens was over they buried them by the
fountain Clebach, making for them a round grave or *ferta*,
according to the ancient custom of the Scots.   But we call
it, says Tirechan, a "*relic*," from the relics of the dead
which are therein.   And that graveyard, or ferta, with the
bones of the saints, was given to God and Patrick and to his
heirs for ever.   They also built a church of earth in the
same place, and it was called Sendomnach Maige Ai, and
was given to Patrick for all time.

There can be no doubt that this ancient church is that
whose ruins, though of later date, still stand close by Clebach's
Well.   It is called " Ogulla "—the Church of the virgins
—and has given title to the parish.   At first sight it might
seem that the well is too far from Cruachan, somewhat more
than a mile, to be the well where the maidens were wont
to wash.   But the Druids with their charge may have lived
nearer to it, and it is certainly the only fountain on the eastern
slopes of Cruachan which answers the description in the
text.   The name, too, of Ogulla is peculiar and convincing.

CHAPTER XIX

FORGETFUL OF THE WAYWARD SPEED IT HAD, THE Oughterard river begins to hush its freshets as it goes through the little town and, gathering to itself all the wildness of its mountain loughs, becomes composed and stilled and deepened to enter without motion the great Lough Corrib which is its wide congenial home.

The boat was ready, but I was not. The river here was deep and high. It was not a foot below the reedless, grassy margin that curved as it came, to distinguish it from a mere man-made canal. The light lay on the water in an indescribable hue, a brown limpidity that flowed into the mind and made it one with the water and at peace. Over there, but not on my side, yellow water-lilies rose and raised heads of unblown blossom aslant for two inches or so into the air. They were all the same age—not one was either faded or overblown. Their flat shields lay beside them on the lake ; and lake and river here were the same. How shall I name it ? What colour is the river ?

" Your boat, sir."

That interjection excuses me. I can now interject something myself far-fetched or exotic rather, by way of a comparison when I try to answer, " What colour is the stream ? " It is as dark and as clearly brown as the brownest and loveliest brown in the world—that which is in the pupil of a giraffe's eye. " A dear gazelle " may have a slow, dark eye, but I have never

seen a gazelle, whereas I have seen a giraffe: I am a
life-member of the Zoo.

"Oh, all right." I suppose I must get into the
thing. It is evident that unless the lake freezes—and
I have no time for that—it will not be easy to cross
the five miles to Inchagoill without a boat. A man
came along in a motor-boat and made it fast as we set
out. He made me envious.

"That's a pleasant patch of land just there by the
water's edge."

"An Englishman bought that."

And no wonder, I thought. He had an eye for
what is beautiful. Then I began to suspect that
perhaps it was the salmon-fishing that interested him,
and not the loveliest water in the world. He was
about to become diminished in my mind when he
became again an object of interest.

"But it went back to the owner."

"How was that?"

"It was summer when he bought it, sir. When he
came back to build his cottage in the Spring the river
was up a bit, and he couldn't find the field. So the
farmer got it back and had the money."

Rather than lose such a site I would have built
my house on stilts as the Lake-Dwellers of Berne and
other places did, or lived in a stranded submarine.
But I could hear the endless "explanations," and the
Englishman, finding that it was no one's fault, or,
rather, not being able to find whose fault it was, sooner
than be the next to blame, throwing up the sponge
in disgust. Perhaps the river was right. It wanted

no red-tiled bungalows. It was content to go on reflecting for ever O'Flaherty's tall grey keep.

Very soon I grew restless as I sat in the back of the boat. I hate to be a passenger. We had five miles to go, and that would take an hour. I felt it was hardly fair to have myself rowed without giving a hand. The Connemara man who rowed me belongs to a rare type: to the tall, thin, fatigueless men of the West. They all look heavy, in their great-coats and damp homespuns, but not one of them outweighed me on a market day in Clifden when we were round a scale. Their average weight was eleven stones. I could give them a stone and a half, and this reflection made me feel that it was all the more unsporting to sit idle in the back of the boat. In spite of the fact that I should no longer be able to keep my eyes on the cone of Croagh Patrick thirty miles away, I said:

"Give me a thole-pin and one of those oars." Unhappy words! I had not rowed since I "went backwards down to Iffley" years ago. Oh, ah! I was forgetting the funeral of George Moore, who was buried on Castle Island on that lake of brilliant water which is coloured like amber, for its bottom is white limestone, and there is no peat round Moore Hall. His sister sat in the end of the boat and held his handful of grey ashes in an urn of brown clay, fashioned after the fashion of the ancient Gaels. In the clear air the island looked nearer than it was. And I, as one of the three outside the family who was invited to attend, volunteered and, which is so like myself, without taking thought.

First off came my silk hat, the frock-coat and . . .

" I presume you will retain your braces," his sister said.

Never again, I had vowed, will I be stroke and bow together.

But here I was (only barring the lady) in a worse predicament.   I had begun by doing so well that—well, not only my braces, but I could open my shirt.   Soon I was opening my hands, which were beginning to blister.

" If you keep them open as you go forward, they will keep cool."

That was slight consolation.   We might interpose a little ease.

" What is that island over there ? "

" That's covered with slugs, and they come out on the rocks to bask."

We passed the sluggish island.   I thought that it was beginning to rain.   What a release that would be !   The boat would be water-logged, and I could get an excuse for resigning my oar.   But it was not beginning to rain.   I was beginning to . . . shed " drops of onset,"—as the politest of poets puts it— from my brow.

" Am I coming back too far ? "

" No, everything is all right."

Is it ?   Well, every stroke is shifting her six feet, anyway.   And two yards into five miles is . . . Well, that has finished my left hand.   I had too tender a palm . . . " palmam qui meruit ferat."   It seems that I am beginning to rave, to become somewhat delirious.

I must take a pull at myself. But myself was taking too many pulls—that was the trouble . . . hic labor! After all I am doing this for St. Patrick. His nephew had a much worse skiff than this to make the journey and when he did make it he had to remain. But I will be coming back, back in the back of the boat. That much was certain.

" Have we far to go ? "

" We're well over half way."

" Are there any interesting islands en route ? "

" Sorra one."

Inwardly I groaned.

" His grandfather was Odisse." I liked the little marginal remark on the edge of the manuscript of the Confession. The scribe had put it on record that the grandfather of St. Patrick was Odisse. The short for Odysseus ? Of course, " I am Odysseus." There's a wave that lifts, breaks and hisses in the name of that sea-tossed wanderer. Sitting well in order, Smite! That was cheering. I would stick it out. His grandfather was Odisse! And his nephew was Lugnaedon the pilot. I loved St. Patrick for his sea-worthiness, to apply that word in a new way. I mean that he never complained of the sea ; and what journeys he must have had, not to speak of the raid. . . . His grandfather was——

" Here we are, sir. Yer a great man to pull."

" Nothing, nothing at all, my man. In fact I would row you back but for a slight blister . . ."

" Mind yerself now."

After all it would never do to let him lift me out
of the boat.

*   *   *   *   *

The air was warm with the sense of growing things
as we went into the thick growth of the rich island.
Not a hundred yards from the shore we came to a well-
mottled style of ancient stone, shaped like a narrow V,
to keep cattle from the sacred enclosure. We passed
an ancient ivy-grown church with a door that leant in
like the door of an Egyptian temple or the " Treasury
of Atreus " at Mycenæ. But it was the much later
church, with nine or ten, not twelve, faces carved around
the arch of its door, that would be more likely to interest
antiquaries. Lugnaedon's stone, a standing stone of
grey and greenish micaceous sandstone, caught my eye.
" That's it."   It stood in a little ferny dell beside one
of the oldest and best-preserved (by reason of its isola-
tion) graveyards in the country. This was Lugnaedon's
stone. It rose to a height of about three feet. Its base
broadened where the lettering ended near the ground.
It was engraved with four very ancient crosses, such as
those which may be seen at Glendalough : equal-armed
and rectangular. I felt the stone, and found that
though it could be made slightly to shake, its fifteen
hundred years had hardly weathered it. It was as perfect as in the days when, after much loving labour, the
mason's work was done and Lugnaedon laid to rest in
the midst of shining waters. I hoped that I stood
beside the standing stone of the man who, judging
nicely, steered St. Patrick and his companions, both
Frankish and British, to Strangford Lough, and ran

through the Symplegades of the ocean river of Inver Brenea.

Long I looked at the old Gaelic lettering that made a grace of whatever irregularity it had, a grace in freedom unknown to the Greek.

Let him not be forgotten, though he lies amidst milder waters, for the seas he mastered and the man he steered safely to our land. It was his to grasp the tiller. St. Paul was a tailor of tents.

As we were about to return, my guide beckoned me into the older of the little roofless churches. On a rough altar stood a basin, or rather bowl, of what seemed to be old sandstone. It was about half as large again as a football, and roughly shaped without, but quite smooth within. A baptismal font? It held about a pint of water.

" That water never dries up."

I looked at the great damp boughs that roofed the little fane. They could hardly be the source of supply. There was no connection by pipe or such with the ground, for I lifted the bowl in my arms and found it free. Before I touched it, I noticed that there was a rim of wet in a ring about two inches wide over the water it held, as if the water had suddenly subsided, or as if somebody had rolled or trolled the bowl before our arrival. But even the caretaker was away. I asked what it would be like at the end of a hot week in summer.

" Just the very same as you see it now."

It was worth coming to see that. I am enamoured of things incredible, as I have confessed before. And

here was a perennially watered font. I should not
say " here was," for it is there still. And the next
time I go, I will go in a motor-boat, not with the idea
of taking the font by surprise, but for other reasons.
Maybe one of these is to save time!

CHAPTER XX

THE ASCENT OF THE CROAGH PATRICK

THERE WAS ONE STAR OUT AT SEA HIGH UP OVER A DARK
wall of cloud, like the last fruit on the bough in some
heavenly orchard, when I rose to begin the journey to
Croagh Patrick mountain, thirty miles distant from the
place where I lay. Under the two stars Croagh
Patrick or the Reek as we call it, was invisible but I
could see it in my mind's eye which had been taught
to see it as Augustus John saw it when he turned a
sycamore panel into a panorama rimmed with mountains showing Croagh Patrick in the distance and
stippled it with sea. The Reek looks best from the
ridge of Renvyle near the old coastguard station about
a mile from the hotel.

Away to the north, thirty miles away, it stands with
its cone lucent and silvern, far-seen, recessed in light
like a mountain in Elysium. In the middle distance
the great mole of Muilrea looms to the east across the
bay which it forms by extending one long low limb to
the west over which the cone appears. Muilrea looms
lambent and purple like the substance of a dream.
And the substance of a dream or of a vision it is for
did not the artist's poetic brain take in the scene with
all its light and colour and project it again transformed
by that creative imagination of his until the mountains
seem to be lit from within and the sea to shimmer
timelessly as if made of the very substance of a dream.
It is this pervasion of purple that makes the distant
silver cone seem to be lost in another world. From

Q

the south all is bright and blessed, no hint of the dark chasm, Lugnaghoul, on its north-eastern side wherein were cast all demons and reptiles. It was three o'clock of a July morning. The moon was still bright and the sky cloudy but not misty. " A merrier man than I am, one lives not in Chrisende," I said, quoting Little John to cheer myself. Was there a prospect of a clear sky from the top of the Reek ? But half-way on the journey, in the region of the Partry mountains, all changed, and low clouds came down and shut out Croagh Patrick from the south. I hastened as fast as the road would hold, and turned off to the left without going into Westport, the little, overcrowded, far-away town into which 'bus-loads and train-loads of pilgrims had been pouring for two days. Some of these pilgrims were sleeping in railway-carriages, some in motor-cars, barns and any available covering, for the houses were full. Many had made the ascent during the long summer evening, and were now gathered on the summit of the Reek. It was four o'clock in the morning by the time I reached its foot.

Long fields of heather slope gently upwards at first, and then they become plateaux filled with large heather-bells and delightful little yellow sessile roses. But soon the rock breaks through and the mountain bares its arms. I sat to get my breath when I had climbed about eight hundred feet. It was almost dark. Blankets of thick fog obscured everything. The silence was full of rest. It was doing me good. But a strange sound met my ear. It was not the noise of wind, for the air was windless ; nor of running

water.   It was a weird and an unexplainable noise—
a kind of clicking, but blunted, and not sharp.   It
was high in the air overhead.   What could it be?
Was the Holy Hill haunted?   The thing to do was
to rise and investigate.   At another few hundred feet
I sat down again, and now to the multitudinous
clicking noises were added the whispers of voices, voices
of the pilgrims in endless procession shuffling up along
the precipitous path, which was composed of loose
stones, grey and greasy with the fog.   It was the rattle
of these stones that had caused the weird noises.   I
had been approaching from the hillside at right angles
to the track.   This was a shorter route than the one
which led up the eastern col; and a far easier route than
the traditional path on the north which leads up from
Murrisk and the shores of Clew Bay.   Soon I was
in the procession of men and women who leant forward,
bowed against the hill.   The road was about ten feet
wide, and the stones of grey-green slate were irregularly
shaped, like some distorted curling-stone.   Added to
this, they were greasy and slippery.   Here and there
a climber fell forward, but not far, for the hill was
becoming somewhat perpendicular.   I withdrew from
the human stream and sat down on a wet rock.   I
looked on the people as they passed.   Country
people for the most part, and here and there a country
girl spoiled by some absurd fashion from the ready-
mades of England that looked wholly out of place in
this environment.   Will no one tell the country girls
that nothing is more becoming than a shawl and that
bare feet are better than cheap, high-heeled shoes?

It would not be of the slightest use. Fashion dominates both dame and dairy-maid.

" I will arise and go now."

In the middle of the second hour I was still toiling upwards, when I heard a shout in the darkness over-head :

" In the name of God ? "

" Amen."

" In the name of God what are you doing here ? "

It was Fr. Paddy, a fine figure of a man as he stood over me with his great ash-plant, like Pantagruel or the Angel Victoricus.

He asked again : " What has you here ? "

" Out of my way ! " And I tried to shout " Excelsior."

He gave me a helping hand.

" ' A banner with a strange device.' And, faith, it was strange," he reflected.

" Let me sit down," I said, " till I get my second wind."

" What have you done with the first ? You'll want half-a-dozen yet. What ails you ? "

" I am ' Gone with the Wind.' But tell me why that device on the banner which the youth bore through snow and ice was so strange."

" Because there's no such word in Latin as ' Excelsior.' It may have been ' altius ' Longfellow was trying to say."

The sliding stones displaced by pilgrims were coming about our seat.

" It's a great thing to have made this ascent, although we can see nothing."

" Have you come up for the view ? "

I had forgotten about the pilgrimage. I had a staff, but I had forgotten the cockle-shell. It would have amused my friend.

" Have we far to go ? "

" When you have put that Mount Everest look out of your face, I'll tell you. Then you can exchange a face of pride for one of martyrdom. You're only somewhat more than half-way up."

Inwardly I groaned. " If this mountain endowed a man with a wish and made it come true, I'd wish I were one of the sheep I met in the heather and that you were an Archbishop with a crozier to haul me up to the top."

" And there'd be more joy in Heaven than for the ninety-nine ! Come on ! "

Once he gets up he will stride relentlessly to the top, so at all costs, unless I am to have a permanently dilated heart, I must play for time.

" Just a moment. Suppose there were no mist, what could one see from here ? " I knew the scene well, but I liked to hear about it.

His Reverence began to describe the invisible panorama. The 366 islands in Clew Bay, Granuaile's Castle on Clare Island with its table mountain where there is now an unaccountable fresco which recalls the tapestry of Bayeux, the mountains sweeping round to culminate in Achill Head, hills that looked as if some awful symphony had become petrified and

manifest. A visible Götterdamerung. Afar to the
north-east a mountain more symmetrical and as clear-
cut as Croagh Patrick. And what was more *à propos*,
" You could see Murrisk Abbey which stands in
Murrisk Aigli. This mountain of old was called
Mount Aigli, and Murrisk Aigli is below. And
extremest western limit of the Saint's journey is
Cahir Island, a long, green wedge between Inis Turk
and Clare island—a two hour's row at least."

" I've seen it from near Murrisk at sea level," I
answered.

(*O dass ich war da!*)

" That's where St. Patrick buried his charioteer."
And Fr. Paddy quoted out of his wealth of lore from
Tirechan :

> " And Patrick journeyed to Mount Aigli to fast on it
> forty days and forty nights, observing the discipline of Moses,
> Elijah and of Christ. And his driver died in Murrisk Aigli,
> that is the plain between the sea and Mount Aigli. . . ."

" I could understand that if he had got half-way up."
But I was ignored, and quite rightly. He went on :

> " And he buried Totus Calvus the driver and he heaped
> stones around his tomb."

(How accurate that was I knew, for I had seen the
grave of the All Bald One who cared for the horses
of the Saint. It lies in a lovely and desirable place,
in the most beautiful grave-garden in the world, beside
a singing brook and immediately in front of a well.
It is marked by six or eight stones arranged circle-
wise and not heaped. These are all but overgrown.
I could see three and feel a few more with my foot.)

Observing me moping, his Reverence touched me with his stick.

". . . and he buried Totus Calvus, the driver, and he heaped stones around his tomb, and he said, ' May it remain so for ever. And it shall be visited by me in the last days.' "

" Totus Calvus " caught my mind's eye. " Totus Calvus ? " I queried.

" Yes. The auriga or driver of Patrick's chariot was called Totmael : 'totus' means 'all,' and 'mael' 'bald.' "

" All-Bald," I translated. I could see Totus swinging the natty cobs into the plain of Murrisk with the pole rattling as he trotted them in. And the locals criticising the Connemara ponies—if they were Connemara ponies in those days before the Spaniards brought in the Arab horses. The Bishop's driver must have been a respected man. The Saint buried him with his own hands. I remembered that that was the third driver the Saint lost. I wondered what killed him.

" What happened to Totus Calvus ? "

" Come on now, if you're coming on at all. If you took less soda-water you'd have better wind. There's refreshment on the top—tea and spirits."

He rose. I lost his great figure as it towered into the gloom. The crowd streamed past. And now they began to make way for some who were descending along the same track. They came down slipping and laughing, followed now and then by little avalanches of stones.

It grew lighter. I could see the bare feet of a girl some yards ahead at the level of my face. I had to avoid the pebbles her toes shot back.

It is a beautiful thing to see a human foot in action : the elasticity and grace of the arch as it takes the strain, and the response of that cable which is called the *tendo Achillis*, which accepts the weight and rises with it.   Her long, bare feet with their wet and pallid soles made light of the difficulties of sharp rock and irregular surface.   She too was soon beyond me overhead.   I noticed that though the young girls had clear and lovely complexions, the backs of their legs were red and shining.   This was invariably the case. Then I realised that the redness was caused by the flip-flap of the skirt against their calves, over their ankles for hours in the climb.

I took another rest.

This is no place for seniors or middle-aged men, or even for those " in their early maturity "—Augustus John's correction for my use of " middle age."   I reflected that there must be few weak hearts for forty miles about the sacred mountain.   I reflected also that any modest ambitions I may have entertained of achieving *angina pectoris* became more and more hopeless as I gained height.   Which wind was I using now ?

What was that ?   Was it a horse neighing on the Murrisk plain—one of the pair of Totus Calvus making ghostly neighings far below ?   No, it was only one of my lungs complaining at being rudely awakened by the morning air at three thousand feet or so.   Otherwise I was going well.   But there were hundreds of feet yet to climb.   The heart was sound enough, but I was giving out in the wind.

" Tristram was stronger, but Lancelot was better breathed." I think I will just sit down again and wait for my second wind. It seems a long time coming. Perhaps I have used it up before. Well, then, I must wait for my third wind. You are supposed to come up for the third time, so there may be a third wind. *Excelsior*! or rather, *Altius*! We must be up and doing. That stone was well fielded, considering I did not see it until I got it on the knee.

If this pilgrimage goes on at this rate, with all these careless people about, in a few years there will be no mountain. They shall have pitched all the stones away.

" Only three hundred yard, Mister!" a laughing youth shouted. No wonder he was laughing. He was coming down. O Lord! I will do my best: only three . . . "And they buried Baldy!" How I envied him lying at Glaish or phonetically " Glosh," a mile from the Croagh Patrick Hotel! He was at sea-level, anyhow. But look at me. If he were where I am, he would not have turned a hair. The Dead have the best of it: they have broken the tape.

" Where is the refreshment, Father?" I asked when at last I had made the necessary height. " You spoke of spirits."

" I did. And when your spirit is refreshed, it will be time enough to think of your body."

" In the name of—— !"

" Amen," said Fr. Paddy.

" The Druids were right!" said I.

The pilgrims were making the last stations about the

little chapel on the summit.   This little chapel seems
to have no door, but to stand open to the winds.
It was bare of decorations ; a poor little fane—save
for this inscription from the sayings of St. Patrick
which was painted on the wall opposite the door :
" Ut Christiani ita ut Romani sitis."   A priest and
a lay brother were officiating.   Outside you could
hear the tapping of pilgrims chipping stones from
Patrick's Bed.   I went over to a booth for a cup of
tea and a sandwich.   These were expensive items,
but when the woman of the booth told me that even
the water had to be brought up on asses to the mountain-
top the day before, not to mention turf for heating and
all the tackle of a camp, it was not unreasonable.   I
bought a little well-written pamphlet on the ascent
of the hill by Alice Curtayne.   I always like to have
authority before I realise an experience, like the
Monk in the Inferno who said, " In our monastery
the Devil is reported to be the Father of Lies."
Centuries of personal experience told him nothing.   The
pamphlet showed the Saint with a modern mitre and
wearing a long white forked beard.   Had St. Patrick
a beard ?   He has in the popular eye, but this only
means that he owes his beard to Leonardo da Vinci, who
by painting the disciples at the Last Supper as middle-
aged, bearded men made the imagination of Europe
come to see eye to eye with Leonardo when it imagines
an Apostle.   If the men of Europe were not to benefit
by the genius of such a creative imagination as was
Leonardo's, then I would have cause for complaint.
And I do not complain.   Raphael has influenced that

imagination perhaps more strongly than da Vinci. What need is there, it may be asked, to run counter to the popular idea of the Saint? Only this, that if the imagination of the multitude which owes its origin to the quattro cento is to dominate the fifth century, all attempts at research and all consideration of the practice of the time of the Apostle must be foregone. The fifteenth century must not be permitted to dominate the fifth. But we are fifteen hundred years behind this convention, and about a thousand years behind the Tuscan who had in mind the ikons of Byzantium and mosaics of Ravenna and of Monreale, majestic in their presentations of the All-Father.

The Saint had barbers about him, barbers as self-effacing, scissor-sounding and as devoted as those of my Lord Beaverbrook who go circlewise genuflecting, snipping while he sits awful, remote and sheeted, upon a dais in Stornoway, who were ready to tonsure his converts. "And his head was shaven" is almost a formula to the account of the reception of a chieftain into the Church.

To return to the older practice should not be considered an innovation. Whether it be or not, it is better to see our Saint as his contemporaries and his converts saw him, than as they see him who take their historical perspective from times when there was little historical perspective at all.

And the stone at Killadeas on which an Irish bishop is represented as beardless, bears out unmistakably the practice of Rome. Not to mention the four effigies of the Saint all beardless on the Cross of King

Flann. May I be forgiven for dispelling another fallacy, and that is the representation of the Saint bedight in modern chasuble, mitred and senile, going about the country? His energy must have been as terrific as his endurance, so *pace* our artists, for all their piety I cannot see the Saint as they see him, frail, elderly and emaciated; but rather do I call him up to the mind's eye as an active man between forty-five and sixty, in the full vigour of his years. And most of all I think of him as a man of commanding presence. Whether you agree with me or not (and I know that Dr. Healy might not until he had given me a hearing), I see him as a stalwart and even a tall man. How else could he have impressed the Ancient Irish, who even to this day in their descendants will not respect even a doctor unless he be the " full of a door "? I know all about McCartan, St. Patrick's strong man who was employed to carry the Saint over fords and stepping-stones. If the Saint were a dwarf, it would not take a strong man to act as a St. Christopher. What we must beware of—and all the more because it is characteristic of those who promulgate it—is a denigrating conception of the Saint. " He was a little man." He speaks of himself as " homuncio." All this is to decry and to disparage the idea not only of the Saint, but also of divinity. Our Divine Lord has had this " legend " spun about Him by the Jew Josephus. Neither of these were under-sized, which is the next thing to being under-reverenced. This is a subtle heresy, for it is aimed at belittling God and Man. Beware of a dwarf presentation of the Saint.

To return to this excellent little pamphlet. I read :

We made the ascent during the night, and this may be the reason why it seemed so hard.

I should tell you that neither my two companions nor myself had ever made this pilgrimage before. I should add too, perhaps, that we were all three town-bred, therefore not inured to rough ground. Our first difficulty was to persuade ourselves that the black jagged rocks dimly discernible at our feet were meant to be climbed at all. They jutted out at such precipitous angles that several times we had to scramble upwards on hands and knees. Also the sound of running water disturbed us : we seemed in imminent danger of tumbling into some unseen torrent. After some ten minutes' peering and blundering, we found that there was a rivulet running down each side of the rocks, and therefore ours was indeed the path. On we went then, with frequent pauses to sit down and pant, for the incline is very steep. Our sticks were an encumbrance (their use is more obvious when coming down).

Every time we sat to rest on a rock, the crowd of ascending pilgrims streamed past us : slipping, stumbling, often sprawling, they persisted in their dogged onslaught on this climb made holy by Patrick fifteen hundred years ago. It would be unnecessary to recommend silence on this journey, so thoroughly do conditions enforce it. The physical distress is too acute, the breathing too laboured for conversation.

By the time we have climbed the precipitous scaur at the base of the ascent, we became aware of two alleviations : we had got our second wind, and our eyes were growing more accustomed to the darkness. While we could not yet see anything of the prospect before us, at least we could see a few feet ahead. And this considerably relieved the tension.

The scaur gives place to very steep broken ground leading to the halt known as the First Station. Here there is the poorest sort of wooden cross and a huge bank of flint stones that look as though they had been tipped out of a mason's lorry. At this point the pilgrim must suspend his climb while he says seven *Paters*, seven *Aves*, and one *Credo*, walking seven times around the Station. Where the pilgrimage exercise probes to the quick is in this rule of *walking*: it is hard, because the climb seems so much, without adding to the tax on one's feet.

On leaving the First Station, the path turns into a sort of little gully, choked with boulders. Sometimes the sides of this little channel rise in such a fashion that it looks like the ravine bed of a dried-up river. Soon we remarked with joy that the sky was lightening by imperceptible degrees, and the gully appeared to end in smooth ground that invited our blistered and aching feet.

But when we came to this smooth ground, we found that its softness was the unpleasant yield of a quagmire. It was black and boggy and oozy; our feet landed in it with an ominous squelch. Heels had a tendency to stick to it, as though one were walking on pitch. We had been looking forward to a rest on this smooth part, but there was no chance of repose here. So we floundered and laboured onwards and upwards, and when the bogland turned once more into a boulder-choked ravine, we welcomed the ruder conditions with gasps of relief.

The sky was now paling, and we could see our watch-faces. We had been climbing for nearly three hours, and we calculated that we were less than an hour's distance from the summit. (Dear reader, do not take this as an index of your own progress. No doubt, you can do better.) This heartened us, for indeed our feet seemed swollen to twice their normal size, and, moreover, weighted and clamped with iron; our thick stocking were torn; our knees and hands bruised; our clothing clammy with perspiration. We could also see the mountain peak now, standing up, dark and solemn, to our right.

Is there anywhere in the whole world a more toilsome prayer, a more punishing prayer, a more gruelling or a more humbling prayer than this annual appeal to Patrick?

And is there anywhere a more fearful mountain? I say this without disrespect for its sacred associations of antiquity. From base to summit, it seems savagely to forbid the pilgrim who would trespass on its ancient side. There is never the relief of even the briefest patch of vegetation, nor even a few feet of passable groundway. Whatever this strange mountain was made for, normally it was surely never meant to be climbed. A landmark of striking beauty for all the west of Ireland, apart again from its sacred associations, the Reek has no beauty on close acquaintance. Indeed, the word that occurred to us most frequently during that night climb was the word, *savage*. Nothing ruder than this journey can possibly be imagined: it demands everything the pilgrim has; the last shred of his resolve, the last ounce of his physical reserve, the last gasp of his wind, the uttermost of his capacity for prayer.

But the pilgrimage is a great experience, and leads one to meditate on Patrick from many a new angle. The Saint who selected this remote peak for a place of retirement certainly desired solitude in its most absolute sense. When he expressed a love of seclusion, he meant it. And what is more, he made sure of it. Saint Francis of Assisi, too, was a lover of solitude, but La Verna has amenities compared with Croagh Patrick.

Evidently she is much younger than I. If it took that much out of her, what must it have taken out of me? But, then, so many things in my life are " taking things out of me " that I have come to regard the process as a kind of beneficial phlebotomy to down pride and blood-pressure.

In keeping with the pace of my ascent, I found my mind slow on the uptake, for only now I realised why it was that the descending pilgrims were so cheerful and merry. It was not wholly because they were going down, but because they had made the pilgrimage. It was time I went down too, that I went down to Murrish Aigli.

Diverted by my short cut—I really had no time for a short cut—by gullies and scaurs, I at length reached the bottom of the hill. And now a rather unusual

and therefore a noticeable thing claimed my attention.
Everyone I met hailed me graciously. It was almost
inexplicable. I who recoil from popularity in any
form, I was quite distinctly and unmistakably popular.
I was becoming alarmed; for popularity, if carried
to its extreme, would land me in the position of a ward-
heeler or a political Boss. And that would be the
worst turn I could do to the kindly Irish. But
these salutes and " Nice mornings " had to be in-
vestigated. What had made me popular and hailed
and well-met? The situation was becoming serious.
It was causing me grave concern. I might as well
be a . . . Suddenly illumination! I had climbed
Croagh Patrick. I had made the pilgrimage. I had
become a worthy person through no fault of my own.

Now I began to realise what St. Patrick had done for
our country. I realised how true was the quotation
from the Latin of the unknown poet which prefaces
this book.

> The outlying parts. . . .
> You drew to better things and civilised.

The amelioration of manners, the kindliness, the
good nature that mark the Irishman, how far were
they due to him? And I began to realise how great
were the hearts that could take the lesson so practically
to themselves and make the ascent of a mountain a
true ascent to the spiritual heights of charity and
goodwill to all men.

The Saint's strong soul was reigning influence still
over all of us after fifteen hundred years.

" A spirit communicated is a perpetual possession."

CHAPTER XXI

MURRISK AND CAHIR ISLAND

SEEN FROM MURRISK ON THE SEA LEVEL, THE MOUNTAIN takes on a sinister appearance because of the dark profound of its ancient crater, which forms a great bowl to the north-east of the conical summit. Apart from the wealth of legends in which it abounds, Murrisk shows signs of having been a centre of Druidical ritual. In a pleasant meadow to the north of the road that leads west to Louisburg only a furlong from the Croagh Patrick Hotel, stand two pillar-stones about fifty yards apart. They are thicker than most pillar-stones, and though in the course of time they must have sunk in the earth, they still show about four feet above it. They are older than the Ogham writing, and though from the grain of the stone of which they are composed there appear to be faint scorings, these are not made by man, but by the Architect of the Mountain. What interested me most—for I had not seen its like before, unless what I took to be a fallen pillar on Mag Slecht be one—was a large oblong slab of dark brown stone lying with a very slight slant from head to foot not twenty inches above the grass. It was marked with two or three round punched-out holes which would admit two fingers or a thumb. This evidently was a great table used in Druidical rites. When questioned, an old man told me that it was very old—more than five hundred years. On it, he said, the old Druids skinned the bullocks they sacrificed. It was interesting to hear the word skinned,

R   257

for it suggested that there was no waste of food, but rather a distribution of the sacrifice among the congregation. Set beside an ever-peaceful bay, it was a lovely place for an altar. Two trees and an old grey garden wall broke the monotony of the view, if a view which looked over an inlet from Clew Bay to the hills of Mullaranny which were beginning to turn to amethyst could be called monotonous.

I went into the hotel to gather more information. Murrisk abounds in legends of St. Patrick and his companions. There is a field behind the school house, which is a hundred yards from the hotel, a sacred field that knows well how to preserve itself from desecration. It appears that it was the site of the refectory of those who accompanied the Saint on his mission. From this the deduction seemed justified that Murrisk was a centre of Druidism, and that St. Patrick abode in it for some considerable time. After a fatuous story of a wild bull (not fatuous if it were some metaphor dimly remembered), which was presented to the community by " some old pagan king," having its bones put together by the Saint after its flesh had been consumed, and having been brought to life again, but with a shin bone missing, to cure it from stampeding, I was told that the field could not be ploughed. An old man had told me that, and he grew very reserved, as countrymen will, when asked for an explanation. He preferred to keep the mystery to himself. Perhaps he felt that virtue would go out of him if he divulged it. Perhaps he mistrusted me as a fitting receptacle of the information. But the woman of the house said that when they tried recently to plough the field, the horses went wild and could not be forced to work. Whatever the explanation may be (and who wants things like these explained ?), the fact that Murrisk was rife with legends and that they were fresh and freely offered to the stranger gave me not a little pleasure. It is something in times like these to have a field which keeps itself unprofaned in honour of St. Patrick.

The Saint must have remained a considerable time in Murrisk. West beyond it by a mile to the left of the road there is a remnant of a little stone-built chapel. The stones with which its gables are built are larger and better set than the stones in the only gable that remains of Saul in Mag Inis. It is by this little chapel that the mountain stream comes down beside which Totus Calvus awaits his master's promise. The spot is lovely enough to make a poet " half in love with easeful death." He lies in a *ferta* or grave surrounded by stones in a circle like the grave that holds the lovely girls who died so young by Clebach's Well. And I thought of another stream fragrant with wild roses which comes from a distant hill which looks conical seen from the north. It was a long journey from Slemish to Croagh Patrick.

From Murrisk the hardy men of the curraghs doubtless rowed the Saint out to visit lonely Cahir Island, which lies between Inis Turk and Clare Island ; the first and last of these must have been, as to-day they are, fairly populous. But Cahir was as it is now, deserted and, far more than Lerins, " withdrawn into the sea." The Saint, who was not a hermit, may have settled on the lonely island one of his companions who wished to emulate his Master's master Honoratus.

It takes two hours to reach, and it is a risky journey, not so much from the chances of being shipwrecked, but from the quite possible eventuality of being marooned. Besides, it is hard to land on. Only a shaly and very rough beach gives access from the sea on its lee side. The island contains " nitials " and the remains of an early church. The " nitials " are possibly intended to mean " initials "—that is, inscriptions, on its stones.

When I visited this island, which lies like a wedge with its raised base oceanward, I sailed in an eighty-ton yacht with a stout Diesel engine. I felt that it was hardly playing the game, but otherwise there was the possibility of becoming marooned by the rising seas.

Not a few of these islands in the Atlantic have ecclesiastical remains, but they are, according to Father Kelly, who knows them well, remains dating from the time of Dermot McMurragh.

The story that the Saint sailed to Cahir will stand no contradiction, in Murrisk, at all events. And it may have been as a result of his visit that even some time afterwards—not necessarily in his life—a hermit or some monks set up a tiny monastery amid the rocks of the Western Ocean.

What the feelings of a party of devout men might have been, I could not imagine. The island cannot support more than one family, if that family had time to attempt to cultivate it. Fresh water I could not find, apart from a small surface well, and this was thick with green

slime.   Fish and sorrel would be all one would have
to support life, unless the island was not " self-
contained," but was still in touch occasionally with
the mainland.   What the urge was to the monastic
life in the first quarter of the fifth century in Murrisk
I do not know.   St. Patrick, though a great ascetic,
was no hermit.   So it must have been after the wave
of monasticism had reached our shores from Lerins
and Monmartier that Cahir Island was occupied.
And that was decades after St. Patrick.

CHAPTER XXII

ST. PATRICK'S PURGATORY

In Connaught is St. Patrick's Reek
His Purgatory in Ulster seek.

ST. PATRICK ASCENDED THE MOUNTAIN ON SHROVE Saturday, and descended from his stony bed on its summit after forty days' fast. This is recorded by Tirechan, whose zeal for thaumaturgy has diverted the minds of his readers from the significance of the great episcopate. It would be easy to say that it has done more harm than good This is not so, but it has covered unmistakable facts with clouds that are not always clouds of glory; and it has disseminated legends where the local traditions, could they be heard on the spot, would be more valuable. It is now difficult to weed out the local traditions from memories of the latter part of the Tripartite Life.

Not that the Tripartite Life is not of inestimable value to us, preserving as it does countless place-names full of the natural poetry of the land—the Lake of the Sloe Bushes, the Ford of the Two Swimming Birds, the Field of Spring, the Clear Well of the White Stone—but it would have been better had it kept to the style with which the earlier part of it was written.

From the traditions which I gathered at the foot of Croagh Patrick, it is no precarious conjecture that the Saint remained at Murrisk and in the vicinity of Aghagower for the better part of a year. His journeys through the island seem to have taken twenty years. It was the ninth year of his episcopate when, on

Shrove Saturday, he ascended the mountain to begin his fast of forty days. This was the year when the calumny and envy of his religious brethren in the Britains reached their height, and an unfavourable report on the conduct of his mission was sent to Rome. Not alone did these men see a man less scholarly than themselves succeeding when none had the initiative to venture, but they felt that their own lack of missionary zeal was rebuked by the successful courage of the Saint. " Why does this fellow thrust himself into danger among hostile people who know not God ? " That—we have the Saint's own words for it (*Confessio* 46)—was what they exclaimed. That was what galled them. St. Patrick may have been " suspended " pending inquiry as a result of this report, which had the authority of those who were nearest to Ireland of any of the Christian communities of the Roman Empire. And so they might be presumed to have definite information. And here was a report that the new Bishop was winning an immense See for himself in unapproachable and virgin territory. In his youth, when St. Patrick seemed to be friendless and helpless, he strengthened himself by fasting and by prayer. May this betrayal not have been the reason for his terrible forty days' penance on the summit of the Reek ?

" When Patrick was in Cruachan Aigli he sent Munis to Rome with counsel to the Abbot of Rome, and relics were given to him."

What significance lies behind that statement, what unexpanded history ! The Saint must have sent a

letter longer and more detailed than the *Confessio*,
which he wrote in old age at the end of his mission, a
letter of which the *Confessio* itself may have been only
a faintly remembered echo.   What would we not give
to see that letter ?   Perhaps one day it may be discovered in the Vatican, for it is unlikely that he
entrusted Munis to be his sole counsel without the
support of his own written deposition.   There is
another possibility—namely, that St. Patrick himself
may have journeyed to Rome.   True, he states that he
never left Ireland, but he said that in a connection
where to leave it would have been to abandon it.   If such
a journey were occasioned by duties arising out of clerical routine, he would no more have counted it as leaving
Ireland as he counted it necessary to mention his own
qualifications or his ordination for the mission.   Whoever went, the result was prosperous.   The Annals of
Ulster record under the date A.D. 441 " Leo ordained
42nd Bishop of the Church of Rome, and Patrick the
Bishop was approved in the Catholic faith."   So his
vigil and prayers on Cruachan Aigli during the spring
of that year were blessed by the Pope.   But the date
is doubtful.

The deductions Bury makes lead him to the conclusion that the Saint did actually visit Rome in the
second year of Leo's Pontificate.

> The ordination of Leo is wrongly placed in the Annals
> in 441; it belongs to 440.   But its close association with the
> notice of St. Patrick's *probatio* shows the meaning of the
> words *probatus est*; and in fact there is no conceivable mean-
> ing than formal approval by the Church, and the only form
> that approval was likely to take in such a case was the

approval of the Church's chief representative, the Bishop of
Rome. Such approval might have come in the shape of a
formal epistle from the Roman Bishop to the bishop in
Ireland. But when we find in our seventh century authority,
Tirechan, a statement that Patrick was in Rome accompanied by Sachellus, and when we find that in his time there
were relics of Peter and Paul and other martyrs at Armagh
procured by Patrick; and seeing that there is nothing improbable in these records, and that, on the contrary, a visit
of Patrick to Rome is antecedently probable; we may
venture, I think, to combine these testimonies and conclude
that Patrick did visit Rome at the beginning of Leo's pontificate. The tradition of Secnall has all the appearance of
being genuine; and Tirechan in this passage was using an
older written document, as is proved by his uncertainty about
a numeral (cum viris viii aut viiii).

And may not the fact that he was in a position to
urge every church that followed him to sing " that
praiseworthy hymn *Kyrie eleison*," which had just been
introduced at Rome *before* it was introduced into Gaul,
point to a new arrival from Rome ?

Tradition in Murrisk points to a college or community of the companions of Patrick. This in its
turn suggests a permanent foundation. And the
voyage to Cahir Island bears it out. It took time to
organise.

Why did he make the venturesome voyage to Cahir
Island ? It may have been that he heard that the
islands of Inis Turk, Inisbofin and Clare Island
" ultimi habitatores mundi " all of which are near it,
were inhabited, as they are to this day. And before
he could testify, as he did testify proudly in his last
years, " Behold we are witnesses that the Gospel has
been preached to the limit beyond which no man

dwells " (*Confessio* 34), it was necessary to visit these outlying islands. But if he visited one before the other, how would he be received in that which was temporarily passed over when he came to land on it? Was it not the wisest course, if rivalry and jealousy among the islands were to be avoided, to summon a hosting of all islanders to the central and neutral Cahir Island? No other reason seems to be apparent for the preference of this uninhabited island to the others; and if he preached there, he had certainly reached the limit beyond which no man dwells. It is hard to land on, and was probably uninhabited, for there were no hermit Druids. The tradition from all around the coasts from which that wedge-shaped island, which looks like a springboard or a bootjack lying on the sea, can be seen, is that the Saint landed on it. Of the duration of his stay there is no information, but you will receive little sympathy and obtain little further information if you doubt the possibility of the landing or pursue your questioning too far.

So Cahir Island marks the most westerly point of the Saint's long journey. It was nine years since he set out from Tara before he sailed the endless waters of the West. He was probably the first man born in Britain who had ever seen that weltering waste that bathes the setting sun, let alone sailed over it. Could the courage of those " dominicati rhetorici," those highbrow dons, the lordly rhetoricians who, in spite of their vaunted superiority, tried to humiliate him, break his spirit and undo his work, have equalled that of the " poor unlearned orphan " who was a Columbus of the Faith to the Gael? Which of them would have dared to travel constantly at the risk of his life and to endure betrayals and bondage in order to bring the Gospel "*usque ad extremas partes*" of the fabulous world to a set of poor fishermen and herdsmen living in the sea-shaken islands of the West?

He had spent half the time of his missionary journey going thus far. He had about eleven years of travel still to do before the Church was established and put on an organised basis throughout the land. It was doubtless some time on his return from Murrisk that he visited that dark lake in Donegal whose island of penance bears his name.

Next to the Peak of the Eagle in Mayo, Lough Derg in Donegal is closely associated with the Saint's austerities.

It would be futile to discuss St. Patrick's Purgatory without a study of that most erudite book which Shane Leslie, the landlord of the territory wherein the lake lies, has compiled. This volume represents years of the most painstaking and scholarly research through the libraries of Europe, from Trinity College to the Vatican Library, from Dublin, Edinburgh, London, France, Italy, Spain to Rome. Its erudition is astonishing. It is the canon of St. Patrick's Purgatory.

If we follow Tirechan, from whom we may infer that the Saint was in the habit of spending Lent in retirement, we may put the date of the Saint's visit to the cave on Saints' Island to a Lent. This would be after the year 442, for we must allow him at least a year to visit and to return from Rome before the outset of his journey through the North-West.

From Templecarne the road passes the south-western shore of Lough Derg, and was known afterwards as the Pilgrims' Tochar, or road to the Holy Island.

What attracted the Saint so far out of his way? Long before he came to our country there was a cave in one of the islands of Lough Derg. Like Glendalough in Wicklow, the lake is dark and bright, and, what is more strange still, there flows from it no peculiar emanation or sense of subterranean influences such as one feels at Glendalough. It can be as lovely a lake as any of the ever-changing mirrors of heaven in Ireland when the sun sets in a golden tower behind Croagh Breac. An ancient poem bears out its association with Fenian heroes: "Fionn loch Deirg was the name of the lake at the beginning, O Patrick!" To this St. Patrick came, for he could not well leave behind his lines a citadel of Druidism unreduced. The ancient Lives do not mention his visit, but local folk-lore, whether *post hoc* or not, is strong and circumstantial. We cannot speak with certainty about anything save the history of St. Patrick's Purgatory, the part it played in European literature—a part excelled by nothing that came out of Ireland before or since—if we except the momentous foray of the Irish sea-kings that brought Patrick in, and the missions of the religious men who kept the light of Christianity alive in Europe during its collapse and relapse into darkness.

What is St. Patrick's Purgatory? Next to the Reek, it is the site most closely associated in Ireland with the Saint, but in the romantic literature of Europe it is the best known of any Irish place or story.   For, like to the way Odysseus went and Æneas after him, it gave entry to the underworld, where an intrepid man, while still in the flesh, could meet the dead and experience, in response to the urge of curiosity which has beset mankind since the world began, the plight of those in the world below.

At Lough Derg St. Patrick becomes subordinated to his Purgatory.   His visit to the island in the lake is of less importance than the observances and the results of the spiritual exercises which are carried out in his name.   Be that as it may, what is of European importance is the history and inspiration of St. Patrick's Purgatory.   From immemorial times down to the days of Homer, Virgil and Gregory the Great, man has sought to penetrate behind the Veil and to still the obstinate questionings of Fate.

The Descent of the Knight Owen was one of the famous romances of Europe.   The Knight Owen has been identified with Evain, one of the knights of King Arthur's Round Table.   He slew the husband of the lady he loved and then he left her.   Like Tannhauser, he found that absolution was hard to obtain.   He undertook at St. Patrick's Purgatory to endure the direst penance in the world, which was nothing less than to pass across the bridge of terror and to seek the bourne from which few return.   He entered the Cave and underwent experiences and beheld in vision things not to be recounted.

A certain Knight, Hœnus by name, who served many years under King Stephen, obtained the King's leave to set out to his native land in Ireland to visit his parents. When he had tarried some time in that land he began to think over his disgraceful life: how from his cradle he had wasted his time in arsons and rapine, and, what he grieved over the more, how he had been a violator of churches and invader of ecclesiastical property, besides many sinful enormities lying in his breast. The Knight was accordingly led by penitence to approach the Bishop of that place. When he had duly recited his sins in order, the Bishop scolded him seriously, asserting that he had over offended the divine clemency. The Knight was much grieved and planned to perform worthy penance. When the Bishop wished to enjoin him the penance that seemed just to him, the Knight answered: Since you assert I have so seriously offended my Creator, I will undertake the penance which is heaviest of all penances, and that I may deserve the remission of my sins, I wish to enter St. Patrick's Purgatory.

Thus Shane Leslie translates from the Latin of Matthew Paris's History.

And with a courage almost inestimable to us now, the Knight entered the Cave and visited the under-world, and, sustained by his own stout heart, undertook that penance which is heaviest of all.

Scholars of mediæval literature may interest them-selves in research and in computing how the Visions of Tundal (1149) and of Turkill (1206) contributed to the grandest Vision ever beheld by the inner eye of man, that Vision which is the *Divina Commedia*; but what fills one with romance is the fact that it interested Marie de France, who was the inspiration and the Queen of Troubadours, so that she translated the Latin version of St. Patrick's *Purgatory* into a French lay. Here are six lines of Marie de France's long rhyme of 2302 verses. It is her signature and her colophon.

Jo, Marie, ai mis en memoire
Le livre de l'Espurgatoire :
En Romanz qu'il seit entendables
A laie genz e convenables.
Or preiom Deu que pur sa Grace
De nos pechiez mundes nus face.

This is how she sings of the foundation of the *Purgatory* of St. Patrick. There is something strangely satisfying to see his name in the old French Rhime.

El tens Saint Patriz par licence
Pristrent li plusur penitence :
Quant il esteient absolu
Si vindrent la u li us fu ;
Enz entrerent seurement
Mult sufrirent peine e turment,
E mult virent horrible mal
De la dure peine infernal.
Apres icele grant tristesce
Virent grant joie e grant leesce.
Co qu'il volstrent cunter e dire
Fist Seinte Patriz iluec escrire.

Thus the Purgatory came to Provence !

It would be fashionable at this point to pause so as to wonder what ennui, what world-weariness possessed a Queen of the Court of Love so that she was attracted by the thought of dire penitential pains. It might be good literary dilettanteism, but it would be sheer affectation and poor historical psychology. Marie of France translated the long account of the adventures of the Knight Owen because he was a stout fellow, and his exploits, and possibly his record and the reasons for his penance, appealed to her. Or, as Dunsany would phrase it, " Because she would." Let us leave it at that ! She dedicated her poem to Richard Cœur de Lion.

A barge that holds at least one hundred and fifty pilgrims at a time puts out from shelter-houses beside a wooden jetty to Station Island. On this island there is a fine basilica designed by the late architect, who, like so many great architects before him, bore the name of Scott. Before his death he lamented to me that his idea of setting thousands of circular pieces of glass in the roof of the cupola had been rejected by the authorities. It would have made a glistening dome that would have sent its rays scintillating far over the shining Lough. Even without this unusual embellishment the design is worthy of the master who built the lovely little Celtic church at Spiddal.

There is no need for me to describe a pilgrimage to Station Island. The Franciscan Fathers conduct one annually from Merchants' Quay, Dublin.

It was on Station Island that I first heard the Lorica or Corslet, or, as it is more commonly called, The Breastplate of St. Patrick, recited in modern Irish. It was recited by a pilgrim who was visiting on his knees the circular stations. As it is an authentic composition of the Saint and a powerful prayer, it may be of interest to reprint a translation derived from the translations of three scholars. It reveals his spiritual personality and recalls his address at Clebach's Well to the two princely daughters of King Laoghaire, Eithne and Fedelm. Its intense devotion would be sufficient to mark it as St. Patrick's even if it lacked the internal evidences which are his signature.

It is a pity that some of our poets do not put rhythm and rhyme on it, for, as they stand, the translations

I have seen not only limp on heavy feet, but hobble like a man shuffling on his knees. It is one of the strongest prayers in the world. Me it attracts mightily, for I heard it in my childhood, and it brings the awe and wonder of the ancient world about me still.

ST. PATRICK'S LORICA

I

I arise to-day :
> in vast might, invocation of the Trinity ;
> belief in a Threeness ;
> confession of Oneness ;
> meeting in the Creator.

II

I arise to-day :
> in the might of Christ's Birth and His Baptism ;
> in the might of His Crucifixion and Burial ;
> in the might of His Resurrection and Ascension ;
> in the might of His Descent to the Judgment of Doom.

III

I arise to-day :
> in the might of the Cherubim ;
> in obedience of Angels ;
> in ministration of Archangels ;
> in hope of resurrection through merit ;
> in prayers of Patriarchs ;
> in predictions of Prophets ;
> in preachings of Apostles ;
> in faiths of Confessors ;
> in innocence of holy Virgins ;
> in deeds of good men.

IV

I arise to-day :
> in the might of Heaven ;
> Splendour of the Sun ;
> whiteness of Snow ;

S

  irresistibleness of Fire ;
  the swiftness of Lightning ;
  the speed of Wind ;
  Absoluteness of the Deep ;
  Earth's stability ;
  Rocks' durability.

V

I arise to-day :
  in the might of God for my piloting ;
   Power of God   for my stability ;
   Wisdom of God for my guidance ;
   Eye of God   for my foresight ;
   Ear of God   for my hearing ;
   Word of God   for my word ;
   Hand of God   for my guard.
   Path of God   for my prevention ;
   Shield of God for my protection ;
   Host of God   for my salvation ;
    against every demon's snare ;
    against all vices' lure ;
    against concupiscence ;
    against ill-wishes far and near ;

VI

I invoke all these forces :
  between me and every savage force that may come upon me,
   body and my soul ;
  against incantations of false prophets ;
  against black laws of paganism ;
  against false laws of heresy ;
  against idolatry ;
  against spells of women and smiths and druids ;
  against all knowledge that should not be known.

VII

Christ for my guard to-day :
  against poison, against burning,
  against drowning, against wounding,
 that there may come to me merit ;
Christ with me, Christ before me,
Christ behind me, Christ in me,
Christ under me, Christ over me,

Christ to right of me, Christ to left of me,
Christ in lying down, Christ in sitting, Christ in rising up,
Christ in all, who may think of me !
Christ in the mouth of all who may speak to me !
Christ in the eye, that may look on me !
Christ in the ear, that may hear me !

I arise to-day :
    in vast might, of the Trinity prayed to :
    believing on a Threeness ;
    confessing a Oneness ;
    meeting in the Creator ;
Domini est salus, Domini est salus, Christi est salus ;
Salus tua, Domine, sit semper nobiscum.

That is the famous Lorica or Corslet of St. Patrick.
It is the canticum Scotticum which was attributed to
St. Patrick before the ninth century.

Is St. Patrick the author ? This is Professor
Atkinson's report :

> It is probably a genuine relic of St. Patrick. Its uncouth-
> ness of grammatical form is in favour of its antiquity. We
> know that St. Patrick used very strange Irish, some of which
> has been preserved; and the historians who handed down
> *mudebroth* as an ejaculation of his would probably take care to
> copy as faithfully as they could the other curious Irish forms
> which the Saint had consecrated by his use.

> If it can be proved that some of the forms in the *Lorica* could
> not have been used by a native Irish writer this would be a
> very strong argument for its composition by St. Patrick. It
> seems possible that St. Patrick's expression *Mudebroth* was
> remembered as the solecism of a foreigner.

When one examines the text in Old Irish of the
Lorica one notices a change in the verse-length and
arrangement of assonance. There may be Celtic charm-
forms older still out of which the *Lorica* grew. And

these spells have been interpolated. The forces of
Nature appear.

Nuirt nime,	Might of Heaven,
Soilse grene,	Splendour of the sun,
Etrochta snechtai,	Whiteness of snow,
Ane thened,	Irresistibleness of fire,
Dene lochet,	The swiftness of lightning,
Luathe gaethe,	The speed of wind,
Fudomna mara,	Absoluteness of the deep,
Tairisem talmain,	Earth's stability,
Cobsaidecht ailech.	Rocks' durability.

When we remember that King Loiguire swore by the
Sun and Wind and what happened to him for becoming
foresworn, the significance of the list of the elements
will be apparent. And then when we come upon a
prayer against the spells of Druids, women and smiths,
what are we to think? Can the Saint have believed
in such things and composed a prayer against their
influence? Or is it not more likely that these were
added by someone who, unconscious of what they would
betray to generations yet to be born, regarded the
machinations of the three estates, Druids, women and
smiths, as real and living dangers, and provided against
them by allying his prayer to the powerful *Lorica* of the
Saint?

" *Fri brichta ban ocus goband ocus druad.* From the
spells of women, smiths and Druids." I for one believe
in them. Think what you like, but can any man
regard himself as totally beyond the reach of woman's
white magic? And would it not be a sorry day for
Ireland if they could no longer weave a spell? And
as for smiths, they controlled fire and bent the stubborn

metal to their will. It was miracle enough in those days : to me it is a miracle still when the engine devours distance or scales the blue sky. And as for Druids' spells, their "*feth fiada*" to which reference has been made already, was a spell which could hide things in an envelope of vapour. In this too I am a believer : I have *heard* the vapourings of our modern Druids when they were spell-binding at the hustings and elsewhere.

But the *Lorica* ? It was also called the *Feth Fiada*, or *Deers' Cry*. This refers to a miracle recorded by Muirchu in his Life of St. Patrick when the Saint transmuted himself and his companions into eight deer and a fawn. This was done in order to escape an ambush of the treacherous High King.

> And when they had parted the king went a little way and called St. Patrick with deceptive words intending to slay him. But Patrick knowing the intentions of the villainous king blessed his companions eight men and a boy and advanced towards the king. The king counted them and as they came and, suddenly, they were no where to be seen: gone from the king's sight. And the heathens saw nothing but eight stags and a fawn going towards the forest.

Now, this, told by Muirchu, is not alone incredible but, as Macalister points out, absurd. The absurdity arises from the ignorance of the biographer who wrote as far away from the days of St. Patrick as we are from the days of Queen Anne. There were, it appears, in the state of primitive civilisation in our country secret societies which can only be compared for barbarism with the modern Ku Klux Klan, who childishly spell it with a K instead of a C: Kondor, Klux, Klansmen and all the rest of it. The Irish Klansmen were known as The Stags; but being almost illiterate they too probably thought of adding to their mysteriousness by a play on sounds. Be that as it may, the *Faeth Fiada* or *Deers' Cry* has been identified with the *feth fiadha* or spell by pronouncing which Druids and poets rendered themselves invisible: so these "Stags".

They were in the direct line of descent from the sorcerer whose painted effigy, tricked out with stag's horns attached to his head, has been posturing for ages and ages on the wall of the wonderful prehistoric picture-gallery called *Caverne des Trois Frères* in Ariège. In their deer-disguise these mysterious personages might be expected to come to sing spells for the victory of a host to whose interests they were favourable. . . .

No one would with full knowledge dream of accusing St. Patrick and his companions of evading their enemies in a disguise so cowardly, ridiculous and heathenish. This must be said as clearly and emphatically as possible, to avoid the least chance of misunderstanding. His ancient biographers have told us, almost in so many words, that they did so; but that is a very different matter. These people (the biographers) knew not what they said: that must be their condonation. When they wrote, the college of deer-dancers, its members and their antics belonged to the dead and forgotten past. But here and there, in a literature now lost to us, they found how this one or that escaped from a tight corner in a "cloak of concealment" and in the form of a deer. The original writers knew what this meant: their later readers did not; and, not realising its implications, they thought that it would be a picturesque incident to adapt to their own purpose. It would have been especially appropriate to the St. Patrick story, for the song said to have been chanted by the Saint bears the name *Faed Fiada*; and whatever the real meaning of these mysterious words may be, they can be understood as signifying "The Cry of the Deer."

Thus does a great scholar rationally exonerate the Saint from the miracles of his biographers: which goes to prove, as in the case of the Saint's " lep " recorded by the lad on Skerry Hill, that one should not scoff before he understands. Understanding leaves no excuse for treating the past with irreverence.

The pilgrim on Station Island stopped so soon in his recital that I guessed that he had gone over but a part of the prayer. Whether he had done so correctly or not, I was in no position to judge. Even if I were a scholar, I could not be sure. Few scholars are agreed as to the translation of the *Lorica*. One glance at the opening line is enough. " Atomriug indiu." O'Donovan began with " At Tara to-day "; Stokes went one better with " I bind to myself to-day," which sounds magnificently appropriate to one doing on a corslet. Archbishop Healy follows with " I bind to myself to-day," which is the same as Stokes. And the hymn-writers have adopted it. Since my visit to Lough Derg I wrote on the subject of the *Lorica* to my friend the great Gaelic scholar Dr. Best, who is Director of the National Library. He writes : —

Ascoli discovered the real meaning as " I rise." *Je me lève*, a reflexive verb: *atomriug*. I think you can follow White. Miss Eleanor Knott made a very acute emendation in the last line of the first stanza which has been variously translated. According to her brilliant suggestion it should read *i ridulemen dail* = '*i ndail duleman*, " with or towards the Creator . . . ." Again, Thurneysen has corrected in the penultimate stanza for " Christ in breadth, Christ in height, Christ when I lie down, Christ when I rise up."

So the translation here given is a blend from many scholars.

Thus I leave St. Patrick's Purgatory.

But while the thought of translations from the Irish is in my mind, I may remark that no language is in greater need of scholarly and sympathetic interpretation.   The very genius of the language gives it no chance with the formulæ of the tongues of the present day.   How can a language abounding in imagination, poetic licence, adjectives and appositions be done into any of the prosaic current tongues ? Their very construction is antithetical, contradictory. Before this immense thesaurus of poetry, proverbs, history and immemorial wisdom has its golden dust buried under the slag of modern languages which are translating themselves into Irish words, a halt should be called and scholars be endowed—or if unendowed, then honoured for their patriotism—so that the living heritage of our country be saved before it is disguised and dissipated for ever in heaps of opprobrious slang.   As a century hence it will be impossible to realise either truth or history behind the distortions and caricatures of the cinema, so far sooner will it be impossible to get a Gobhán Saor to draw down the living stream of procreant water in his hand, or a poet to reinvigorate and re-inspire the race from its ancestral voices.

CHAPTER XXIII

ST. PATRICK AND USHEEN

You who are bent and bald and blind
With a heavy heart and a wandering mind,
Have known three centuries, poets sing,
Of dalliance with a demon thing.

" St. Patrick to Usheen." Yeats.

SOON THE RUDE ASCESIS OF THE PILGRIMS CEASED TO
interest me, and mindful of the way the legends of Finn
merged with those of the Saint, I found myself thinking
more of poetry than of purgatory, and of that great son
of Finn, the warrior bard Usheen, who dwelt for three
hundred years in the Land of the Ever Young. The
legend that associates the pagan with the Saint and
makes Patrick for his love of Song take pity on the old
poet, broken with the weight of all his years which
falls suddenly upon him because he touched earth again,
is one of the most dramatic and romantic feats of the
Gaelic imagination. It is comparable to the legend
that made Plato journey to Sicily to experiment with his
Republic under the tyrant Dionysius. Whoever
thought of it must have felt some restlessness with the
new regime and a longing for the old. The contrast of
the holy with the heroic life embodied in the legendary
conversations of saint and pagan has been eagerly
treated by our poets Yeats and Stephen Gwynn. The
first composer of the legend got over the difficulty of
Usheen having lived three hundred years before the
Saint by using what was ready to hand, the wonderland
off our western coast. He puts Usheen safely into
what can by no means be called the cold storage of Tir

nan Oge. It was far from being cold. A faery bride brought him there, having sought the poet at his father's house. Finn asks !

> Was there no better than my son
> That you through all that foam should run ?

And Niam answers :—

> I loved no man though kings besought,
> Until the Danaan poets brought
> Rhyme that rhymed to Usheen's name,
> And now I am dizzy with the thought
> Of all that wisdom and the fame
> Of battles broken by his hands
> Of stories builded by his words.

And so with the white lady Usheen rides

> To shores by the wash of the tremulous tide,
> Where men have heaped no burial mounds.

But at last a longing for the Fianna, his old companions, overpowered him even in that happy place. He cried :—

> O Niam ! O white one ! if only a twelve-houred day
> I must gaze on the beard of Finn, and move where the old men and
>   young
> In the Fenians' dwellings of wattle lean on the chess-boards and play.
> Ah, sweet to me now were even bald Conan's slanderous tongue.

Reluctantly he is permitted to depart, but he is warned that if he dismounts from his faery steed and but touches earth ever so lightly, he will never return :—

> But weep for your Niam, O Usheen, weep ; for if only your shoe
> Brush lightly as hay-mouse earth's pebbles, you will come no more to
>   my side.

He returns to Ireland only to find the Fenians gone and

a weak race in the heroic fields.   He sees two men struggling with a sand-bag, and he leans from the gem-studded saddle of his faery steed and flings it five yards with his hand ; but the girthings break and he touches earth.   His horse flies off and the weight of three hundred years suddenly descends.   It is at this stage that the Saint takes pity on the obdurate old man.

Since the Poems and Ballads appeared and caused all that ado in Victoria's day, no poetry came with such freshness and beauty as the poem from which the extracts have been made.   Yeats' " Wanderings of Usheen " was published in 1889, and in his poet the older bard finds a fitting successor.

It was hard.   It must have been difficult to prevent the imagination of poets from making Patrick meet Usheen just as Greek imagination made Plato meet Dionysius.   In an old drawing woodcut in Peter de Navalibus's " Catalogue of Saints " the Saint is represented as demonstrating Purgatory.   By a pass of his crozier he describes a circle, and as through a glass, purgatory or the infernal regions are seen.   It must have been Hell that was shown to Usheen when he refused to desist from enquiries about the Fenians' fate and the fate of Bran the Hound of Finn and the great war-dogs Sgeolan and Lomair.

On the flaming stones without refuge the limbs of the Fenians are tost ;
None war with the masters of Hell, who could break up the world in
    their rage ;
But kneel and wear out the flags and pray for your soul that is lost
Through the demon of Love in its youth and its godless and passionate
    age.

Stephen Gwynn, in a ballad which appears to me to be the best ballad on the subject ever written, and one of the best ballads ever written on any subject, treats the old man differently. He proves how the lesson is lost which the Saint gave him when he showed him the Fenians condemed to endless and fruitless warfare against the demons in Hell. The poet has graciously given me permission to reprint it, and this is done at length, for no one could follow St. Patrick were he to omit this legend of the Saint.

I make no excuses for the amount of poetry that I have included in this volume. After all, our land, if it be anything, is a Land of Song, and its imagination insists that the Saint was himself a lover of song, and that this brought about his meeting with Usheen. And who am I to curtail poetry and parch the meadows ? Ireland is either a Land of Song or a Land of Slugs with a trend to become a Land of Shylocks. Let Song save it ; and let the Warrior Bard, Stephen Gwynn, twang now for the company. He did not refuse a world fight even when a Nestor. I tried hard to shorten this magnificent War Song, but I could not remove a line without loss of power. And what a powerful song it is ! Why cannot we appreciate what we have before searching for what shall never be sib to us ?

A LAY OF OSSIAN AND PATRICK

> I tell you an ancient story
>   Learnt on an Irish strand,
> Of lonely Ossian returning
>   Belated from fairyland

To a land grown meek and holy,
  To a land of mass and bell,
Under the hope of heaven,
  Under the dread of hell.

It tells how the bard and warrior,
  Last of a giant race,
Wrestled a year with Patrick,
  Answering face to face,

Mating the praise of meekness
  With vaunt of the warrior school,
And the glory of God the Father
  With the glory of Finn Mac Cool.

Until at last the hero,
  Through fasting and through prayer,
Came to the faith of the Christians
  And turned from things that were.

When the holy bread was broken,
  And the water wet on his brow,
And the last of the fierce Fianna
  Had spoken the Christian vow,

In a sudden glory Patrick,
  Seeing the fierce grown mild,
Laughed with joy on his convert,
  Like father on first-born child.

" Well was for you, O Ossian,
  You came to the light," he said ;
" And now I will show you the torment
  From which to our God you fled."

Then with a pass of his crozier
  He put a spell on the air,
And there fell a mist on the eyeballs
  Of Ossian standing there.

Shapes loomed up through the darkness,
  " And now," said the saint, " look well :
See your friends the Fianna
  And all their trouble in hell."

Ossian stared through the darkness,—
  Saw, as the mist grew clear,
Legions of swarth-hued warriors
  Raging with sword and spear,

Footmen huge and misshapen,
  Stiffened with snarling ire;
Chariots with hell-black stallions
  Champing a spume of fire;

And all of the grim-faced battle,
  With clash and yell and neigh,
Dashed on a knot of warriors
  Set in a rank at bay.

Ossian looked, and he knew them,
  Knew each man of them well,
Knew his friends, the Fianna,
  There in the pit of hell.

There was his very father,
  Leader of all their bands;
Finn the terrible wrestler,
  Gripping with giant hands;

Oscar with edged blade smiting,
  Caoilte with charging lance,
And Diarmuid poising his javelin,
  Nimble as in the dance;

Conan, the crop-eared stabber,
  Aiming a slant-way stroke,
And fiery Lugach leaping
  Where the brunt of battle broke.

But in front of all by a furlong,
  There in the hell-light pale,
Was the champion, Gull MacMorna,
  Winding a monstrous flail.

And still the flail as he flung it
  Sang through the maddened air,
Singing the deeds of heroes,
  A song of the days that were.

It swung with the shrilling of pipers,
    It smote with the thud of drums,
It leapt and it whirled in battle,
    Crying, " Gull Mac Morna comes."

It leapt and its smote, and the devils
    Shrieked under very blow;
With the very wind of its whistling
    Warriors were stricken low.

It swept a path through the army
    Wide as a winter flood,
And down that lane the Fianna
    Charged in a wash of blood.

Patrick gazed upon Ossian;
    But Ossian watched to descry
The surf and the tide of the battle
    Turn, as in days gone by.

And lo ! at the sudden onslaught,
    The fighters of Eire made,
And under the flail of Mac Morna
    The host of the foemen swayed,

Broke, and Ossian, breathless,
    Heard the exultant yell
Of his comrades hurling the devils
    Back to the walls of hell.

And the sword-blades reaped like sickles,
    And the javelins hissed like hail,
And louder and ever louder
    Rose the song of the flail,

As whirling in air the striker
    Sang clear or thudded dull,—
When, woe ! the tug on a sudden
    Snapped in the grasp of Gull.

Hand-staff and striker parted;
    The song of the flail was dumb—
On the heart of Ossian, listening,
    Fell that silence numb.

And oh ! for a time uncounted
   He watched with straining eyes
The tide of the devils' battle
   Quicken and turn and rise.

He watched the Fianna's onset
   Waver and hang in doubt,
He watched his leaderless comrades
   Swept in a struggling rout.

But Gull, with a shield before him,
   Crouched on the battle-ground,
And there in the track of the slaughter
   Tore at what he found,

Until in the crash and tumult,
   And dashed with a bloody rain,
He had knotted his flail together
   With sinews torn from the slain.

Then as the grasping Fianna
   Felt their endeavour fail,
Chanting their ancient valour
   Rose the song of the flail.

And again in the stagnant ebbing
   Of their blood began to flow
The flood of a surging courage,
   The hope of a crowning blow.

And the heart of their comrade watching
   Stirred with joy to behold
Feats of his bygone manhood,
   Strokes that he knew of old.

Again he beheld the stubborn
   Setting of targe to targe,
Again he beheld the rally
   Swell to a shattering charge :

And surely now the Fianna
   Must slaughter and whelm the foe
In a fierce and final triumph,
   Lords of the realms below,

As they leapt in a loosened phalanx,
    Climbing on heaps of slain :
And again Gull's wizard weapon
    Flew on a stroke in twain.

For a time and times uncounted
    Ossian endured the sight
Of the endless swaying battle,
    The ebb and flow of the fight.

His face grew lean with sorrow,
    And hunger stared from his eyes,
And the labouring breath from his bosom
    Broke in heavy sighs.

Patrick watched, and he wondered,
    And at last in pity spoke :
" Vexed is your look, O Ossian,
    As your very heart were broke.

" Courage, O new-made Christian :
    Great is my joy in you :
I would like it ill on a day of grace
    My son should have aught to rue.

" Therefore for these your comrades
    I give you a wish to-day
That shall lift them out of their torment
    Into some better way.

" Speak, be bold in your asking,
    Christ is strong to redeem."
—Ossian turned to him sudden
    Like one awaked from dream.

His eye was fierce as an eagle's,
    And his voice had a trumpet's ring,
As when at the Fenian banquets
    He lifted his harp to sing.

" I ask no help of the Father,
    I ask no help of the Son,
Nor of the Holy Spirit,
    Ever Three in One.

T

" This for my only asking,
    And then let might prevail,—
Patrick, give Gull Mac Morna
    An iron tug to his flail."

*   *   *   *   *

Patrick is dead, and Ossian
    Long to his rest is gone;
But the words and the deeds of heroes
    Linger in twilight on,

In a twilight of fireside tellings
    Lit by the poet's lay,
Lighting the gloom of hardship,
    The night of a needy day.

And still the Gael as he listens
    In a land of mass and bell
Under the hope of heaven,
    Under the dread of hell,

Thinks long, like age-spent Ossian,
    For the things that are no more
The clash of meeting weapons,
    And the mad delight of war.

Yes; war must have been a form of sport in ancient Ireland. One has only to look at the richest of all the collections in the National Museum to realise that our chief industry was spear-making.

The tradition of that Long Ago lingers on, and there may be a trace of it in the resentment with which we meet any reflection on our physical courage and the pains we take to suggest its existence unimpaired and to flatter by implying it to a friend.

" Courageous energy is always valued and remembered, and though the highwayman and others often used their energy wickedly, they still used it and risked their lives to use it," as my friend the great Poet Laureate remarks. We catch one or two glimpses in the

Confession as to what the times were like when they were only two classes in a country, where manslaughter took so long to decrease. It may have accounted for the delay in missionary work from Britain for nearly two hundred years before the advent of the Saint. It is echoed in the complaints of the jealous rhetoricians there who murmured against him. But all this is irrefutable evidence of the courage of the man who, as poets hold, converted Ossian " After his long dalliance with a demon thing."

CHAPTER XXIV

THE SAINT'S VISIT TO DUBLIN

IN ST. PATRICK'S TIME THE SITE OF WHAT IS NOW THE city of Dublin, the Seventh City of Christendom, was called the Ridge of the Hazels. Hazels, as we have seen, were largely distributed over the land, and they formed the principal woods : thus, *Silva virgulti* on the shore of Strangford Lough, the Wood of the Wattles, which were so useful for house-building as it was practised in the Ireland of old. The wattles or laths were woven between upright poles and plastered with clay. This made the " lime-white mansions," and the roofs were thatched. *Silva Virgulti* is one of the alternate readings to the much-discussed *Silva Focluti*, which has driven so many biographers off the Apostle's track. And do not let us forget that this *virgulti* is of the same root as the name of the :

> " Wielder of the lordliest measure
> Ever moulded by the lips of man "

the poet Virgil. Later maybe, perhaps contemporaneously, what is now Dublin was called Ath Cliath, Hurdle Ford. Archbishop Healy writes :

> The Ford of the Hurdles, which gave its Irish name to Dublin, was a rude bridge over the Liffey, somewhere near the head of the tide near Kingsbridge.

This, as I have reason to know, is somewhat inaccurate. The Liffey is tidal right up to Island Bridge, where the weir at the boat-house of the Dublin University Rowing Club holds back and deepens its stream.

The Ford of the Hurdles was at the end of the great
road which ran south from Tara through Batterstown
(a corruption of Boher, the road) and crossed the Liffey
where the Ridge of the Hazels was highest, and where
afterwards the ships could find fair harbourage on the
north side of the river at the Dark Linn. This Black
Pool or Dark Linn was at the junction of the little
river Poddle with the Liffey, and from it Dublin derives
its name. The road from Tara crossed the river there,
and as anyone who lives in Dublin can see, the river
must have been fordable at low tide through any point
of its course through the city. This is so even now,
when its current is gathered so well by the great granite
walls built by Grattan's Parliament.

The road from Tara crossed the Liffey at the Hurdle
Ford, and the road from Tara, passing through
Batterstown, reached Stonybatter (again the Irish for
road is seen in " batter ", *i.e.* " boher "), and crossed
the water at the Hurdle Ford to go on to Bohernabreena, where the public hostel or caravanserai of the
Derga was at Bohernabreena, the " Road-House " or
hostel of Da Derga on the river Dodder. This is the
Archbishop's account of St. Patrick's visit to our city.

Here we must pause to consider the question whether or
not Patrick really visited the place called in his time Ath
Cliath, but known as Dublin to the Danes or Ostmen. We
have already referred to the brief and suspicious reference in
the Homily on St. Patrick in the Lebar Brecc to this alleged
visit of the Saint to Ath Cliath. But Jocelyn gives a much
fuller account of this visit, which, in substance, is as follows :—
Patrick in his journey from Meath to Leinster, having
passed a certain stream called Finglas, came to a hill about

one mile distant from Ath Cliath, which is now called Dublin
(Dublinia).   Looking towards it, he blessed the place, and
foretold that though now a small village, it would one day
become the capital city of the kingdom, a prophecy which has
been manifestly fulfilled.   He then came to the Ford of
Hurdles.   On his entry into the town (villa), the people, who
had heard of his wondrous miracles, received him with great
joy.   The Saint then healed the only son of the ruler of the
place, who was on the point of death, and restored him to his
father; whereupon all the people believed and were baptised
by Patrick.   Moreover, as the tide made the river water
brackish, the matron in whose house the Saint lodged complained of the want of sweet water; upon which Patrick,
striking the earth twice with the Staff of Jesus, caused a most
abundant spring to gush forth from the earth, whose waters
are not only sweet, but powerful to heal diseases.   Seeing this,
all the people greatly rejoiced; and the fountain has ever since
been fitly called St. Patrick's Well.

Here we have at least a simple narrative; but immediately
follows another chapter which gives an entirely different and
wholly inconsistent account of Patrick's reception in Dublin.
We are told in chapter seventy-one that Patrick came on his
missionary journey to a famous city called Dublin, inhabited
by Norwegians and natives of the Isles, who, however,
recognised the King of Ireland, in an uncertain fashion, as
their Suzerain.   It was a city steeped in the filth of idolatry
and wholly ignorant of the true God.   Just then, however,
it came to pass that the son of the King died suddenly in his
marriage bed, and his sister was drowned in the river Liffey;
but Patrick, the miracle-working prelate of Armagh, restored
both to life, to the great joy of King Alphinus and all his
people.   The maiden, who was brought to life by Patrick,
was called Dublinia, and gave her own name to the city.
Both King and people, too, were baptised by Patrick in a well
on the south of the city, which issued from the soil where
Patrick struck the earth with his crozier.   Moreover, the
whole city agreed to pay large offerings to Patrick's church of
Armagh for ever, and built a church in his honour near the
well, which was outside the city, and another within the walls
in honour of the Holy Trinity, close to which they also assigned

a mansion, or residence, to Patrick and his successors for all
time."

This ridiculous story seems to be an interpolation in the
original text of Jocelyn, and is, of course, utterly worth-
less.

But the first account seems to have been really written by
Jocelyn, and must be taken as his version of a living tradition
in the time of the writer.   Yet we cannot attach much
historical importance to the narrative.   It is not corroborated
by any of our annalists, nor is anything like it found in any of
the ancient Lives of our Saints.   There is no reference to
Patrick's visit to Ath Cliath, or to Dubh-linn, in either the
Tripartite or the Book of Armagh, nor in any of the other
Lives published by Colgan.   We know, indeed, that at a
later period a monastery was founded by St. Mobhi on the
banks of the Tolka, near Glasnevin, which is not far from
Finglas.   Dubious references are also made at a much later
period to St. Livinus and St. Rumoldus as bishops of Dublin;
but these Lives were written on the Continent by scribes who
knew little or nothing of our domestic history, and it would
seem, after the Danish occupation of Dublin.

To protect their shipping they built a dun or castle
on the high ground just over the pool, and thenceforward
—that is from about the year 835, when the Danes made their
first permanent settlement there—the place came to be called
Dublin.

Yet the presence of St. Patrick's Well, and the dedication
even by John Comyn of his great church outside the walls in
honour of St. Patrick, as well as the narrative of Jocelyn in
chapter 69, go to show that Patrick did visit the place, coming
through Bregia to Finglas, and crossing the river at the Black
Pool.

Such a visit, though not explicitly referred to, either in the
Tripartite or the Book of Armagh, is not excluded, and is
expressly referred to in the Irish Homily from the Lebar
Brecc already quoted.   We know, too, that Patrick on his
journey southward passed, not through Meath (Midhe), but
through Bregia, which included north Dublin to the Liffey;
and if he were, suppose at Dunshaughlin, it would be very
easy for him to turn aside for a little, and visit Finglas on the

north, or even the pagus or village between the Poddle and the south bank of the river.

It is true we have no account of any royal dun near the Hurdle Ford; but still ancient authorities represent the place as one of considerable trade from the earliest times. Our annals tell us that the fact of the northern shore of the Liffey being more frequented by ships than the southern shore, was one of the causes that gave rise to the great strife between Conn the Hundred Fighter and Eoghan Mor. The ancient Life of St. Kevin of Glendaloch describes the place, which is called in Irish Dubh-linn, as a powerful and warlike city. We think, however, although Colgan seems to differ from us, that this description was written by one who knew it after Dublin was occupied by the Danes. St. Sedulius also is described as Abbot; but here, too, the writer uses a term that was not in use, so far as we can judge, in the time of St. Kevin, and being a foreign writer, he was probably unacquainted with the true history of the city. We can only say, therefore, that the story of St. Patrick's visit to the ancient Ath Cliath is very uncertain, although the presence of his well there, and the ancient church dedicated to him, go far to prove that Ath Cliath was visited by our apostle.

Having read this, I knew that the extraordinary allure water has for me would set me on a quest for St. Patrick's Well, that well " on the south side of the city " where its citizens were baptised. I had learned enough about wells to know that they need not necessarily have been caused to spring miraculously from out of an arid place by the Saint. It is not necessary to make him an imitator of Moses. At Elphin, where there is a great gush of water, three inches or more across, the well got its name from the fact that the Saint only rested by its side. And as he had to baptise the nation, and as wells were the only sources of water-supply except rivers, it came about that thousands of wells in Ireland are called

St. Patrick's wells.   There is even a village by that name in the County Limerick.   But it was a well in Dublin sacred to the Saint that held my interest. Where was it ?

The answer to that question may be summed by another question : Which way do you want it ?   That is, which way do you require that a well should be St. Patrick's Well ?

In the days when the only water-works a hamlet knew were wells, these were all-important.   They had an added importance for the Saint because they supplied the water for baptism.   But as we have seen that in Elphin the story goes that he merely rested by the Water of the White Stone to make it his well forever, almost without any exception whatever well he used in Ireland became his well.   Then there was the custom of changing the name of wells from their pagan association, just as we change the names of our streets to rid them of political memories, and calling them after St. Patrick.   But this was naturally after his return as a saintly bishop.   But could there not have been another reason why a well became his ?   Had he rested by one in the days of his escape and been refreshed by its water, or been directed on his way by some kind water-carrier, and recounted the incident long after to some friend, that would be sufficient. There were three wells in Dublin called after St. Patrick.   That by St. Patrick's Cathedral has disappeared since 1756.   The one in the Provost's garden cannot compare with the gusher in Nassau Place.   Whichever well it was, let us give the chief palm to the one with the

purest and most generous supply of water.   And it is
on the south side, and, what is more important, if it is
to be considered as a refreshing agent on his journey,
it is on the path of his escape to the port in Wicklow.
Even now the road to Booterstown and the coastwise
way passes its rich spring.

It is somewhat thoughtless to pronounce
authoritatively that St. Patrick never visited Dublin.
His visit is made hypothetical by the absurdity of the
historian, and it is uncertain only because of the absence
of local legend or tradition.   But what can you expect
of a city that has been subject to so many takings and
re-takings, rulers and vicissitudes ?   What can you
say of a city that was not there at the time—to put it
characteristically ?   It may have been only a hamlet.
But the wells were on the site and about it.   And there
is one going strong to the present day—a fact that
borders on the miraculous when one comes to think of
all the changes, both to the surface of the ground
through pavement and to the ground far down
through drainage.   Even if the whole city of Dublin
were to be roofed over, it would make no difference to
St. Patrick's Well in Nassau Place, a few yards from
the highway, for it owes its freshets to no surface water.
Its sources are fed by invisible rivers as far under-
ground as the hidden waters of Rome.   Lately another
source was tapped at a depth of five hundred feet,
which goes to show how independent of what may
happen to surface waters is the well owned by the
Mineral Water Distributors, the inventors of table
waters.

CHAPTER XXV

"HIS INDWELLING SPIRIT"

HERE AT LAST I CAN LEAVE THE FIELDS OF CONJECTURE and reconstruction and tread on the firmer ground of my own experience. At the outset it was stated that this book would be confined to an account of the places visited and of the legends listened to in following the Saint's journeys from the place of his capture in Wales to Slemish in Ulster and the route of his escape, sojourn abroad and return to our country and its ultimate islands in the Western Ocean, while it attempted to build up the historical background of his truly adventurous and hazardous life, a background which, if it could be reconstructed in detail, would prove to be the most significant and interesting in the history of the British nation.

I do not propose now to exceed that limitation ; but it was impossible to visit the many places which he had made famous and to talk to the many people who, after their different fashions, from intimacy to reverence, held him dear, without finding that a definite portrait of the Saint was beginning to form itself on the canvas of our country. I could not follow St. Patrick without knowing St. Patrick as he lives to-day in the general heart of his people.

I had begun by tracing a vague, historical figure through the dimmest century of European history ; I end by meeting a definite living force and a spiritual personality unique in the Calendar of the Saints.

His boyhood, spent in a time of unending terror for

those who dwelt by " our sea " on the outer edge of the Roman Empire, is lost to us.   His growth to maturity from the date of his escape at the age of twenty to the date of his return an eager volunteer to Ireland is almost as concealed.   And the certainty of his sojourn for twenty-three years in Gaul and Britain makes the lack of information tantalising in the extreme.   One word of his—a name, a city, a mountain or a stream—might have illuminated the century.   We know little, and that little is uncertain.   He breaks silence only when his religious life is concerned.   He ignores the mundane.   We do know that wherever he was he learnt the Scriptures so thoroughly that they became for him almost a medium of communication.   It was not until about the year 460 that the monasteries set themselves to become centres of scholarship.   Before that time whatever scholarship was brought into them came with the retired rhetoricians and men of consular rank who, like Honoratus, forsook the crumbling world.   But what he was taught, St. Patrick mastered.

When he comes to Ireland, though the scene changes totally, there is no change in his habit of reticence.   He will not voluntarily mention a name.   When he does—as, for instance, when he defends his flock against the apostate Picts who under Coroticus "forsook their baptism " —he leaves the identification of that petty tyrant to become a puzzle to scholars.   And when he tells of one of his most important converts, this is her only title to fame through the ages : " Once especial there was one blessed lady of Scottic parentage, noble, most lovely, nubile, whom I myself baptised."   But who was she ?

His model for this reticence was not the Gospels, for
they, though devoid of any record of the personal
characteristics of Our Lord, are full of names of people
and places. He followed no model, but he refrained
from details, either because he did not wish to give
particulars which might be seized upon and distorted
by his absentee detractors in Britain, or, as is more
probable, he wrote with complete self-effacement ; even
the twelve tribulations to which he was exposed and
the life-long dangers amid warrior kings are left
undescribed, as if these mattered nothing compared to
" the one thing necessary," the defence and furtherance
of his mission and the protection of his Irish sons and
daughters in God. We know that he experienced
betrayal on the part of the guides he had hired and the
chieftains to whom he had paid for safe-conduct " the
price of fifteen male slaves." He was reared and
lived in unremitting danger, and he can say even as
his mission was drawing to its close " For daily I
expect either slaughter, or to be defrauded or reduced
to slavery, or an unfair attack of some kind." This last
was his lot. But of God's grace he will not be silent :
" Let him who will laugh and mock, I will not be
silent nor conceal the signs and wonders which were
shewn to me by the Lord many years before they came
to pass since he knows all things even before time
began." But beyond this he makes the reason for
his silence abundantly clear. In an illiterate country
rumour and gossip are the only news. There is no way
of checking their accuracy or of limiting their mischief.
So, lest he raise a persecution against his converts, the

Saint kept his counsel to himself as if sealed with a seal of confession. And for another reason " that the heathen might receive me and my ministry on one ground or another; and that I should not in the smallest matter give occasion to the unbelievers to defame or to disparage."

That he was a man, first of all, of the highest courage is an outstanding fact, and this in an age when physical courage was a prerequisite of existence. Secondly, that he was a silent man who kept his own counsel and one in whom his converts could confide and on whom rely is beyond doubt. The first impression he must have made on the heathen chieftains was that of a man unintimidatable and devoid of fear. Had he been otherwise he would not have gone far with them nor would they have respected his teaching. They understood courage. Rome awed them, and he was the nearest emissary they ever chanced to meet. He gained men's respect however hostile they were and however humiliating were the conditions with which at times he was surrounded. Like Socrates pausing in his retreat from Delium, he impressed his victorious enemies by the majesty of his lofty manhood. He was in their power, but they hesitated to pursue. He was dignified, a man of worth. He must have had a strong spirit, for in all the twenty years or so that it took to found the Church we hear of no Irish apostates during his lifetime. And he had no locum tenens while absent in Rome. In Rome, where the tradition of our remoteness still lingers, he may have heard such words of appreciation of this island and such a tribute to his work as I heard from the present Pope, who granted us an audience 1500 years but three after the visit of the Saint :—

" Insula remotissima sed fidelissima et cordo meo carissima."

The most faithful island of all !

It was then as it is described to-day.   It is to-day as it was when Paulinus of Nola paid tribute to Our Apostle :—

> Per te
> Barbari discunt resonare Christum
> Corde Romano.

There is no Saint in any country who is so familiar to the inhabitants, and I may say, using it in a secondary sense, with whom the people are so familiar.   What does St. George mean to the Prime Minister of England?   An heraldic figure ; a design on an obsolete coin.   And St. David is not much of an inspiration or a comfort to the miners of Wales.   It is not about him they joke.   He is dated and dead.   But with St. Patrick it is different.   He is not dead.   He is everyone's " familiar."

As I went by Rocheford Bridge on the road to Tyrrell's Pass, I stopped to look at " the green smooth Hill of Croghan."   A countryman was walking his fields.   I asked him the name of the hill.   He told me that it was Croghan.

" Is it famous for anything ? " I asked.

" It's famous for a well on the other hill beside it."

" Whose well ? "

" St. Patrick's.   You can see the print of his knees

on the stone where he knelt down to drink.   And the print of his horse's hoof."

I was glad to have another witness to the tradition that the Saint travelled in a chariot.   But I kept on to the hill.

" Is there anything to be seen on the bigger hill ? "

" Not much."

I had flown over Croghan Hill twice at different altitudes without sighting anything that could be taken for the remains of earthworks or a tumulus.   Dr. Macalister too was disappointed, as far as I remember, with the results of excavations on this hill.   But the Saint had visited it when it must have been a centre of authority or influence after his long mission through the land.   From it he could see the watershed of the noble river at whose mouth he landed to have audience of the High King twenty-one years before.   Once the Saint was mentioned I was all alert.

" So the Saint was there ? "

" Indeed he was.   He preached from there.   He's hard put to it keeping them in order now, I'm thinking."

" He's hard put to it now ! "   A living presence !

After a short discussion about the present-day problems that confront the Saint, I found that I had made a friend.   I forgave him for attributing the fame of Croghan Hill to the one next to it.   After all, it was the proximity of the Saint that had made us friends— something beside ourselves !

This is where one can be on certain ground : the realisation of the omnipresence of the Saint in our

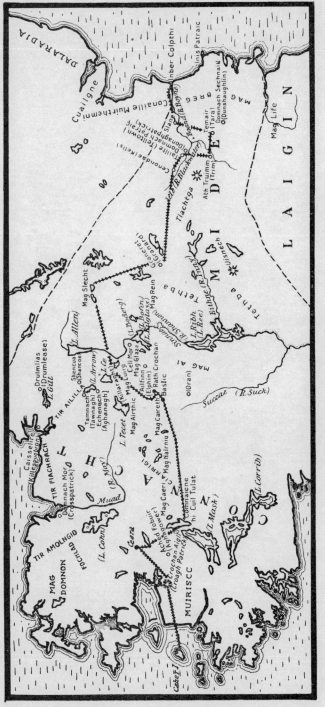

MAP OF THE CONJECTURAL JOURNEY THROUGH MEATH AND CONNAUGHT

country. His presence is a bond, a common heritage, an obligation of goodwill. So intimate with the country has its Patron become that the people in a mood of hypocoresis can patronise their Paudeen without loss of reverence. Be the history of the fifth century what it may, the immanence of St. Patrick to-day in Ireland is a fact beyond hypothesis or conjecture. He has become Ireland. He lives in the people that he made.

Therefore it is interesting to work back and to inquire how far the character of the Saint can be deduced from the character of his people. It is the same thing if we inquire how far the Irish people have taken after the Saint.

What are the characteristics of the Irishman? Primarily he is a sportsman and an agriculturist. He is quick to anger : " *celer iratus*," like another Roman who might be taken in some sort for his archetype. He is a lover of Song in the Land of Song. His physical energy is prodigious, and he is capable of asceticism, as the numbers of our monks witness. He is full of ardour and proud of nobility. Here it may be timely to turn aside to rebutt those who mock at St. Patrick's claims to nobility, and who take it for granted that he drew them from the station of his father and grandfather. These were *decurions*, and *decurions* were, it is argued, debased in the latter days of the Empire. But who ever drew patents of nobility from the profession of his parents ? Rather from their family and birth. In all likelihood both his mother and father were related to that Roman prefect of cavalry Q. Calpurnius

U

Concessinus who distinguished himself in a skirmish at Hexham when the Saint was a child. (St. Patrick's father was Calpurnius and his mother Concessa.) Furthermore, Irishmen were never treacherous : they forsook not their baptism while the Saint lived, while he " endured insults from unbelievers and heard the reproach of his going abroad." (*Confessio* 37.)

Now, these traits might be traits of the Saint himself. He was given to fishing and gardening—a Roman accomplishment. He was impatient in his zeal. But the identity of the Saint and his people needs no better proof than the many thousands who are called by that patrician name of his. The clear springs, the streamy hills, the mottled rocks themselves testify, as if animated, to his identity with this island which has become as sanctified as the islanders have been transmuted by his personality. This is as it should be, and in a way it is inevitable, for we grow like the ideal which we conceive.

But Patrick was more, apart from his religious genius, than we can be said to be as a race. He was " a steadfast and unchanging man." That is the verdict of a contemporary witness—and the same a king—on him. The story arises from the fact that the Saint had set his heart on founding what was to be the headquarters of all his church organisation on the Height of Macha, the present Armagh. Not far from his own dwelling at the eastern foot of the hill King Daire granted him a little holding, on which a circular space was marked out one hundred and forty feet in diameter, and ramparted round with an earthen wall.

Within were erected a Great House, a kitchen and a little oratory, according to what seems to have been the plan of the primitive establishments of the Saint and his company. But the Saint wanted the site of what was to be his chief ecclesiastical city on the heights. At first the King refused to grant a space on the summit. He fell ill, but was restored to health by holy water which the Saint had blessed. Then the King paid a visit to the lowly settlement and presented the Saint with a bronze cauldron brought from over the sea. "*Gratias agamus*," said the Bishop; but he said it rapidly (a man of his temperament must have spoken rapidly), in the Latin of the colonies, and it sounded in the way it has been preserved for us phonetically, "*gratzacham*." This was not enough for Daire. His three-gallon cauldron acknowledged by but one word, and that unintelligible! He sent his servants to bring back that which the Bishop apparently could not appreciate. And these reported that all the Saint said as it was being taken away was "*Gratzacham*."

"What?" said the King, "*Gratzacham*? He said that when it was being given and he says it when it is being taken. It is a strong spell that is used for getting and losing. I will give him back his cauldron." And the King came with it and presented it in person :

"Keep the cauldron, for you are a steadfast and unchanging man."

And he gave him the land which was his heart's desire.

This is as near as we can get to history, but it may cover the real facts of there being at first a small foundation at the foot of the hill which later was increased on

the larger space of the hill-top.   The older foundation
became in later days the Temple of the Graveyard.
Thus was Armagh elevated above the churches of
Ireland by him to whom a king witnessed as a " steadfast
and unchanging man," a man whose peace was in the will
of God and to whom earthly goods were of no account.

If we lack steadfastness as a nation, the deficiency is
made good by that Roman Briton who knew not fear
and whom nothing could dissuade.   As for endurance,
compared to the conditions which men of nearly every
century but the last few endured, we have nothing to
endure.   In the times in which the Saint lived there
was in the outlying parts of the Empire a condition of
things which, seen in the light of the social standards
of to-day, was almost incredible.   Never in the world's
history were the poor subjected to greater oppression,
never was there less relief.   Houseless, unsanitary
(even in the palaces this was the state), unsegregated
from maniacs and leprosy and lupus, half-naked,
untreated for even the simplest maladies, subject to the
terrors of witchcraft, the poor, devoid of hope and
ignorant of better things, were used as chattels to be
bartered for cattle or sold to the brothels of Europe as
Coroticus sold the Christian virgins whom he seized
after their baptism by St. Patrick.

To these slaves he brought a soul, and to their kings
he gave a conscience.   Though it took centuries to
blossom out, the sentiment which made for the respect
for women and amelioration of their lot was inculcated
by him.   To a savage culture he introduced civilisation.

He did more than this.   Inherent in the religion

which he taught were ideas which, when translated into
the secular world, were of inestimable advantage for the
nation. These were ideas which were to release the
country from a system of tribal sub-divisions, and in
the end to emancipate the country's mind from a petty
parochial outlook and unite it to the civilisation of
Europe. While the Imperium Romanum was going
down in chaos, those who were to become the Irish
nation and the saviours of what was left of Christian
civilisation were being brought into one fold in Ireland
by the Saint. Relapses to political narrowness there
have been now and then, but generally the far-flung
Irish race is inseparably identified with Roman Christianity the world over. The personality of the Irishman has gained amplitude from it, and there is certain
friendliness in the idea of a Paddy. He is as a person
whose general characteristics are well known. He is
approachable wherever he is. He is not despised as a
prig or avoided as a bigot: there is something wide and
uninsular about him. This he got from the univers-
ality of that Empire which the Saint represented
spiritually when it disappeared secularly before the
wild tribes who resented its peace.

Put in another way, the personality of St. Patrick,
which every Irishman shares to some extent, may be
measured negatively—if there be a way of measuring
things negatively (and I am sure there is among mathe-
maticians, who were the first to invent minuses and put
a value on the non-existent)—by considering his
opposite. How would it have been had the land been
converted gradually and by half a dozen apostles

instead of one ?   Or by a few of the lordly rhetoricians who resented the showing up of their lack of missionary zeal by the success of a colleague whom they affected to despise, but who was about to restore missionary ardour to the Church ?

Now that the question is put, it will be seen that it is unthinkable.   Nevertheless we can see what a loss of personality it would have implied.   It comes to this, then: that an Ireland without St. Patrick is unthinkable.   Every person in our island shares something of the personality of that steadfast and enduring man who is spoken of more frequently with affection than with awe.

He sentenced himself to a life-long and barbarous exile for our sake.   He travelled with but little inter-mission throughout the country, faced its manifold dangers and founded single-handed an organisation " which in the last times he had excellently and kindly planted," and which is as enduring as the man himself, and as quick to-day as he himself is alive in the hearts of the people.   He met savages and made them Christians who to this day owe to him largely that which makes them kindly Irish.   He is a man after their own hearts: unmiserly, fearless, sudden and unafraid to denounce what he disapproved.   He got nothing for himself for his service and self-sacrifice except detrac-tion from Britain.   Is it any wonder that so many of our people keep alive the image and likeness, and do not hesitate to call themselves by the high patrician name, which means a Roman noble, of the noblest Roman of them all ?

FINIS

APPENDIX I

THE CONFESSION

Here Begin the Books of Saint Patrick the Bishop :

1. I, PATRICK, SINNER, AM THE MOST ILLITERATE AND inconsiderable of all the Faithful, and am despised in the hearts of many.

I had for father Calpurnius, a deacon, one of the sons of Potitus, a presbyter, who belonged to the village of Bannavem Taberniæ ; for he owned a small farm hard by, where I was made a captive.

At the time I was about sixteen years old. I had no knowledge of the True God, and I was led to Ireland in captivity with many thousand others, according to our deserts, because we departed from God and did not keep his commandments, and we were not obedient to our priests, who were wont to admonish us for our salvation. And the Lord poured upon us the fury of his anger, and scattered us among many gentile nations, even unto the ends of the earth, where now my littleness may be seen among stranger folk.

2. And there the Lord opened the understanding of my unbelief, so that, though late, I might summon my faults to mind and turn with all my heart to the Lord my God, who regarded my low estate, and pitied my ignorance and youth, and kept watch over me before I knew him or had attained discernment or could distinguish good from evil, and fortified me and comforted me as a father his son.

3. Therefore I cannot now maintain silence (nor would it be fitting) as to the great favours and the great grace which the Lord vouchsafed to bestow on me in the land of my captivity. For this is the return we make : that after our chastening and our recognition of God we shall exalt and praise his wondrous works before every nation which is under the whole heaven.

4. For there is no other God, and never has been, and never will be hereafter, except God the Father unbegotten, without beginning, from whom is all Beginning, who holds all things, as we say, and his Son Jesus Christ, whom we witness likewise to have been ever with the Father, spiritually existing in the

311

Father before the origin of the universe, begotten inexpressibly before all beginning.

And by him were made things visible and invisible.   He was made man, and after triumphing over death was received up to the Father in heaven.   And he gave to him all power above every name of things in heaven and things in earth and things under the earth; and let every tongue confess to him that Jesus Christ is Lord and God in whom we believe.

And we look for his Coming any day now.   He the Judge of the quick and the dead, who will render to each man according to his deeds.   And he shed on us abundantly the Holy Ghost, the gift and pledge of immortality, who turns those that believe and obey into the Children of God and Joint-heirs with Christ, whom we confess and adore as One God in the Trinity of the Holy Name.

5. For he himself declared through the prophet, " Call upon me in the day of trouble; I will deliver thee, and thou shalt glorify me."   And again he says, " It is honourable to reveal and confess the works of God."

6. Yet, faulty as I am in many ways, I desire my brethren and kinsfolk to know what manner of man I am, so that they may be able to understand the dedication of my soul.

7. I know well enough the testimony of my Lord, who witnesses in the Psalm, " Thou shalt destroy them that speak a lie."   And again he says, " The mouth that belies kills the soul."   And the same Lord says in the Gospel, " The idle word that men shall speak, they shall give account thereof in the day of judgment."

8. Therefore I ought exceedingly, with fear and trembling, to dread this sentence in that day when no man shall be able to absent himself or hide; but all of us, every man of us, must give account of even his tiniest sins before the judgment seat of the Lord Christ.

9. Consequently I have long considered a written statement, but till this moment I have hesitated.   For I feared to come under the censure of men's tongues, because I am not learned as others are, who have imbibed in the most approved ways both Law and Holy Scripture in one draught, and who from their infancy have never changed their speech but instead went on bringing it to ever greater perfection.

For my speech, my style, is translated into a strange tongue, as can easily be perceived from the flavour of my writing the degree of my training and instruction in the matter of words. For, says the wise man, " By the tongue will be discovered understanding and knowledge and the teaching of truth."

10. But what use is an excuse however nigh the truth, especially when joined to presumption? seeing that now I myself, in my old age, strongly desire that which in my youth I did not acquire; because my sins stood in the way of my mastering what I had previously read over. But who believes me even if I repeat what I have said in my prefatory remarks?

A youth, scarcely indeed a boy, I was made a captive before I knew what I should strive for or what I ought to shun (in language). And so today I blush and am exceedingly afraid to show nakedly my inexperience, because through lack of education I cannot express myself with brevity. For as the Spirit yearns, the disposition discloses the soul and the understanding.

11. But even had I had the same opportunity as others, still I would not keep silent, on account of the reward. And if perhaps it should appear to many that I am thrusting myself forward in this matter with my ignorance and my slow tongue, yet it is written, " The tongue of the stammerers shall quickly learn to speak peace." How much rather should we covet to do this, who are, he says, the Epistle of Christ for salvation unto the ends of the earth, although not a learned one, yet ministered with all strength, written in your hearts, not with ink, but with the Spirit of the living God. And again the Spirit witnesses, " And husbandry (or rusticity) was ordained by the Most High."

12. Whence I, at first illiterate, an exile, unlearned as is one who does not know how to provide for the future—yet this I do know with full certainty, that before I was afflicted I was like a stone which lies in the deep mire; and he that is mighty came, and in his mercy lifted me up, and set me on the top of the wall. And therefore I ought to cry out and render somewhat to the Lord for his benefits so great both here and in eternity, which the mind of man cannot estimate.

13. Therefore, be you filled with wonder, you that fear God, both small and great, and you lordly rhetoricians, listen and search it out. Who was it that called me up, fool as I am, from

the midst of those who seem to be wise and skilled in the law and powerful in word and in everything?

And me, too, the abhorred of this world, did he inspire beyond others, if such I were, only that with reverence and godly fear and unblameably I should faithfully serve the gentile people to whom the love of Christ transferred and presented me, as long as I live, if I should be worthy: that in humility and truthfully I should serve them.

14. So it is right that according to the rule of faith in the Trinity, I should define doctrine and make known the gift of God and everlasting consolation, without being held back by danger, and spread everywhere without fear, confidently, the name of God; so that even after my decease I may leave a legacy to my brethren and sons whom I baptised in the Lord, many thousands of men.

15. And I was not worthy, nor such a one, that the Lord should grant this to his poor slave after calamities and such great difficulties, after captivity, after many years: that he should grant me so great a grace towards that gentile people—what formerly, in my youth I never hoped for or pondered.

16. Now after I came to Ireland, daily I pastured flocks, and constantly during the day I prayed. More and more there grew the Love of God and the Fear of him, and my Faith increased, and my Spirit was stirred up, so that in a single day I uttered as many as a hundred prayers, and nearly as many in the night, so that I stayed even in the woods and the mountain. Before dawnlight I used to be roused to prayer, in snow, in frost, in rain. And I felt no harm, nor was there any slothfulness in me (as I now see), because then the spirit in me was fervent.

17. And there verily one night I heard in my sleep a voice saying to me, "You fast to good purpose, soon to go to your fatherland." And again after a very little time I heard the Answer speaking to me, "See, your ship is ready." And it was not near, but was far off about 200 miles. And I had never been there, nor had I knowledge of any person there.

And thereon shortly afterwards I took myself to flight and left the man with whom I had been for 6 years; and I came in the strength of God who prospered my way for good, and I encountered nothing alarming until I came to that ship.

18. And on the very day I came, the ship sailed from its anchorage. And I declared that I had to sail away with them. And the shipmaster was displeased, and replied harshly with anger, " On no account seek to go with us."

When I heard this, I departed from them to go to the hut where I was lodging; and on the way I began to pray. And before I had completed my prayer, I hear one of them. He was shouting loudly after me, " Come quickly, these men are calling you."

And they began to say to me, " Come, we accept you in good faith. Make friends with us in any way you like."

And on that day I refused to suck their breasts through fear of God; but nevertheless I hoped that some of them would come into the faith of Jesus Christ, since they were gentiles. For that reason I stayed with them; and straightway we set sail.

19. And after three days we reached land, and for 28 days we travelled through a desert; and food failed them and hunger overcame them. And one day the shipmaster began to say to me, " How is this, you Christian? you say your God is great and almighty. Why then can't you pray for us? We're in danger of starvation. Hardly are we like to see a human being again."

Then I spoke plainly to them.

" Turn in faith and with all your heart to the Lord my God, to whom nothing is impossible, so that he may send you food today for your journey until you can eat no more, for everywhere he has plenty."

And, by God's help, so it came to pass. Lo, a herd of swine appeared on the track before our eyes; and they killed many of them and spent two nights there, and were well refreshed, and their dogs were fed full, for many of them had fainted and were left half dead by the way.

And after this they offered the fullest thanks to God, and I became an object of honour in their eyes, and from that day on they had food in plenty. They even found wild honey and gave me a piece of it. But one of them said, " This is offered in sacrifice."

Thanks be to God, I tasted none of it.

20. On that very same night I lay a-sleeping, and powerfully Satan assailed me; which I shall remember as long as I am in

this body.   He fell upon me like an enormous stone, and I was stricken nerveless in all my limbs.   Whence then did it come into my unscholarly spirit to call upon Helias ?   At once I saw the sun rising into the dawnsky, and while I kept invoking " Helias, Helias," with all my strength, lo, the Splendour of the Sun fell over me and instantly shook all the heaviness off from me.

I believe I was succoured by Christ my Lord and that his Spirit even then was calling out on my behalf.   And I trust that it will be so in the day of my trouble, as he says in the Gospel. " In that day," the Lord testifies, " it is not you that speak, but the Spirit of your Father which speaks in you."

21.   And a second time, after many years, I was made a captive.   And so on that first night I remained with them.   I heard the Answer of God declaring to me, " For two months yet you will be with them."

So it came to pass.   On the sixtieth night after that, the Lord delivered me from their hands.

22.   Moreover, on our way he provided us with food and fire and dry weather every day until on the tenth day we reached our journey's end.   As I explained above, for 28 days we travelled through a desert.   And on the night on which we finished our journey we came to the end of our food.

23.   Again, a few years later, I was in Britain with my kin, who welcomed me as a son and in good faith besought me that now at least, after the great tribulations which I had endured, I would not ever again go away from them.

And there verily I saw in the night visions a man whose name was Victoricus, coming as it were from Ireland with countless letters.   He gave one of them to me, and I read the beginning of the letter, which was entitled, "The Voice of the Irish "; and while I was reading out the beginning of the letter, I thought that at that very moment I heard the voice of those that lived beside the Wood of Focluth, which is near the western sea. And thus they cried out, as if from one mouth, " We beg you, holy boy, to come and walk among us yet again."

And I was deeply broken in heart, and could read no further, and so I awoke.   Thanks be to God that after a great length of years the Lord dealt with them according to their cry.

24.   And on another night, whether within me or at my side,

I cannot tell, God knows, in words of the utmost eloquence, which I heard but could not comprehend until the end of the prayer, he spoke thus, " He who laid down his life for you, he it is who speaks in you." And so I awoke with heart of glee.

25. And another time I saw him praying in me, and he was as it were within my body, and I heard him over me—that is, over the inner man. And there he was praying, mightily, with groanings. And meanwhile I was wonderstruck, and marvelled and considered who it was that prayed within me; but at the end of the prayer he spoke out that he was the Spirit.

So I awoke and remembered how the Apostle says, " The Spirit helps the infirmities of our prayer, for we know not what we should pray for as we ought; but the Spirit himself makes intercession for us with groanings which cannot be uttered, which cannot be expressed in words." And again: " The Lord our Advocate makes intercession for us."

26. And when I was assailed by several of my elders, who came to urge my sins against my toilsome episcopate—certainly on that day I was sore thrust-at that I might fall both here and in eternity. But the Lord graciously had mercy on the stranger and sojourner for his name's sake; and he helped me stoutly in that humiliation, so that I did not fall badly into disgrace and reproach. I pray God that it may not be laid to their charge as sin.

27. For after thirty years had passed they found as an occasion against me a matter which I had confessed before I became a deacon. In my anxiety, with sorrowing heart, I disclosed to my closest friend what I had done in my youth on one day, no, in one hour, because I had not then triumphed. I cannot tell, God knows, if I was then fifteen years old, and I did not believe in the living God—nor had I believed from my infancy; I remained in death and unbelief until I was thoroughly chastened and humbled in truth by hunger and nakedness, and that daily.

28. Towards Ireland I did not stir of my own accord until I was almost worn out. But this was all to my good, since thus I was amended by the Lord. He fitted me to become something which was once quite beyond my grasp; he made me take for my care and busy myself about the Salvation of others, whereas at that time I did not even think about myself.

29. Accordingly, on that day when I was rejected by the aforesaid persons whom I have described, during the night I saw in the night visions. There was a writing without honour over against my face. And meanwhile I heard the Divine Answer speaking to me, " We have seen with wrath the face of So-and-so." (I suppress the name.) He did not say, " You have seen with wrath," but " We have seen with wrath," as if in that matter he linked himself with me.

As he said, " He that touches you is as he that touches the apple of my eye."

30. So I thank him who has enabled me in all things, since he did hold me back from the journey on which I had resolved, and from my labour which I had learned from Christ my Lord; but rather I felt in myself no little virtue proceeding from him, and my faith has been approved in the sight of God and of men.

31. Therefore I say boldly that my conscience does not blame me here or hereafter. I call God to witness that I have told no lie in the matters which I have recounted to you.

32. Rather do I grieve for my close friend that we should have deserved to hear from God such an Answer. A man to whom I trusted even my soul! And I discovered from some of the brethren before that contention—at which I was not present; at the time I was not in Britain at all; nor will the story originate with me—that he, this friend, had fought for me in my absence. He had said to me with his own lips, " You are the man to be raised to the rank of bishop." Of which I was not worthy.

How then did it occur to him after to shame me in public, before everyone, good and bad, with regard to an office which previously of his own accord and joyfully he had conceded to me, and the Lord too, who is greater than all ?

33. I have said enough. Still, I ought not to conceal the gift of God, which he bestowed upon me in the land of my captivity; since then I zealously sought him, and there I found him and he kept me safe from all iniquities (as I believe) because of his indwelling Spirit, who has worked in me till this day.

Boldly again I speak. But God knows if man had said this to me—maybe I would have held my peace for the love of Christ.

34. Hence therefore I render unwearying thanks to my God

who kept me faithful in the day of my temptation, so that today with confidence I offer sacrifice to him, as a living victim, even my soul to Christ my Lord, who saved me out of all my troubles so that I may say, Who am I, O Lord ? or what is my vocation that you have opened so great a source of divine aid ? so that today among the gentiles I should constantly exalt and magnify your name wherever I may be; and that not only in prosperity, but also amid afflictions; so that whatever may happen to me, whether of good or bad, I ought to accept it with equanimity and always give thanks to God who showed me that I might yield him endless trust as one that cannot be doubted; and who heard me, so that I, ignorant as I am, and in the world's last days, should proceed to take up this work so holy and so wonderful; so that I might to some extent imitate those whom the Lord long ago prophesied would proclaim his Gospel for a witness unto all nations before the end of the world. Accordingly, as we see, this had been so fulfilled. Lo, we are witnesses that the Gospel has been preached to the places beyond which no man dwells.

35. A long task it is to narrate in detail the whole of my labour, or even parts of it. I shall briefly tell in what manner the most gracious God often delivered me from slavery and from the Twelve Perils by which my soul was beset, besides many plots and things which I am not able to express in words—lest I should tire out my readers. But for voucher I have God, who knows all things even before they come to pass, as the Divine Answer frequently warned me the poor starveling uneducated orphan.

36. Whence came to me this wisdom which was not in me, who neither knew the number of my days nor had a taste of God ? Whence after came to me that gift so great and so salutary, to know God and to love him, only that I should put aside my fatherland and my kindred ?

37. Many were the gifts proffered to me with wailing and with tears. And I displeased them, and also, against my wish, some of my elders. But, through God's guidance, in no way did I acquiesce or surrender to them. Not my grace was it, but God who conquered in me and resisted them all, so that I came to the Irish heathen to preach the Gospel and to endure insults from the unbelieving, so as to hear the reproach of my going

abroad, and to meet many persecutions, even unto bonds; and so that I should give up my free condition for the profit of others.

And if I should be worthy, I am ready to give even my life for his name's sake, unhesitatingly and most joyfully; and there I desire to spend it until the day of death, if the Lord would grant it to me.

38. Because I am greatly a debtor to God, who afforded me such great grace that through me many people should be regenerated to God and afterwards confirmed, and that clergy should everywhere be ordained for them—for a people newly come to belief, whom the Lord took from the ends of the earth, as he promised of old through his prophets:

" The Gentiles shall come unto thee from the ends of the earth, and shall say, As our fathers have got for themselves false idols and there is no profit in them." And again: " I have set thee to be a light of the Gentiles, that thou shouldest be for salvation unto the ends of the earth."

39. And there I wish to wait for the promise of him who never disappoints. As he promises in the Gospel, " They shall come from the east and west and from the south and from the north, and shall sit down with Abraham and Isaac and Jacob "; as we believe that believers will come from all over the world.

40. For that reason then we ought to fish well and diligently, as the Lord forewarns and teaches, saying, " Come ye after me, and I will make you to become fishers of men." And again he says through his prophets, " Behold I send fishers and many hunters, saith God, and so forth."

Therefore it was urgently necessary that we should spread our nets to take a great multitude and a throng for God, and that everywhere there should be clergy to baptise and exhort the poverty-stricken and needy folk, as the Lord in the Gospel warns and teaches, saying:

" Go ye therefore now and teach all nations, baptising them in the name of the Father and of the Son and of the Holy Ghost; teaching them to observe all things whatsoever I have commanded you: and lo, I am with you always, even unto the end of the world."

And again he says: " Go ye therefore into all the world and preach the Gospel to every creature. He that believeth and is baptised shall be saved; but he that believeth not shall be damned."

And again: "This Gospel of the kingdom shall be preached in all the world for a witness unto all nations: and then shall the end come."

And in like manner the Lord, foretelling by the prophet, says: "And it shall come to pass in the last days, saith the Lord, I will pour out of my Spirit upon all flesh: and your sons and your daughters shall prophesy, and your young men shall see visions, and your old men shall dream dreams: and on my servants and on my handmaidens I will pour out in those days of my Spirit; and they shall prophesy."

And Hosea says: "I will call them my people, which were not my people; and the one that hath obtained mercy which had not obtained mercy. And it shall come to pass, that in the place where it was said, Ye are not my people, there shall they be called the children of the living God."

41. Whence Ireland, which never had the knowledge of God, but up to the present always adored idols and abominations —how has there lately been prepared a people of the Lord and the name given to them of Children of God? The sons of the Scots and the daughters of their chieftains are seen to become the monks and virgins of Christ.

42. But once especial there was one blessed lady of Scottic birth, noble of line, very lovely, and of full age, whom I myself baptised; and after a few days she came to me for a certain purpose. She disclosed to us that she had received from God a private admonition, and it warned her to become a Virgin of Christ and live closer to God.

Thanks be to God, on the sixth day after, most worthily and zealously she snatched at that vocation, as all the Virgins of Christ do in like manner; not with the consent of their fathers; no, they endure persecution and lying reproaches from their kindred, and yet their numbers increase all the more and we cannot tell how many of our race are thus reborn there, besides widows and the continent.

But the women who are held in slavery are in the worst toils. They constantly endure even unto terrors and threats. But the Lord gave grace to many of my handmaidens; for, although they are forbidden, they resolutely follow the example of the others.

X

43. Therefore, even if I should wish to depart from them, and thus proceeding to Britain—and gladly ready was I to do so —as to my fatherland and kindred; and not that only, but to go as far as Gaul, to visit the brethren and behold the face of the saints of my Lord—God knows that I used to yearn deeply for it—yet I am bound in the Spirit, who witnesses to me that if I should do this he would mark me as guilty; and I fear to lose the labour which I have started off—no, not I but Christ the Lord who bade me come and be with them for the rest of my life, if the Lord so will, and if he should guard me from every evil way, so that I may not sin in his sight.

44. Now I hope that this is my course of duty; but I do not trust myself as long as I am in the body of this death. For he is strong that daily strives to turn me away from faith and from the chastity of a religion without fiction, which I have resolved to preserve till the end of my life for Christ my Lord. But the flesh our enemy forever drags us towards death; that is, the baits of pleasure which can be enjoyed but only in woe.

I know in part wherein I have not led a faultless life; but I confess to my Lord, and I do not blush in his sight, for I tell no lie: From the time that I learned to know him in my youth, the love of God and the fear of him grew in me; and to this day, with God's favour, I have kept the faith.

45. Let who will laugh or insult, I shall not keep silent or conceal the signs and the wonders which were furnished to me by the Lord many years before they came to pass, since he knows all things even before the world began.

46. Therefore I ought without pause to render thanks to God who often pardoned my folly and my negligence—and that not in one place only—so that he was not passionately angered against me who was given as a fellow-labourer; and yet I did not speedily acquiesce in accord with what had been revealed to me, and as the Spirit brought to my remembrance. Thousands of times the Lord showered mercy upon me, because he saw that I was ready but did not know what I should do in response, situated as I was with many men forbidding this embassage.

Behind my back they were talking among themselves and saying, " Why does this fellow push himself into danger among hostile folk who know not God ? " Not for reasons of malice; but it did not seem sensible to them, as I myself bear witness I understood, on account of my illiteracy. And I did not quickly recognise the grace which was then in me. Now I see the right course which I ought to have seen before.

47. Now, then, I have with simplicity made these disclosures to my brethren and fellow-servants who have believed in me, for the reason which I told you before and foretell you to strengthen and confirm your faith. Would that you too would imitate greater things and perform acts more potent for good! That will be my glory, for a wise son is the glory of his father.

48. You know, and God also, in what manner from my youth onwards I have lived with you, in faith of the truth and in sincerity of heart. Even towards those gentiles among whom I dwell I have kept faith, and will go on keeping it. God knows, I have defrauded none of them; nor do I think of doing so, for the sake of God and his Church, lest I should raise persecution against them and all of us, and lest the name of God should be blasphemed through me. For it is written, " Woe to the man through whom the name of the Lord is blasphemed."

49. But though I be rude in all things, still I have sought in some degree to keep watch over myself, both for the Christian brethren and the virgins of Christ and the devout women who used of their own free will present me with their little gifts and threw on the altars various of their adornments, which I delivered back to them. And they were scandalised against me because I acted thus. But I did it out of my hope of immortality, that I might keep myself cautiously in all things, that the heathen for one reason or another might accept me or the ministry of my service, and that I should not, even in the smallest detail, give pretext to the unbelievers to defame and disparage.

50. Maybe, then, when I baptised so many thousands of men, I hoped from any one of them even as much as the half of scruple? Tell me and I shall restore it to you. Or when my trivial self had been the Lord's instrument for the ordaining of clergy on all sides, and I gave them my ministrations for nothing, if I required from any one of them even the price of my shoe, tell it against me and I shall restore you the price and more.

51. I spent for you that they might receive me; and both among you and wherever I travelled for your sake, through many dangers, even to outlying regions beyond which was no

man, and where nobody had ever come to baptise or ordain clergy or confirm the folk, I have, by God's bounty, done everything diligently and joyfully for your salvation.

52. At times I used to give presents to the kings' besides the wages I paid their sons, who went round with me; and yet they siezed me once with my companions. And on that day they most eagerly desired to slaughter me; but the time was not yet come. Everything which they found upon us they plundered, and myself they bound with irons. And on the fourteenth day the Lord freed me from their power; and whatever was our property was restored to us for God's sake and the sake of the near friends whom we had provided beforehand.

53. You know also from your own experience how much I paid out to those who were Judges throughout all the districts which I more regularly visited; for I calculate that I distributed to them not less than the price of 15 men, so that you might enjoy me and I might enjoy you ever in God. I do not regret it, nor consider it enough. Still I spend and will spend more. The Lord is mighty to grant me afterwards to be myself spent for your souls.

54. Lo, I call God for a record upon my soul that I lie not; nor was it that there might be an occasion for flattering words or covetousness that I have written to you; nor do I hope for honour from any of you. Enough for me is the honour which is not yet seen but is believed in the heart. And faithful is He that promised; never does he lie.

55. But I see that already in this present world I am exalted beyond measure by the Lord. And I was not worthy, nor am I such that he should grant me this gift, since I know with full certainty that poverty and affliction become me better than riches and luxuries. Why, Christ the Lord was a poor man for our sakes. But I, wretched and stricken, possess no wealth even if I should wish for it; nor do I judge mine own self. For every day I expect either a violent death or to be defrauded or to be reduced into slavery, or some such disaster. But none of these things move me, on account of the promises of heaven. I have cast myself into the hands of Almighty God, for he rules everywhere, as the prophet says: "Cast thy care upon God, and he shall sustain thee."

56. Lo, now I commit the keeping of my soul to my most

faithful God, for whom I am an ambassador in my lowliness, only because he accepts no man's person and he chose me for this office, that I should be his minister, one of the least of them.

57. Therefore I shall render unto him for all his benefits towards me. But what shall I say or what shall I promise to my Lord? For I see no worth except what he himself has given to me. But he tries the hearts and reins, and knows that abundantly and strenuously do I desire, and have long been ready, that he should grant me to drink of his cup, as he has granted to others who love him.

58. For which reason may it never happen to me from my God that I should ever lose his people whom he purchased at the ends of the earth. I pray God to grant me perseverance and deign that I may render myself a faithful witness unto him till the time of my passing hence, for God's sake.

59. And if I ever accomplished aught in the cause of my God whom I love, I beseech him to grant me that I may shed my blood with those strangers and captives for his name's sake, even though I should lack burial itself, even though the dogs and the wild beasts most wretchedly should rend my corpse limb by limb or the fowls of the air should devour it. With perfect certitude, I think, if such should be my fate, I have gained a soul as profit with my body. For beyond all doubt we shall rise on that day in the crystal brightness of the sun; that is, in the Glory of Christ Jesus our Redeemer, as sons of the living God and joint-heirs with Christ, conformed to his image which is to be. For of him and through him and in him we shall reign.

60. For that sun which we behold rises by God's command on our behalf every day. But it will never reign, nor will its Splendor endure; but all who worship it, wretched men, shall stumble upon their punishment. Whereas we, who worship and believe in the True Sun, Christ, who will never pass away— nor will anyone who doeth his will; but he will abide for ever, as Christ will abide for ever, who reigns with God the Father Almighty and with the Holy Spirit, before all worlds, and now, and for all the ages ever to come. Amen.

61. Lo, again and yet again I shall briefly set forth the words of my confession. I testify in truth and in glorying of heart before God and his holy angels, that I never had any cause

except the Gospel and his promises in ever returning to that people from whom I had before with difficulty escaped.

62. But I pray those who believe and fear God, whosoever has deigned to scan and to take this writing which Patrick the Sinner; verily of no education, composed in Ireland, that none shall ever say it was my ignorance which achieved whatever tiny success was mine or whatever I showed in accordance with God's will; but make your judgment, and let it be most truly believed that it was the Gift of God.

And this is my Confession before I die.

Translated by Jack Lindsay, with acknowledgments to Newport J. D. White's and Archbishop Healy's versions.

APPENDIX II

Acknowledgements

AFTER BIP PARES, THE ARTIST WHOSE EXCELLENT COMPOSITIONS illustrate this volume, and Jack Lindsay, the scholar whose translation of the *Confession of St. Patrick* is part of it, there remain many who have in various ways helped me generously. I name them in alphabetical order:

Mr. J. H. Ardill.
Gordon Bottomley.
Lynn Doyle.
Mr. Foley.
Mr. Garaghan.
Liam S. Gogan, Esquire.
Philip Graves.
Stephen Gwynn.
Mr. James Hornell.
Mrs. and Miss Hyde.
Doyle-Jones.
Shane Leslie.
The librarians of Trinity College, The National Library, and the Library of the National University.
Professor Macalister.
The Marquess and Marchioness of Londonderry.
Frank Owen.
Kevin Smith.
Colin Still.
Donal O'Sullivan.
Seumas O'Sullivan.

And to many in Wales, Ireland, Scotland, England and France who after much questioning helped me to attain to "the one sure track of history" in spite of what the Saint's first biographer, Muirchu, calls "the extreme difficulty of story-telling," in spite of "conflicting opinions and the very many surmises of very many persons," much thanks is due and gratefully returned.

INDEX